THE SCOPE LOGIC APPROACH TO CLASS ANALYSIS

The Scope Logic Approach to Class Analysis

A study of the Finnish class structure

RAIMO BLOM
MARKKU KIVINEN
HARRI MELIN
LIISA RANTALAIHO

Avebury

Aldershot · Brookfield USA · Hong Kong · Singapore · Sydney

Published by
Avebury
Ashgate Publishing Limited
Gower House
Croft Road
Aldershot
Hants GU11 3HR
England

Ashgate Publishing Company
Old Post Road
Brookfield
Vermont 05036
USA

A CIP catalogue record is available from the British Library and the US Library of Congress.

ISBN 1 85628 350 X

Printed in Great Britain by
Athenaeum Press Ltd, Newcastle upon Tyne.

Contents

Raimo Blom: cpts 1 and 2, 3.1., cpts 5 and 6
Markku Kivinen: 3.2., 3.3., 3.7., 4.1., 4.3., 4.6., cpts 5 and 6
Harri Melin: 3.2., 3.4., 3.5., 3.6., 4.1., cpt 6
Liisa Rantalaiho: 3.7., 4.1., 4.2., 4.4., 4.5., cpt 6

List of tables and figures

Acknowledgements

The research work for this book was done at the Department of Sociology and Social Psychology at the University of Tampere, Finland. It represents the Finnish contribution to the International Project on Class Structure and Class Consciousness, which has been led and coordinated by Erik Olin Wright from the University of Madison. The Finnish project leader is professor Raimo Blom. We are indebted to all the people whom we met in the course of the project and at its many meetings.

Introduction

The question of social classes has been discussed by social scientists from a number of different perspectives. In this study we are concerned to elaborate a class theory in its broadest sense: rather than contenting ourselves with quantitative analyses of class structure and stratification, we aim at a more comprehensive understanding of the relationship between class location and social action.

It is our intention to show that what we call the 'scope logic' of class analysis is essential to resolving the problems concerned. Our main argument is that the relevance of class theories and classes must be tested systematically through different stages. First, following a basic description of class structure, we must determine the structuring role of class location in the work and reproduction situation. This represents the first level or cycle of class analysis. On the second level, we must proceed to determine the impact of the interrelationship between class location and class situation on class consciousness. Finally, the question of how class subjects are related to the state can be regarded as the most concrete level of class analysis, which cannot be tackled until we have gone through all these mediating steps.

Our study is based on Marx's class theory: we consider classes as being determined by the relations of production. Having said that, we do not believe that the relative strengths of different research traditions can be determined without a serious comparison of these at all levels of class analysis. Also, although Marx's concepts of the theory of capitalism provide an important starting-point for class research, it must be borne in mind that Marx himself does not present a systematic elaboration of class theory in his own production. Therefore it is necessary in our concrete research work to combine different theoretical approaches and empirical lines of argumentation.

Empirical class research is not and can never be theoretically neutral; its results inevitably reflect its theoretical premises and its basic conceptual and methodological solutions. Nonetheless we believe that the empirical consequences of different theories can be meaningfully compared. Although an empirical comparison of this kind always involves some measure of subjective interpretation, it cannot be directly subsumed to theory. It is important that our choice of research approach also allows for the possibility that different kinds of class theories are relevant at different stages of the research process. What we hope to demonstrate is that the approach adopted here enables exactly that.

Our study is part of E.O. Wright's *International Comparative Project on Class Structure and Class Consciousness*, and it is within this framework that we have collected the present empirical data. The project has also played an extremely important role as a forum for inspiring and critical debates. However, the theoretical starting-points of the present work lie in the Finnish team's own concepts and interpretations of Marxist class theory. Likewise, our notion of the successive 'cycles' of class analysis is not found within the international project. The Finnish team has been on very different lines than the international project especially in its conceptualizations and empirical analyses of work situation and consciousness: we have taken a critical stand on Wright's theory, particularly on the theoretical and empirical validity of his analysis of class structure and on his theorizing concerning class interests and class consciousness.

Finland's semiperipheral position on the world's 'geotheoretical' map has, paradoxically enough, also brought some important advantages to us (though we are of course painfully aware of the many drawbacks). Finnish scholars are not captive to one mainstream tradition in the same way as social scientists in the English-speaking world. In the case of the present work, this combines at least three different class-theoretical traditions: Anglo-Saxon structuralist class research, the German capital-logical tradition, the French school which started from a critique of state-monopolist theories of capitalism by Poulantzas and others.

In a study such as ours which approaches the problems of social classes from a very broad perspective, it is obvious that we must also take into consideration theoretical developments which are not directly related to class theory. In the present work such theoretical discourses that proved relevant were the labour process debate, the theory of class consciousness, and attempts to conceptualize hegemonic projects.

2

1 Social classes and social research

1.1. Theoretical traditions and new challenges

Class theory and class research tend to mean different things in different contexts. Classes may be described at the level of production relations as bearers of the functions of capital or wage labour; as categories or strata determined by statistical criteria such as educational level and income; or as categories based on purely subjective criteria.[1] Furthermore, there are descriptions of classes that draw on market and consumption criteria rather than production relations; this difference underlies the fundamental distinction between Weberian and Marxist class theories. The present project represents the latter tradition. More specifically, its theoretical background lies in the class theory proposed by Erik Olin Wright, a theory essentially based on the relations of appropriation and domination prevailing in production.

Within Marxist class research we can also identify several different theoretical schools. A major influence in recent years has been the West German debate, whose contributions have largely been neglected in the English-speaking world and which has rarely been confronted with the work of Poulantzas, Wright and other representatives of the Anglo-French tradition. In this book we try to bridge this gap.

One of the most important lines of theorizing in the Federal Republic is represented by the 'capital-logical' school. Starting from the class theory presented in *Capital*, its aim has been to elaborate the concepts of Marx's critique of political economy and on this basis to produce definitions applicable to the class structure of advanced capitalist society.[2] There are three distinctive features

3

in this theory:

(1) Boundaries between classes and class groups are determined on the basis of the form determinants (*Formbestimmungen*) of capitalist production relations. Projekt Klassenanalyse (PKA), for example, uses form and source of income as its main criterion here.

(2) Theoretical derivation (*Ableitung*) is also applied to the analysis of forms of consciousness.[3] PKA writes: 'In order to find out how the given societal relations of productive workers are reflected in their minds, we need only to analyse economic form determinants' (1973, 220; see also Bierbaum et al. 1977). A central distinction in the statistical analysis of class structure has been between the appearances or surface forms of capitalism and its essence. The aim has been to demystify such statistical and judicial categories as 'manual workers', 'white-collar employees', 'civil servants', to prove that all these categories actually include several different class positions.

(3) Finally, detailed analyses have been presented of the relevance of the 'laws of capitalist development' to the economic position of wage workers (Vonrerach 1974, 62-102; Bader et al. 1975, 237-260). In these works the main focus has been on the general laws of capital accumulation and on the tendency for the rate of profit to fall, i.e. on their consequences from the working class's point of view.[4]

A direct challenge to the 'capital-logical' project can be found in the work of the Institut für Marxistische Studien und Forschung (IMSF),[5] whose class analyses are built upon the theory of state monopoly capitalism. IMSF has been concerned to determine the place of different class groups within the context of the coercive mechanisms of monopoly capitalism. In the analysis of the internal differentiation of wage workers, this perspective leads to three basic propositions: First, the top white-collar employees of state and private capital are classified under the state monopoly bourgeoisie. Second, the primary criterion with which the working class is distinguished from other groups is the extent to which labour power has transformed into a commodity, i.e. the extent to which the position of a given wage worker group is subordinated to the laws of capitalist development. Finally, IMSF proposes the concept of *wage-labouring middle strata* to describe the heterogeneous intermediate categories located in the middle ground between the bourgeoisie and the working class. We revert to the German debate in greater detail later.

As we just mentioned, there has been very little dialogue between the German and Anglo-French traditions; both have been building their class theories very

4

much independently of each other. At this point it is useful to single out two features that distinguish the theoretical goals of the latter tradition from those of the former. First, a central concern in its analyses of the internal differentiation of wage workers has been with the methods of control of the labour process and with the position of different worker groups in the production process (or the extent to which these groups bear the global functions of capital).[6] These questions are of central interest to the sociology of work, most particularly to those strands concerned with modes of control in different types of work and Taylorism, the development of wage workers' skills and qualification requirements, and Fordist and neo-Fordist reproduction.[7] The second major focus that distinguishes the Anglo-French tradition from its German counterpart is the study of class struggle and class relations. In particular, Poulantzas and his followers have invested considerable energy in elaborating concepts for these purposes.

In France, Poulantzas concentrated on developing his theory of what he called the 'new petty bourgeoisie'. His aim was in fact not only to elaborate criteria and definitions for a new theory of class structure, but he was also out to challenge the idea entertained by monopoly capitalism theorists that the coalition of the proletariat, the wage-labouring middle strata and the intelligentsia are a central revolutionary force. Another significant French contribution to the international debate on class theory has been made by Serget Mallet[8] and Alain Touraine, who drew attention to the changing role of the 'new working class' and the technical intelligentsia in the social structure. Mallet and Touraine argued that the scientific and technical intelligentsia (the 'new working class') will be in the vanguard of change in the era of automation, because their position in production gives them a ringside view on both the shortcomings and potentials of the prevailing production system. More on these questions later.

The main concern of class theory is not only with changes in the class structure. Another problem that is high on the agenda of class theorists is the constitution of classes into conscious and active subjects.[9] This issue brings us into a realm where we encounter such distinctions as those between 'class in itself' and 'class for itself' (Marx); trade unionist and political class consciousness (Lenin); the working class as object and subject (Vester 1970); the sphere of production relations, civil society and the state; and to the question of class as an 'agency' and as something that constitutes itself through learning.[10]

It is therefore obvious that class theory, in its broadest meaning, intersects with other problem areas that are also relevant to class research. Although it may be impossible to define the exact boundaries of these areas, we shall attempt to evaluate their relevance to class research in general and to our study in particular at different stages in this book. Under section 1.4., we outline a theoretical scheme of what we call the scope logic of class theory: a scheme that describes the relationships between different stages of class research and between different problem areas, proceeding from the simpler to the more complex levels of analysis.

Among the most significant recent theoretical debates relevant to class theory are those concerned with the questions of *subjectivity, hegemony and organization* and, on the other hand, the question of *culture and ideology*. These debates have above all been critical reassessments of the old theoretical and methodological frameworks, and themselves been marked by *anti-objectivism, anti-reductionism and anti-economism*. At the same time, however, they have arisen from a practical social and political background. One central aim has been to better understand the dynamics of new social movements and in general the principles guiding social action in the sphere of civil society.

A major influence behind these new trends is the anti-economist, anti-empiricist and anti-historicist theory of Louis Althusser (see Althusser 1969). For Althusser, social structure is a totality where the different elements and levels of the social formation (economic, political and ideological) are preconditions for each other's existence, although each area enjoys relative autonomy from the others. The economic area is the 'overdetermining level', but only 'in the last instance': each historical conjuncture is the result of a number of determining factors. Althusser's attack on economism and the related concept of 'expressive totality' has given a positive impulse to the development of Marxism, but this impulse can only be translated into definite progress by transcending the conflict in his work between the emphasis of the primacy of class struggle and certain functionalist tendencies; that is, by concentrating on the study of the specific historical articulations between various instances and practices. Although often marred by latent reductionism, studies of wage-worker socialization provide a good example.

Notwithstanding their differences in orientation, all studies of wage-worker socialization[11] tend to emphasize the reciprocal relationship between the socialization process and the capitalist production process, i.e. they focus on the changes occurring in subjectivity with the development of the capitalist mode of production. Along with changes in the mode of production, there also develop

6

new action requirements. One central requirement is 'the internalization of the norms of abstract work' (Krovoza 1976, 74), which implies a change in patterns of time usage: rather than by the rhythm of nature, the use of time is now determined by the clock. Also, people's increasingly fetishized social relations mean they develop new kinds of needs and new forms of self-observation and self-control. The process in which workers are transformed into labour power and instruments of labour leads to the desexualization of the human organism, and in the reproduction of labour power and everyday life the only objective is to ensure maximum efficiency in the production process (ibid., 75-76). Lefebvre's distinction between 'cumulative' and 'non-cumulative processes' highlights the fact that a number of different and even contradictory types of processes and modes of production are combined in the capitalist reproduction process (Lefebvre 1975, 150). Krovoza, in turn, points out that 'socialization processes constitute a sphere with its own inner logic and materiality' (1976, 76), and that 'the transformation of the societal practice of production cannot be divorced from the practice of self-reflection' (ibid., 80). These descriptions can be compared with the world of Elias and Foucault (see Honneth and Joas 1988, 118-150).

Within socialization studies there has been a highly critical response to the inclusion of more or less the whole socialization process in an extended concept of production. The important discovery of studies on socialization to the action requirements posed by the capitalist mode of production is that the capitalism-adequacy, work motivation and obedience of labour power are continuous problems that cannot be solved within the confines of the reductionistic economy/subject couplet. This conclusion is consistent with the results of analyses by sociologists of work (Edwards 1979; Littler 1982).

Another binary code which has significantly structured the debate in the social sciences is the structure/subject couplet. In the context of theoretical class research, the writer who has perhaps most consistently emphasized the spontaneity of the working class and the purposeful action of subjects is Edward Thompson. Thompson stresses the significance of common experiences and a common interest struggle in the definition of the concept of class. Conceding that class experience is largely determined by production relations, he adds that there is always a cultural moment in this experience: 'Class-consciousness is the way in which these experiences are handled in cultural terms: embodied in traditions, value-systems, ideas and institutional forms. If the experience appears as determined, class-consciousness does not. (...) Class is defined by men as they live their own history and, in the end, this is its only definition.' (1968, 9-10) As Anderson has noted, Thompson's concept of the cultural determination of class comes closer to *Erlebnis* than to *Erfahrung*, a moral-existentialistic rather than a practical-experimental experience (Anderson 1980).

Several authors have also attempted to resolve the problem of the relationship between structure and action, chiefly on the basis of various conceptions of 'structuration' (e.g. Giddens). In the theory of structuration, social structure is seen both as a means and as the end of the reproduction of social practices. The intimate connection between production and reproduction means social life has what Giddens calls a 'recursive character'. This alleged resolution to the problem remains highly philosophical, however; it does not provide direct solutions to the problems we encounter at more concrete levels of analysis where we have to deal in real terms with the complex relations between acting human subjects and various social practices and instances. Likewise, it is clear that the illegitimate reduction of 'structures' to a single 'economic structure' poses a serious epistemological obstacle to the elaboration of these specific problems.

Indeed the more recent theorizing on the ideological and the cultural has often set to work on distinctly anti-economistic premises and paid special attention to subject-constituting 'meaning systems'.[12] A particular concern has been to describe the specific features of the cultural aspect of social life. In this difficult task there are two basic types of mistake one can make: either translate all phenomena into cultural ones and refuse to make any abstractions, or trivialize the concept of culture and identify it with leisure pursuits, for example (Johnson 1980, 230). Insofar as the cultural aspect is central to the constitution of classes into active subjects, we must be able to produce a sound theoretical conceptualization of this aspect.

For these purposes the following points that have been raised in the debate on the theory of culture will prove relevant: The cultural primarily embraces those aspects of human interaction in which people engage in purposeful, intellectual and especially artistic activity. The cultural, as opposed to the ideological, is a form of spontaneous horizontal societalization (*Vergesellschaftung*). In theories on the development of culture 'from below', a central concern is with the social and local limitations of culture and the question of whether these limitations must be incorporated in the concept of culture (cf. the historical studies that stress the writing of history at a local level, from below, and the method of 'oral history'). Another significant perspective on the cultural is that of subject-constitution.

8

Here, the most important aspect is a lived experience that cannot be reduced to the structures of reproduction of life, or to structural frames of experience.[13]

Within the confines of the present study it is not possible to discuss the specific problems of the theory of culture and ideology.[14] Instead, we shall continue for some while on the constitution of subjects and on the question of how individual action is determined by class. The former problem has been a focal issue not only in the debate on the ideological and the cultural, but also in reassessments of the concepts of civil society and social power. John Urry (1981) describes civil society as follows: Civil society refers to social practices which are both constituted by and are conditional upon the existence and interaction of human subjects. Although civil society is based on economic circulation and a related area of privacy, it is external to both the state and economy. On the other hand, the sphere of civil society is functional for the reproduction of capitalist social relations. Civil society is one of the areas where actors are constituted as subjects, and the area that is usually described as the effect of the ideological. Civil society is structured not only around production relations (or class position); other important dimensions include the gendered division of labour, religious, national and racial relations, and the differentiation of subjects on the basis of publicity and political organization. From this definition of civil society, Urry draws the following conclusions: First, classes only exist at the level of civil society, i.e. as subjects of civil society (as opposed to economic agents); in structuralist terms, classes are overdetermined by the practices of civil society. Second, *hegemony* is an effect of civil society, a special articulation of the relation between economy and the state. And third, a distinction must be made between the *general democratic struggle* (which is associated with the articulation of civil society) and class struggle (which follows directly from the contradictions in production relations). It is important to notice that the general democratic struggle forms an *already structured* environment for the class struggle.

Neo-Gramscian or discourse-theoretical critique of class theory (see Jessop 1982, 191-210; 1990, 191-272; Becker 1986) rejects the idea that classes are already given as active subjects. Przeworski argues that the class struggle is above all a *struggle for the constitution of class subjects* (1977, 371-373). Thus, as Mouffe and Laclau (1985) point out, subjects are constituted only in ideological practices. Subjects are not given at the level of production relations; and even after their constitution they do not necessarily belong to a given class. The dominant neo-Gramscian theory is that of *the discursive formation of hegemony*, according

9

to which all social relations derive their social character through discursive constitution. Every social practice constitutes itself as such and to the extent that it produces a meaning for actors. Concepts such as 'people', 'maternity', 'competition', 'uniformity', 'nationality' etc., assume a different meaning depending on how they are articulated with other elements of a certain discourse. Hegemony is therefore achieved in the discursive articulation of different subjects, who are constituted through and in the discourse. In this sense, hegemony is the 'discourse of discourses'; it is directed at the discursive mechanisms available to different political forces in their attempt to constitute subjects in a given project. For the 'discourse-theoretical' approach, subjects and political forces are not already class-determined. The meaning of different determinants of subjects depends on how they are associated to a certain socio-political project, such as Reaganism or Thatcherism. Laclau (1983, 43) has argued that the relation between the level where production relations of subjects are formed and the level of politico-social activity has undergone a historical change, in that nowadays 'the relative coherence existing between different positions of the same subject depend more and more on complex and variable politico-discursive articulations'.

The commonest criticism against the 'discourse-theoretical' perspective is that it fails to come to grips with the social preconditions for the production and reception of discursive practices. According to the critics, the theory merely transfers the problem of social preconditions to a new level and also omits to consider the role of material stimuli and physical coercion (Jessop 1982, 202). However, as far as we can see, the main future task here is to link discourse theory to the line of theorizing that emphasizes the structural and objective nature of social relations, a line initiated by Marx in his critique of political economy. Another significant counterargument against discourse theory is that it does not deal with the historical change of the capitalist reproduction structure and the structuration of class situation. It should be clear that an analysis of historical changes in capitalist societalization and in conflict frontiers between classes includes important theoretical mediations that are not present in discourse-theoretical analyses.[15]

Below, we shall take a closer look at the two 'major powers' of contemporary class research: neo-Weberian theories and the Marxist theory of E.O. Wright, which forms the theoretical basis for an ongoing international project on class structure and class consciousness. Through a critique of both, we hope to clarify our own theoretical position, which is presented in section 1.4.

1.2. Neo-Weberian theories

Max Weber's work has provided the basis for most contemporary non-Marxian approaches to social class. Although these approaches usually go under the general heading of neo-Weberian theories, there are in fact many different emphases amongst its representatives. There are two main reasons for this. First, Weber's analyses of class in *Economy and Society* are highly fragmentary. Second, and perhaps more importantly, most interpretations of Weber have been either biased or simply wrong (Clegg et al. 1985, 52).

In the discussion that follows we are concerned with only one aspect of Weber's theoretical work on classes, i.e. the class relations of capitalist society. Apart from providing a critical review of Weber's own production, we shall also comment upon some of the most important neo-Weberian class theories.

We can distinguish between at least five different categories of neo-Weberian theories.

(1) *Status and stratification theories*. Stratification theorists rejected out of hand the economic determinism of Marx and contested his theory on the basis of Weber's concept of status (*Stände*), with which they sought to incorporate various aspects of way of life in a new theory of class. This approach lost much of its theoretical credibility in empirical studies dealing with equalized stratification factors and stratification metrics (the most important contemporary work in stratification theory is *Class, Status and Power*, edited by Bendix and Lipset and first published in 1953; for a representative study in stratification metrics, see Coleman and Rainwater 1982; stratification theory and the use of Weber is also discussed by Wright 1980 and Abercrombie and Urry 1983, 7-8).

(2) *Authority theories*. The best-known example is Ralf Dahrendorf (1958). Class theories that start from Weber's concept of authority are not in fact built upon Weber's work on classes but on his analyses of different types of domination. The starting-point lies in the dichotomy of class relations, with persons endowed with authority on the one hand and those deprived of it on the other. In principle, this distinction is applicable to all communities or organizations (see Abercrombie and Urry 1983, 17-20).

(3) *Market capacity theories*. A significant part of neo-Weberian class theories fall in this category. Class situation is here determined by various marketable goods (property, skill, education). These theories are directly based on the definition of class situation with which Weber begins the Chapter on 'Status

11

Groups and Classes'. The most notable representative of this trend is Anthony Giddens (1973).

(4) *Closure theories*. These are based upon Weber's work on 'Open and Closed Relationships' under Chapter 1 'Basic Sociological Terms' in *Economy and Society*. From these fairly general starting-points, these theories have elaborated different forms of closure in social relationships and types of closure strategies (e.g. Parkin 1979 and Murphy 1985 and 1986).

(5) *Mixed theories*. These attempt to take into account the various aspects of both 'market situation' and 'work situation' in the analysis of class positions (e.g. Lockwood 1958; Abercrombie and Urry 1983).

Weber's contribution to class theory can be evaluated from many different angles, but obviously the key lies in what is considered to constitute the hard core of his theory, or the 'authentic' Weberian class theory. The trends outlined above have different views on this, as we shall see later. It is also useful to evaluate the place and relevance of Weber's class theory at a more general level in the field of social theory: what kind of questions does it answer, what kind of perspectives does it open for further elaborations?

Weber discusses the problem of social class in his book *Economy and Society*; more specifically, under Chapter IV 'Status Groups and Classes' in part one 'Conceptual Exposition', and under Chapter IX 'Political Communities' in part two, entitled 'The Economy and the Arena of Normative and De Facto Powers'. The subtitle of the latter analysis is: 'The Distribution of Power Within the Political Community: Class, Status, Party'.

Weber's definition of class is based on the concept of class situation (*Klassenlage*). Class situation means the typical probability of (1) procuring goods, (2) gaining a position in life and (3) finding inner satisfactions (*des inneren Lebensschicksals*). Class situations differ according to the degree and type of utilizing goods or services, and according to their income-producing uses within a given economic order. In this definition Weber is referring, first, to the *individual* conditions for prospective activity (procuring goods, finding inner satisfaction) and, second, to the relative control (*Verfügungsgewalt*) that can be gained over goods or skills. Class situations are thus determined through a certain type of action, which in other contexts we would identify as forms of rational-instrumental action (Jones 1975, 734).

Class, then, means all persons in the same class situation (Weber 1978, 302). Weber makes a distinction between three different types of class: (1) property classes, which are primarily determined by property differences; (2) commercial classes, where class situation is determined by the marketability of goods and services and (3) social classes, which make up the totality of those class situations within which individual and generational mobility is easy and typical. In the two former categories, Weber further distinguishes between positively and negatively privileged classes; in between these are the middle classes.

Weber's concept of social class is a generalization of his concept of class. It is based on the relative control over goods and skills which can be used on the markets for producing income. An additional criterion is social mobility. There must be a greater probability of individual and generational mobility within classes than between classes; Weber speaks of easy and typical mobility. There-fore, in a sense, the definition of social classes is possible only in a society with a relatively rigid structure.

Weber identifies four social classes: 1) the working class as a whole, 2) the petty bourgeoisie, 3) the propertyless intelligentsia and specialists and 4) the classes privileged through property and education.

The working class, according to Weber, is a relatively uniform class — and is the more so, the more automated the work process becomes. Weber defines specialists as including technicians, various kinds of white-collar employees and civil servants; his central criterion here is the cost of training. He also points out that 'every worker used to aspire to be a self-employed small businessman', but this has become 'less and less feasible'.

The main argument of the following discussion is that Weber's theory of class situation is in essence a general theory of *market capacities*. The decisive moment, Weber writes, is not property or the ownership of economic resources, but the chances of utilizing these resources in the *market*, which present a common condition for the individual's fate. In this sense, he continues, class situation is always ultimately 'market situation'. Further, Weber adds that 'the fact that creates "class" is unambiguously economic interests and indeed, only those interests involved in the existence of the market' (1978, 928). Classes are stratified according to their relations to the production and acquisition of goods (ibid., 937); thus the concepts of economic action and markets provide a central basis for the concept of class. Weber even speaks of an analysis 'within the area in which pure market conditions prevail' (ibid., 928).

Weber's class theory must be interpreted within the framework of his theory of action and, in particular, his analysis of economic action. Economic action acquires its planned and rational nature through its orientation to the market. The power of capital lies with economic enterprises, which are constituted by autonomous action capable of orientation to capital calculation, to calculating the probable risks of loss and the chances of profit. In the last instance economic action is oriented to expectations of prices and their changes as they are determined by the conflicts of interests in bargaining and competition and the resolution of these conflicts. At the same time, economic action concerns and moves the most important classes and class groups, the owners of capital and workers. (For interpretations and critiques of Weber's concepts related to economic action, see Bader et al. 1976, 193-320; Clarke 1982, 204-220; and Gronow 1978.)

There are a number of writers who draw a parallel between the class theories of Marx and Weber on account of their reliance on economic determinants or ownership as central criteria for class differentiation. This, however, is a shallow argument that fails to see some very important qualitative differences between Marx's and Weber's concepts of capital, markets, etc. Additionally, these concepts are built upon very different methodological premises. Weber's notion of 'markets', for instance, is explicitly based on methodological individualism, whereas the main idea in Marx's theory of capitalism lies in the independent role of societal relations.

Weber's scheme implies such a diversity of market positions and underlying goods and skills (market resources) that on this basis an unambiguous determination of class boundaries is impossible; the problem is hardly made any easier by Weber's complex classifications of 'market capacities'. Giddens (1973, 104) says that there 'would appear to be as many "classes", and as many "class conflicts", as there are differing market positions'. Therefore, we need a method for making the necessary theoretical transition from market capacities to the identification of class. Giddens proposes the concept of structuration.

Giddens distinguishes between two main types of structuration: mediate and proximate. The former refers to the distribution of mobility chances within a given society, in which case we have three relevant sorts of market capacity: ownership, qualifications and education. In the latter type of structuration there are three sources of structuration: the division of labour within the enterprise, the authority relationships within the enterprise and the influence of 'distributive groupings'. In other words, the factors in the former category come close to market capacity criteria, the latter come near to determinants of 'social status' and relations of domination in production. The combination of the sources of mediate and proximate structuration creates a class structure based on market capacities. Thus the difference between the middle class and the working class, for example, arises not only from mobility difficulties, but also from different roles in authority relations, the low level of communication between the two groups and neighbourhood segregation.

Giddens proposes a three-class system where white-collar employees form a middle class that is clearly distinct from manual workers. However, there are certain major shortcomings in Giddens's solution to the boundary problem. Like Weber, he uses a number of incommensurate factors from mobility to neighbourhood segregation as class criteria but he fails to show why a threefold class structure is generic to capitalist society (Abercrombie and Urry 1983, 25).

The fundamental counterargument against Weber's theory of class situation concerns his failure to make any distinction between different goods and commodities which provide actors with market capacities. Ownership of land, industrial means of production, education and technical qualifications all carry equal weight as long as they produce control on the markets. Giddens attempts to solve the problem by launching additional criteria, but he too fails to show how these additional factors are translated into differences in market capacity; and even if this were possible, we would not in fact have a theory of class structure that is based on 'forms of structuration' but merely a new version of stratification metrics. As was discussed earlier, a central criterion of control in Weber's definition of social class is 'easy' social mobility within classes. This is no doubt an important criterion but it does not help to solve the problem of how class positions are structured. Before we proceed to a study of mobility, we must be able to define the classes within or between which this mobility is taking place.

In short then, Weber's class theory, as one of class situations, is a general theory of market capacities. Rather than offering criteria for defining social classes, it equates different kinds of 'market resources' and collapses into an analysis of relative control on the market. In fact, the entire theoretical basis suggested by Weber is inadequate for purposes of producing boundaries between distinct classes, because Weber's description of the social structure in conjunction with his analysis of social classes (Weber 1978, 305) does not focus on a historically specific form of social relations.

Neo-Weberian theories of social class have also been developed on the basis of Weber's analysis of *closed social relationships* (ibid, 43). Typically the objective of closure (*Schliessung*) is to gain a monopoly over certain goods or commodities. A social relationship is closed against outsiders insofar as, according to its subjective meaning and its binding rules, 'participation of certain persons is excluded, limited, or subjected to conditions' (ibid., 43).

Weber distinguishes between four types of closure, which correspond to his distinction of different types of social action: (1) traditional (e.g. in family relationships), (2) affectual (erotic relationships), (3) value-rational (religious communities) and (4) instrumentally rational (monopolistic economic enterprises). Within a group or organization, the transition from a state of openness to one of regulation and closure may also be gradual. The principal motives for closure may vary from the securing of prestige and honour to economic interests, and usually they are combinations of various motives (ibid., 46).

Weber's discussion of open and closed social relationships does not provide a very clear starting-point for the elaboration of class theory. It has, however, inspired various attempts to analyse different strategies of class struggle and class *formation*. Parkin (1979, 93-94) suggests a distinction between two reciprocal modes of social closure: (1) exclusion and (2) usurpation. By exclusion, Parkin means the process in and by which a privileged group aims to oust its competitor from the market. Exclusion strategies involve the exercise of power from above, in a downward direction, the aim being to secure the group's advantages. These strategies may lead to fragmentation within classes.

The strategy of usurpation involves the exercise of power in an upward direction. The subordinate classes respond collectively to their exclusion, which results in a strategy of solidarity and, potentially, in a growing sense of unity within the class. This may aggravate the conflict of interests between the higher and lower groups. The dominant class in society usually consists of groups who have acquired their resources through exclusion, the subordinate class tends to consist of groups which resort primarily to the strategy of usurpation (Parkin 1979, 67-93).

Closure may also be either 'dual' (as in the case of the exclusion of working-class women) or even 'triple' (working-class women within different minority groups). Murphy (1985), then, proposes a distinction in his analysis of class and closure strategies between (1) principal forms, (2) derivative forms and (3) dependent forms of closure. Without dwelling on these distinctions any further, it may be noted that they can be helpful at least in two respects: firstly, they bring into focus the differential importance and the mutual dependence of different closure strategies and, secondly, they offer a conceptualization of different resources, possibilities and strategies of closure, which are unequally divided between the ruling and subordinate classes of society (cf. Offe and Wiesenthal 1980).

Parkin's theory of closure enlarges the concept of exploitation from its restricted Marxist meaning to include all exclusion practices. In principle any factor or process that enhances the rewards of one group on the market and closes off opportunities to others, may serve as a basis of exclusion and thus of class boundaries: property ownership, qualifications, race, religion, language, etc. According to Murphy (1985, 37), Parkin's closure theory enlarges the focus of the 'object of closure', first, from the means of production to other bases of domination (knowledge, power) and, second, from the laws of private property to other forms of monopolization and exclusion. It is interesting to note that this kind of attempt to enlarge class theory has many points in common both with stratification theory and with the contemporary debate on the theory of civil society.

In sum, it seems rather obvious that closure theory has not been able to solve the problems of Weber's theory of class situation, even though the explicit objective especially of Parkin's work has been to do away with the 'Marxist one-dimensionality' of class theory and to elaborate upon Weber. The analysis of exclusion and closure strategies and their different uses has most relevance within the problem-area of class formation, the struggle for classes and interest positions.

Neo-Weberian stratification theories have been developed on the basis of Weber's concept of *status*. This is also the point in Weber's class theory that has caused most misunderstandings among sociologists. Status (*ständische Lage*), according to Weber, may rest on various aspects of style or way of life — but that definition is not yet exhaustive.

Weber (1978, 305) defines status as an effective claim to social esteem and social honour. The individual's status position is typically based on his (1) style of life (*Lebensführungsart*), (2) formal education and (3) hereditary or occupational prestige. Weber says that whereas the 'genuine place' of classes is within the economic order, the place of status groups is within the social order, that is, within the sphere of the distribution of honour (ibid., 938).

In social life status honour is normally expressed by the fact that a specific style of life is expected from all those who belong to a certain circle (ibid., 932). Status honour always rests upon distance and exclusiveness vis-à-vis other groups (ibid., 935). Status positions are determined in a different way and in 'different

17

spheres' than class positions, but nonetheless there are certain similarities between them. The formation of status positions, Weber writes, is as such conducive to the monopolization of domination and economic opportunities (ibid., 306). The monopolization of market resources was also a central feature in the formation of property classes.

The points we have raised on Weber's concept of status are significant in that they lead us to a consideration of three aspects that are closely related to this central notion: (1) social esteem and style of life, (2) classes and economic action and (3) general domination (as distinct from domination based merely on the monopolization of economic resources).

Economic monopolization can take place both on the basis of class position and on the basis of status position. These, however, are two completely different processes. The formation of status groups, Weber writes, is the exact counterpart to rational economic action. Capitalist monopolies differ from monopolies of status groups by their purely economic and rational character: they are based upon an entirely rationally calculated mastery of market conditions, but nonetheless they can retain their formal freedom. The formation of status groups, then, represents a threat to free enterprise, fetters the free market and creates economically irrational consumption patterns (ibid., 307).

Weber also puts forward what might be termed a cyclic theory of the significance of class and status situation in different economic conditions: class situation is pushed into the foreground during periods of radical social change and economic transformation, whereas in relatively stable conditions social action tends to be regulated by status position (ibid., 938).

In short, then, we may summarize Weber's discussion of class and status by noting that these two categories are based upon different structural orders, i.e. the economic and the social order. From the point of view of free enterprise and rational economic action, status positions undermine the preconditions for rational economic action and therefore represent irrationality. Class action and status action are based upon different kinds of basic orientations. Although Weber's concept of status has at least three different facets, this does not provide sufficient grounds for the formulation of the concept of stratification. The concepts of class and status have a qualitatively different basis.

In an attempt to enlarge the concept of class through closure theory, some writers have directly linked up Weber's concept of status with his concept of class. Raymond Murphy (1986, 252), for example, defines social class as a global concept which takes into account all the major socially structured mechanisms of domination and exclusion in society.

Murphy proposes the following generalization: 'Social classes in Weber's sense consist of the resultant of the various power vectors of domination in society' (1986, 252). The problem with combining the qualitatively different concepts of class and status, as Murphy does in this interpretation, is that it tends to lead merely to a reformulation of the old stratification theory and, ultimately, to the generalization of class into a concept of power theory. In this case the entire debate on civil society carried on by closure theorists, including Murphy himself, would have been in vain: the whole problematics of civil society would be rendered superfluous.

Bryn Jones draws our attention to an interesting paradox in Weber's concept of class. The mode of action typical of classes, he writes, is in conflict with action to attain class advantages (1975, 738). Class action, as economic action, is a form of rational-instrumental action which aims at appropriation through the markets. But when classes are successful in their monopolizing action and exclude others from a certain economic interest activity, they are actually engaged in 'status activity'. This is because class and status pertain, as was already mentioned, to different spheres. The kind of action which is typical of classes is rational-instrumental activity on the markets; status groups are typically engaged in normative, value-oriented activity.

The implications of the problem are clear when we consider the chances of classes to take political action. If political action is always a priori concerned with normative interests, then, by definition, class action cannot, as a form of non-normative, rational action, extend to the sphere of politics. The concept of class cannot be extended into an instrument of political analysis. Weber writes: 'As a separate structure, a political community can be said to exist only if, and in so far as, a community constitutes more than an "economic group"; or, in other words, in so far as it possesses value systems ordering matters other than the directly economic disposition of goods and services' (Weber 1978, 902; Jones 1975, 74).

For Weber, communal relationships are based on a subjective feeling of the parties involved that they belong together. These relationships are the exact counterpart to economic relationships. Class actors cannot, in any sense, be 'communal actors'.

Weber argues that while status positions usually rest on class positions, the former are not solely determined by the latter (Weber 1978, 306). Accordingly, direct inferences cannot be made from class positions to class actions (ibid., 932). Weber draws a distinction between the 'mass behaviour' of separate individuals as a class and amorphous social action, which may also lead to organization. However, he adds that the change from mass behaviour to social action is dependent on the general cultural conditions, especially on 'those of an intellectual sort'; it also depends on the extent of the contrasts that have already evolved and, finally, on *the transparency of the connections between the causes and the consequences of the class situation* (ibid., 929). Weber's idea of the transparency of social relations resembles in certain respects Marx's discussion of the form of consciousness which is characterized by commodity fetishism, but unlike Marx he does not develop this idea into a full analysis based on the form of capitalist social relations.

Jones suggests in his interpretation of Weber that economic action is in fact the exact opposite of real subjective activity, i.e. value-rational activity. Economic action entails non-normative, individual instrumentalism. Inter-subjectivity of a truly meaningful kind, as the essence of social action, is achieved through the human and the spiritual. This means that behind classes, status and collective action, particularly political action, there is a structural antagonism stemming from Weber's basic concepts. This antagonism makes possible the various areas of Weber's discourse and at the same time makes impossible the simultaneous use of the concepts of class and status in a historical and social analysis (Jones 1975, 743-754).

Jones's ideas are interesting. However, while the diagnosis he makes at the general level of the theory of action is correct, the conclusion he draws with regard to class analysis is not. The anomalies arising from Weber's distinction between 'mass behaviour' and social action and the structural antagonism that Jones refers to in the case of Weber's concepts of class and status, are real and serious problems. The former shows that Giddens not only fails to solve the determination problem of class positions, but in fact that as far as the collectivity of classes is concerned, his approach to the problem is wrong. The latter, then, points to the inevitable theoretical break that exists between class position and 'class action'. However, the solution that Jones offers would merely imply sweeping the problem aside. But there would also be another alternative: to build a theory in a process which advances from one level of abstraction and one stage of analysis to the next, accepting that there are inevitable breaks between these different levels and that it is necessary to resort to qualitatively different kinds of theoretical constructs in this process (cf. Luokkaprojekti 1984). Starting from these premises, we can utilize different types of action in the analysis of the forms and intensity of collective action, of the feeling of belonging together. Of course, in this analysis we do not have to psychologize social action, but develop a theory of action that is more systematic than the one proposed by Weber.

The same criticisms we presented against Giddens's class theory are also applicable to the 'combination theorists' that were mentioned earlier. They too fail to solve the determination problem, and also ignore the question of how the individual's work and reproduction situation is affected (structured) by class position — and thus ignore one real possibility of testing the relevance of class theory. When 'market situation' and 'work situation' are taken simultaneously as the basis of class determination (as Abercrombie and Urry do), this already excludes the question of the differential relevance of class position for work and reproduction situations.

Weber's distinction between communal (*Vergemeinschaftung*) and associative (*Vergesellschaftung*) relationships is particularly helpful in studying the chances of action of different organizations. Communal relations rest on a subjective feeling of belonging together, on affectual, emotional or traditional bases: examples are a religious brotherhood, an erotic relationship or a relation of personal loyalty. By contrast, associative relationships are based upon a rationally motivated adjustment of interests or a similarly motivated agreement.

The internal organization of (status) groups may vary from weak to strong social bonds. Weber's theory provides the basis for a three-fold distinction of forms of organization into amorphous, associational or communal (Murphy 1986, 259). The formation of associations on the basis of pre-existing communities is possible only in the case of *communal status groups*. The existing community is in many respects an important resource with which to organize collective action.

Neo-Weberian closure theorists who are working on the elaboration of class theory are in the final analysis concerned to solve the eternal problem of the relationship of structures and action. In the context of class theory, the problem is crystallized in the question of the mutual relationship of positions within the production process and class consciousness and action. Parkin's (1979; 1980) solution is an anti-structuralist collective-action conception of class. He notes that 'the mode of collective action is itself taken to be the defining feature of class' (1979, 68). This means that classes are no longer determined on the basis of a given group's position in the productive process or in the social division of labour, but on the basis of that group's mode of collective action. This is in itself in conflict with the premises of *structural* closure theory, where class is the resultant effect of the particular combination of (1) 'individualist' (credentials, property) and (2) 'collectivist' (race, ethnicity, religion, sex, etc.) structural relationships of exclusion in force in a particular society. As Murphy correctly points out, Parkin is highly inconsistent in adopting both these class conceptions (Murphy 1986, 248).

One of the commonest criticisms against Parkin's class conception is that it fails to advance criteria for evaluating the primacy of one mode of closure and collective action over the other, and also that it offers no basis for the definition of classes (Murphy 1986, 249-250). The latter remark is particularly important. Parkin's collective-action conception of class presupposes an independently defined structure of positions, but he refuses to present any definition of such a structure; in other words, his conception has no theory of class structure to fall back on. From a methodological point of view, Parkin's solution can be criticized at a more general level as well. That is, he confuses the various stages of class analysis (class structure, class situations, class consciousness and action), which means he is incapable of evaluating the relevance of class theory step by step and of discussing the relationships between the theoretical constructs required at the different stages. Finally, the diffuse unity of structure and action in Parkin's collective-action conception of class knocks the bottom out of any attempt at a clear understanding of civil society.

Our attack on Weber's class theory is primarily directed against his notion of class situation, in which he makes the vague assertion that certain actors or groups succeed in monopolizing market resources while others do not. Weber is a market theorist who fails to conceptualize the capitalist form of economic appropriation, the appropriation of surplus value and the class relations that are based on these processes. Weber's theory also gives no clue as to where we should start our study of the processes of control that are related to productive domination; contemporary sociology of work has much more to offer in this respect. These two cornerstones of class research are both absent in Weber's theorizing. The same criticism applies to Weber as a 'theorist of class consciousness': Weber has no theory of forms of consciousness or organization.

One fundamental distinction we have emphasized in our discussion of Weber's class theory is that between class situation and class action; this is an important vantage point for all class research. Perhaps the main contribution of neo-Weberian theories to the ongoing debate on social classes lies accordingly in its analysis of the mechanisms through which class positions are maintained and occupied, and in its analysis of the chances of collective action available to groups and social categories with a different background. Although these analyses have not directly helped us to solve the central problems of class research, they have provided helpful tools for the elaboration of the theory of civil society and for theorizing on the relationship between class structure and civil society.

1.3. Wright's theories of class structure

Erik Olin Wright's theories of class structure represent the Marxist tradition of class theory and centre on *the social relations of production*. Wright attempts to define his position through a critique extending in two directions: he rejects stratification analysis and Weberian class theories on the one hand, and various Marxian class concepts on the other (Wright 1980; Wright et al. 1982, 3-7).

The fundamental flaw in stratification theories, Wright contends, is that they concern themselves with divisions rather than relations. They tend to pigeonhole groups in this or that stratum on the basis of totally arbitrary combinations of criteria, and at the same time they neglect the structuring role of production relations. Weberian theories, then, take market position or power (or authority) relations as the central basis for class differentiation and adopt 'market capacities', together with ownership and possession of the means of production, as their main criteria. However, as Wright correctly points out, domination is not the only relevant dimension in class relations; of equal importance are the relations of appropriation, which at the same time are relations of subordination (Wright et al. 1982, 6). Further, in a critique of the various conceptions of market capacity, Wright argues that knowledge and skills can link up with production relations (relations of control and authority within production) in several different ways. Knowledge and skills do not automatically give control and authority in production, nor can they be sold in the same way as property.

Wright's critique of Marxian class concepts focuses, first, on those overly simplistic theories that define the working class as consisting of all wage workers or blue-collar workers, for example; and second, on the various conceptions of the 'new petty bourgeoisie', particularly the ideas presented by Poulantzas in *Classes in Contemporary Capitalism* (1976). A closer comparison of Wright's and Poulantzas's theories follows later. Wright also rejects those theories that define contradictory class locations on the basis of functional criteria, notably the conception of Carchedi (1977). We revert to Carchedi's theory and especially his ideas about the class position of the 'new middle class' in our discussion of the internal differentiation of wage workers.

Wright is a representative of the French/Anglo-Saxon class debate, which has developed completely independently of the West German debate. We shall not yet go into a detailed comparison of these two mainstreams, but it is useful to note that there are significant differences between Wright's theory and the work of Projekt Klassenanalyse, for instance. PKA draws upon straightforward derivation and on economic form determinants, which means that it has great difficulty in analysing contradictory class locations. IMSF, in turn, refers to the 'commodity nature of labour power' and — unlike Wright whose argument leads to distinctions between contradictory wage-worker locations — emphasizes the distinctions between the core and periphery of the working class.

Wright sets out in his theorizing from the relations of appropriation prevailing in production, which *at the same time* are relations of domination. He also takes into account the separation of economic ownership and possession in modern capitalism, as well as the functional differentiation of complex hierarchies within capitalist enterprises. Thirdly, a central starting-point in Wright's theory is the existence of different modes of production (capitalist commodity production and simple commodity production). The latter means that the contradictory class locations within production also differ from each other in qualitative terms and that the interpenetration of various modes of production constitutes an essential problem (Wright et al. 1982, 9).

According to Wright, there are three kinds of locations within class relations: (1) basic class locations, (2) contradictory locations within a mode of production and (3) contradictory locations between modes of production.

Basic and contradictory class locations can be determined on the basis of the *structural relations of domination and subordination prevailing in production*. These, in turn, can be specified according to the matter or resource controlled. The bourgeoisie controls (1) the flow of investments and the process of capital accumulation, (2) the physical means of production and (3) labour power. The first of these dimensions is to do with *economic ownership* (control over surplus value), while the two latter are forms of *economic possession* (control over capital and variable capital). Whereas the bourgeoisie has control over all these three resources, the working class is excluded from control of all three resources. The wage-earner groups (from top managers to supervisors) located in-between the bourgeoisie and the working class have control over these resources to varying degrees. It must be noted at this point that these various dimensions of control are not equal in value: control over money capital gives control over physical capital, which in turn gives control over labour power.

There are many problems with describing the class relationship between the bourgeoisie and managers on the basis of the distinction between economic ownership and possession. Firstly, the mechanisms of exploitation and domination are combined in this relationship and, secondly, ownership of the means of production and the functions of capital do not necessarily coincide (cf. Carchedi 1983). Ownership itself has become increasingly depersonalized (Cottler 1984). It has also been argued that in the case of the problem of managerialism, the legal conditions of economic activity have not received sufficient attention (Jonston 1986, 38).

The petty bourgeoisie, Wright continues, is defined by control of the physical means of production and control of investments within simple commodity production. Small employers occupy a contradictory location between the bourgeoisie and the petty bourgeoisie. Semi-autonomous employees, for their part, occupy a contradictory location between the working class and the petty bourgeoisie and, like the working class, they are excluded from control of the three main dimensions of resources. However, in contrast to the working class, they have a high degree of control over their labour process. Table 1.1. presents in summary fashion Wright's class structure typology.

The following critique of Wright's theory, which concentrates on the problems and shortcomings which affect his analysis of the class structure, will necessarily be brief and schematic. However, it should be sufficiently detailed to provide a basis for our later comparisons of Wright's position with the work of other Marxist theorists. We single out eight different types of problems:

(1) The qualitative differences between contradictory class locations. The relationship between the capitalist mode of production and simple commodity production is particularly problematic. Wright proposes that the petty bourgeoisie is a basic class alongside the bourgeoisie and the working class; but surely the position of the petty bourgeoisie (in the same way as that of small employers) is largely determined by the specific relations of subordination and dependence of the capitalist mode of production. In any case these relations of dependence should be taken under careful empirical scrutiny. Additionally, we argue that it is misleading to equate control over the labour process with other dimensions of

Table 1.1.
Wright's typology of class structure

TYPE OF CLASS LOCATION	CLASS LOCATION	Capitalist mode of production				Simple commodity production	
		Ownership relation	Exchange relation	Real exercise of effective property	Authority relations	Ownership relations	Domination relations
Basic class	BOURGEOISIE	Owns means of production	Buys labour power	Makes core decisions over allocation of resources and use of means of production	Directly controls the authority hierarchy		
Contradictory location within capitalist mode of production	MANAGERS	Does not own means of production	Sells labour power	Directly involved in at least some core decisions	Dominant and subordinate		
	SUPERVISORS	•	•	Excluded from all decisions over the workplace	Dominant and subordinate		
Basic class	WORKING CLASS	•	•	•	Subordinate		
Contradictory location between capitalist production and simple commodity production	SEMI-AUTONOMOUS EMPLOYEES					Non-owner of means of production	Substantial direction within the labour process (unity of conception and execution)
Basic class	PETTY BOURGEOISIE					Owns means of production and directly uses them without employing labour power	Complete self-direction within the labour process
Contradictory location between capitalist and simple commodity production	SMALL EMPLOYERS	Owns means of production	Buys limited amounts of labour power	Makes core decisions	Controls authority structure	Owns means of production and directly uses them within the labour process and hires some wage labour	

26

control and authority in production. Wright applies the criterion of control over the labour process to define the group of semi-autonomous employees, yet this is contradictory with his original intention of determining class locations within the general context of the relations of production. Moreover, the group of semi-autonomous employees is in itself rather heterogeneous. Autonomy may be both a 'petit-bourgeois remnant' and 'new autonomy' produced by capitalist development and the enlarged role of the state in society.

(2) There are major shortcomings in Wright's analysis of state employees. In his earlier production Wright argued that state bureaucracy can be identified with capitalist production (Wright 1978, 94-96), but later he has suggested that the state could be treated as a specific form of production relations (Wright et al. 1982, 10). However, it would seem that a relevant class analysis of state employees should take into consideration at least their specific form of income; the nature of their functions as compared with other wage-earner groups; the different position of various state employee groups in organizational hierarchies; and those structuring characteristics of their position which they share with other wage-worker groups. On the whole, the greatest merit of Wright's conception in this context is that it makes possible a class analysis of the relationships prevailing within the state and other organizations. On the other hand, Wright fails to produce a detailed analysis of statehood and the related conflicts of interest. These should be examined before proceeding to an analysis of relations of domination within organizations.

(3) Wright does not consider the special position of the agricultural population vis-à-vis the rest of the petty bourgeoisie, nor does he analyse the internal differentiation of this class group. Furthermore, Wright omits to discuss the forms of vertical and horizontal integration in agriculture; this also applies to his analysis of other petty-bourgeois positions and small employers.

(4) There is no analysis in Wright's work of the ways in which different working-class groups (industrial workers, workers in sales and services, state employees) are subordinated to capital; such an analysis would be particularly useful in the case of those modes of subordination that are not reflected in differences in job autonomy. It follows that Wright is unable to describe the internal differentiation of the working class, which we consider a serious shortcoming.

(5) There are also difficulties in Wright's analysis of the economically non-active population. Wright starts out from the presumption that these groups

(housewives, students, the unemployed, pensioners) occupy a position which, in terms of class content, is mediated. However, he fails to bring this idea to a satisfactory conclusion, ignoring, for instance, the stability of the class positions of these groups and the differences in their degrees of wage-worker socialization.

(6) Although Wright attempts to move towards an historical concept, he still offers a very static description of class relations. His theory has nothing to say about the internal differentiation of the working class; about the proletarianization and dequalification of the 'new middle class' (cf. Carchedi); or about how these tendencies are related to the (economic and political) developments of the capitalist system.[16]

(7) Wright starts from the assumption that relations of domination and subordination are also, at the same time, relations of appropriation. However, it remains unclear exactly how exploitation and domination are interrelated. Ownership of the means of production and the sale of labour power are essentially different kinds of criteria than control and authority on the job. On the basis of the former we can distinguish between the bourgeoisie, the petty bourgeoisie and wage workers, but not describe the internal differentiation of wage workers. For this latter purpose, Wright resorts to criteria of relations of domination. Every wage worker is subject to the domination of the owner of the means of production, but as a result of the differentiation of the functions of capital certain wage earners (hired managers and supervisors) gain control over specific aspects of production and over the use of other workers' labour power.

If Wright's division according to authority positions is assumed to form a 'hierarchic continuum' of contradictory class locations running from the bourgeoisie to the working class, then are we also to assume that it forms a 'continuum of exploitation'? This is hardly an acceptable proposition. Although in empirical research we will probably have to operate with relative indicators, the only relevant criterion in the case of exploitation is qualitative, i.e. the production of surplus value and its (non-equivalent) appropriation — a criterion that is meaningful only in the case of top managers. If the hierarchy of authority is thought to be related to the differentiation of the functions of capital from those of the collective worker, then it is *wrong to assume that there is a linear correspondence between hierarchic and exploitative positions*. Nonetheless, it is important to examine the extent of such correspondence.

(8) Finally, we feel that Wright's *class-determined concept of interest* is far too simplistic. Certain class groups, he posits, have a 'fundamental interest' in

28

socialism, others do not. The concept of interest as a mediating category between class position and class consciousness and action is no doubt useful, but it has to be based upon an analysis of the structuration of class situation, proletarianization, the discursive articulation of interests, etc.

In his recent auto-critique Wright (1985) has discarded his previous concept of the role of historical processes in the formation of capitalist class relations, and also dissociated himself from Braverman. He abandons autonomy as a criterion for class determination in favour of the concept of exploitation; even the relations of domination, which were central to his earlier argumentation, are now linked up with different forms of exploitation. Wright's new theory revolves around three forms of exploitation and three different kinds of assets: capital, organizational and credential assets.

The foundations for Wright's new endeavours are provided by John E. Roemer's theory of exploitation as a causal relationship between different types of social actors and governed by the laws of game theory. Wright modifies and elaborates Roemer's notions about exploitation to produce a more rigorous basis for the concept of contradictory class locations.

According to Roemer (1982, 194-195), a particular coalition of players (S) can be said to exploited if the following conditions hold: (1) There is an alternative, which we may conceive as hypothetically feasible, in which S would be better off than in its present situation. (2) Under this alternative, the complement of S, the coalition S', would be worse off than at present.

Roemer says that in order to understand exploitation, we must first see which alternative game goes together with this or that mode of production. In the case of feudalism the withdrawal rule might be that the player leaves the game with his personal assets rather than with his per capita share of the total assets. The peasants would therefore be better off when freed from all obligations of personal bondage; conversely, the feudal lords would be worse off. This kind of withdrawal rule cannot be applied to capitalism because the workers would be worse off if they withdrew from the game with only their personal assets. In the alternative game for socialist exploitation each player would receive his per capita share of inalienable assets. A certain coalition of players would be characterized as socialistically exploited if it could improve its position by withdrawing from the game with its per capital skills, leaving its complement worse off.

Wright, however, argues that the nature of existing socialist societies cannot be explained on the basis of skill exploitation. In capitalism the organizational resources of individual firms are controlled by managers, whereas in state socialism the control of organizational resources has more far-reaching consequences: responsibility lies not with individual company managers, but with the centralized planning instances within the state apparatus. This means that the material basis of class relations and exploitation is determined by the control of organizational resources.

In capitalism this basis is determined by exploitation that derives from the unequal ownership of the means of production. In addition, there are exploitation relations that are based on organizational position and occupational skill. Wage workers occupying contradictory class locations do not own the means of production, but on the strength of their position in the organization or their credential assets, they participate to varying degrees in these secondary forms of exploitation.

In the new theory that Wright has built upon these premises, managers and supervisors occupy the same position they had in the old one. However, Wright also introduces new distinctions within these groups on the basis of their involvement in exploitation through credential assets. There are two additional groups which only participate in the latter kind of exploitation, i.e. experts and semi-credentialled workers.

As far as we can see Wright's reformulated theory is a step backwards when compared with the old one (see also Carchedi 1986; Offe 1986; Rose and Marshall 1986; for an overall critique of the class theory of 'analytical Marxism', see Blom and Kivinen 1989). Firstly, while in his old theory Wright attempted to move away from the form determinants of work towards an historical concept of capitalism by analysing the relations of domination prevailing in production, in this newer version the class relations of capitalism are emptied of all historical content and the changes in the forms of work organization within capitalism are reduced to mere relationships between different modes of production. This means that class relations are no longer perceived as processes.

Secondly, the concept of exploitation with which Wright operates is narrowly based upon the relationships prevailing in the distribution of products, obscuring from view the relationships prevailing in production (Carchedi 1986, 198-204); this applies particularly to decision-making authority, control and autonomy on the job. Wright's critique of capitalism therefore boils down into a critique of distribution relations. At the level of concrete research, this means that Wright cannot even set the question of how the repression involved in class relations is reflected in the structuration of class situation. At the same time, the idea of privileged wage-worker groups becomes far too simplistic. Wright fails to recognize that there are certain marginal groups of the new middle class (such as craftsmen and careworkers) who have no privileges whatsoever on any dimension of exploitation but whose work situation and content of work differs in essential respects from those of the working class proper.

Finally, the rejection of autonomy as a class criterion in favour of credential assets means that Braverman's problematique concerning the degradation of work within capitalism is replaced by a theory of socialist exploitation. However, if the aim is to build a theory of the development of skills within capitalism, the problems will be precisely the same as when autonomy was in focus: the forms and strategies of organizing work. 'Exploitation based on occupational skill', for instance, cannot be defined without a careful analysis of the power resources and strategies used at the level of the work process.

1.4. The scope logic approach to class analysis

We have seen in the foregoing that there are many different approaches to class research and different views on the levels and concepts that need to be incorporated in an adequate class theory.[17] All the clues contained in the relevant theoretical debates can obviously not be followed up in one single work, but at least we have made it clear that a class reductionist approach to the formation of social forces is not tenable. The analysis of the conditions of and obstacles to the constitution of classes into active subjects must be based on concrete class research. We may further conclude that neither the *discourse-theoretical, the neo-Weberian nor the class-deterministic approach provide a sufficiently rigid basis for class theory*. Instead, the aim in class research should be to uncover the interdependence of class location and other social determinants of subjects, as well as their relationship to consciousness and organizations constituted in hegemonic struggles.

In the following table we outline the scheme which has served as our theoretical guide throughout the project: we call our research strategy the *scope logic approach* to class analysis. Three points are evident in the scheme: (1) the dependence of each level of analysis on the problems and concepts formulated at the previous level (also, we have included in our scheme those aspects of the problems of collectivity and class consciousness which may be thematized at

Table 1.2.

Levels and scope of class analysis

Problem field	Specific problems	Prerequisite analysis	Description	Thematization of collectivity	Thematization of class consciousness
CLASS STRUCTURE	* character and relationships between classes and class groups; the criteria of class boundaries * social composition and homogeneity of classes * class mobility	* historical development (and concept) of class society * structural basis of class constitution ("theory of capitalism")	* qualitative differences and relationships between classes * (quantitative) analysis of class structure, class mobility and changes in class structure * social composition of classes	* structural tendencies towards individualization * compatibility or contradictions between objective relations (interests) of different classes and class groups	* analysis of possible bearers of class consciousness
CLASS SITUATION	* determination and structure of class situation	* basis of class constitution, especially the structuration of class situation	* development of main characteristics of class situation * internal contradictions of class situation	* spontaneous collectivity arising from common problems in class situation and based on close social relations (subcultures) * preconditions created by class situation for higher level of social participation	* preconditions of (class) consciousness, their relationship to objective class situation
CLASS EXPERIENCES & CLASS CONSCIOUSNESS	* determination and structure of consciousness * the problem of capitalism-affirmative vs anti-capitalist consciousness	* forms of consciousness within capitalism * determinants and mediations of consciousness	* experience and consciousness profile of wage workers, its internal contradictions * description of the modes and limits to the formation of capitalism-affirmative (vs anti-capitalist) consciousness mediated/produced by character mask (as a form of subsumption)	* role of average wage-worker consciousness carried by individuals as a subjective mediation of collectivity	* worker consciousness as average individual consciousness * relationship between anti-capitalist consciousness and class consciousness

COLLECTIVE INTEREST ORGANIZATION	* main forms of organization and their structural genetic basis * interest organizations as collective actors with their own goals * interest organizations as apparatuses with an institutional structure and as structures mediating between members' needs and the apparatus and the problems of interest selection and corporatism	* structural genesis and forms of interest organization within capitalism * structural and historical basis and preconditions for the development of interest organizations into independent apparatuses	* presentation of the relationship between non-state political organization and organization through associations, the historical development of their genetic basis and institutional structure * description of structure and development of affiliation to organizations on the basis of class and social structure categories	* forms of collectivity based on mediated interest articulation * problems related to the relationships between "interest articulation at basic level"—"forms of organization as apparatuses"—"publicity/the state"; from the point of view of the formation of collectivity * intensification or weakening of unity and forms of collectivity based on class situation as a result of organization in associations	* class consciousness as a complex entity of average individual consciousness and (class-based) organization * role of institutional practices and related collective learning processes as effective preconditions for worker/class consciousness
CLASSES AND THE STATE	* form of the bourgeois state * the state (and political organization) as an apparatus (organizing interest articulation and class relations) with an institutional structure * formation and reproduction of political power elites, their balance and hegemonic relationships	* reproduction\transformation of precapitalist political forms (institutions, practices) * solution to the relationship between the critique of political economy and the theoretical construct which regards the state as a field of class struggle and organizing class relations	* theory of "the state as state" and as hegemonic apparatus * presentation of the state as an apparatus which organizes class relations and as a field of political groups at the different stages of capitalist development	* the state and formal general interest as social collectivity * relationship between subjects thematized by "economic" classes and forms of collectivity of different levels of interest articulation and unity based on changing balance of power between hegemonic groups	* role of state fetishism in the formation of (mystified) worker consciousness * role of state interest articulation and organization of class relations as effective preconditions for consciousness

different levels); (2) the applicability of different theoretical constructs to the various levels of class theory (particularly the limits of the critique of political economy); and (3) the method of theoretical presentation adopted in our study. Between the different levels of class analysis, we encounter various problems and breaks: the most significant of these appear in the transition from class position to class consciousness and from class consciousness to the analysis of classes (as societal forces) and the state. The problems of mediation will be discussed in more depth under the respective sections and summarized in the last chapters of this book.

Scope logic has significant methodological and conceptual implications. First of all, it means that a synthesis is required of *all* preceding levels of analysis before we can proceed to the next level. That is, in attempting to determine the relevance of class theory, we must start with an analysis of class structure and then move on to the structuration of class situation; a synthesis of these levels will take us to the analysis of consciousness and organization; finally, following a synthesis of the previous levels, we can proceed to the relationship between classes and the formation of social forces. In other words, we cannot jump directly from a study of class structure to class action; the structuration of class situation and the question of organization and consciousness are important mediating levels.

In the study of class structure, we must start by determining the class structure and class locations and then proceed to an analysis of class and reproduction situation. At this first level of analysis, we are particularly interested in whether class situation (which finds expression in work situation, reproduction situation, and in the relationship between work and out-of-work time) is structured by class location.

At the next level of analysis, our concern is with the consciousness and organization of classes. Here we will need additional mediations. Therefore the transition from one level of class analysis to another may also be described as a theoretical break. Consciousness and organization are not directly determined by class location, and it will also prove necessary to employ the concepts of more than one theory.

At the final level of analysis the aim is to describe the relationship between classes and the state and the formation of social forces and hegemonic projects. This level represents a synthesis of syntheses, and also the highest level of class research. Here, we deal with such questions as political and institutional relationships and structures; the relationship of classes and the structuration of civil society in the formation of social forces and subjects; and short and long-term conjunctures, where economic policy serves as a mediating factor.

In the figure below we present a schematic illustration of our idea of proceeding via mediating syntheses through the different levels of class analysis.

Given these methodological premises, we will also have to compare and test the relevance of different class theories at these different levels, because the divisions suggested in a certain theory may prove relevant at one level but not at another. For example, neo-Weberian theories start out from class situation without considering how it is structured by the work and reproduction situation of a given class location. On the other hand, Wright's assumption that class consciousness ('interest in socialism') can be directly inferred from class location is hardly tenable: consciousness is always mediated by collective organization and commitments to political action. These mediations cannot be uncovered through

Figure 1.1.
Levels and mediating syntheses of class analysis

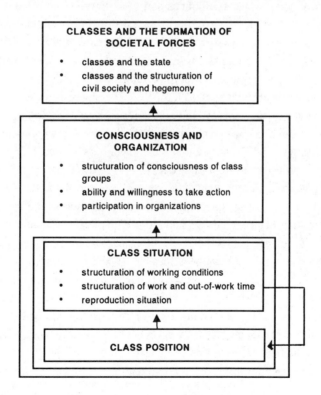

empirical analyses, but only through theoretical work based upon a theory of the state and a theory of collective action. In the comparison of different class theories we do of course need empirical analyses to test their consequences, but nonetheless theoretical work plays the most important part in assessing class theories, their limits, their logic and their relationship to social theory in general.

1.5. Problems of empirical research

The empirical analyses that follow are based upon the survey method, but at the same time they are guided by the scope logic approach outlined in the foregoing. In this final section of Chapter 1, we shall discuss the main advantages and drawbacks of the survey method as well as the empirical implications of our theoretical framework.

In any social scientific study the choice of method is ultimately determined by the objectives of the study and by the wider setting within which it is placed. The present study was carried out as part of an international comparative project on class structure and class consciousness, the aim of which was to produce comparisons between a large number of different countries. It was therefore necessary to use a method that would make such comparisons possible — and to accept the various limitations that followed from this choice.

The survey method was chosen for the following reasons. In comparison with qualitative methods, a survey study does not have to be restricted to one area or to certain social groups or communities. This means we can ensure a representative sample, which is essential when the aim is to draw a detailed picture of the class structure and to compare these across different countries. The same advantages are apparent in quantitative analyses and international comparisons of occupational groups, generational mobility, membership of social organizations, etc. Also, the project's decision to use identical questionnaires to study and compare dominance and authority in different class locations meant that qualitative methods would not have been feasible. In addition to representativeness and comparability, a further advantage of the survey method is that it is far more economical than other methods when extensive data have to be collected and investigated. Finally, in comparison with studies drawing on official statistics, which utilize such categories as 'workers', 'functionaries' and 'civil servants' to determine the boundaries of classes and class groups and which thus fail to analyse relationships of appropriation and domination, for example, the survey method has the advantage that it allows us to conduct our research within a rigid theoretical framework, to follow a set of thought-out theoretical guidelines.

There are of course also certain drawbacks. Firstly, the survey method is not historical; it excludes the possibility of doing qualitative research into culture and consciousness; and it also means we cannot use the biographical approach. Strictly speaking, the first of these limitations is not quite true in the sense that we can of course include retrospective questions concerning mobility between and within generations, for instance. In the present study, however, we have solved the problem differently. We have resorted to existing historical analyses of structural changes in society and conducted separate analyses using statistics and other similar sources on the development of the Finnish class structure and political organization during the present century (Kerkelä 1982).

Our study is also not biographical, although it does contain certain data on each interviewee's (working) life history. However, a proper biographical study should also include many other sorts of data, particularly on important turning-points in the individual's life and on their relative subjective significance. On the other hand, it remains unclear whether biographical sociology should be preoc- cupied with *individual* biographies in the first place, or whether emphasis should be given to typical life histories at the societal level (Osterland 1983).

The use of qualitative methods in the study of culture, consciousness or way of life would have certain important advantages over the survey method, although in the present context of class research these tend to be limited to the analysis of consciousness. In a qualitative study we do not have to restrict our questions to certain aspects of experience, and we can also obtain data on the subjective importance and the intertwining of different elements of experience; these may turn out to be at sharp variance with the researcher's preconceptions. On the other hand, it must be emphasized that — unlike ethnomethodologists and many others like to believe — the use of qualitative methods cannot replace theoretical reflection. During our project we carried out an experiment to determine the 'validity' the 'wage worker's experience profile' which we drew up on the basis of the answers we received to the questions concerning experience and conscious- ness: we compared this profile with the results of qualitative interviews carried out with a sample of wage workers from the Tampere region.

One of the commonest criticisms against the survey method is that it tends to 'objectivate' its subjects. However, this same criticism also applies to qualitative methods and even to action research — which, incidentally, should not be equated with research aiming to achieve social change, in that it is typically restricted to specific groups and communities. In principle, both survey studies and action research may or may not advance certain goals that are valued in society.

The limitations of the survey method are more apparent at certain levels of class analysis than at others. In the case of class location, occupational position (including work history) and organization, the method produces rather reliable data, but in the analysis of consciousness and subjective meanings in general there are serious validity and reliability problems. The formulation of good questions obviously becomes more and more difficult the further away we move from the respondent's immediate experience, and therefore open-ended questions rather than precoded answers are favoured in this department.

These difficulties led us to use a great deal of secondary sources in the analysis of organization and consciousness. This is particularly true of our attempts to explain political activity and alienation against the background of the structure of political organization in society.

We now move on to consider the question as to whether class research using the survey method has anything to learn from qualitative culture studies. On the whole it seems that the role of the cultural has varied significantly in different qualitative studies on the way of life and consciousness of the working class. In a perceptive evaluation of these studies, especially the study by Zoll (1981) on workers' experiences of economic crisis, Mahnkopf (1982) make some useful and interesting comments.

Zoll was concerned in his study with metal workers' awareness of economic crisis and with the obstacles to forming a realistic picture of the crisis situation. He concluded that that picture was far from realistic and described the dominant type of awareness or consciousness as reductionistic. The realistic type, according to Zoll's criteria, was represented by the worker who placed the crisis in historical perspective, evaluated it against a general social theory and seriously weighed its consequences; the unrealistic or reductionistic type was characterized by complete denial of the crisis, a tendency to view the different crisis phenomena as isolated problems and individual strategies of adaptation for reducing anxiety.

Mahnkopf criticizes this kind of approach on two accounts. Firstly, in a direct comparison of workers' consciousness with a theoretical concept of crisis, it is impossible to uncover the materialistic basis of what Zoll calls a 'reductionistic consciousness of crisis'. Secondly, Zoll proceeds too hastily to a discussion of the intrapsychic mechanisms of dealing with the contradictions caused by the crisis.

38

According to Mahnkopf, these critical shortcomings mean that Zoll's work does not qualify as a genuine cultural study, which should contain an analysis of both the materialistic basis and the mediations of consciousness. A basic difficulty with Zoll's approach is that it leads to ignoring the group-specific mediating mechanisms which may be essential for the cultural. The psychic mechanisms through which crisis consciousness is suppressed are real, but on that basis it is not possible to develop any kind of action strategy (e.g. trade union activism).

Mahnkopf holds that studies of the cultural are particularly significant in attempts to describe the internal structural differentiation of wage workers and in investigating the mechanisms through which wage-worker groups distinguish themselves from each other. He illustrates the point by referring to the tendency for the distinction between manual labourers and (lower) white-collar employees to remain more or less unchanged even though the difference between the shopfloor and the office is growing smaller: the emphasis tends to be on the differences in group identity rather than on factual changes in working conditions. A significant factor behind this tendency, Mahnkopf argues, is the conservative craftsman's attitude towards all worker groups who do not do 'honest, hard work': women, young people, the elderly, immigrant workers and other marginal groups. With the increasing segmentation of the labour market, the employer can further enhance this distinction by a personnel policy which marginalizes low-performance and militant workers and which strengthens the group identity of craftsmen.

Mahnkopf's main argument is that crisis experiences acquire their relevance to action and experience only through the process in which group-specific meanings emerge (ibid., 58). These process, Mahnkopf says, represent *quasi-objective lines of internal class differentiation*. The significance of these processes lies in their quasi-objectivity, their real existence as lines of demarcation distinguishing the experience and consciousness of different worker groups. The psychic mechanisms involved, Mahnkopf writes, are 'not so much to do with individual psychic moulding of reality than with a collective self-understanding of specific proletarian milieux' (ibid., 59).

It is clear that the latter emphasis in particular restricts the scope of the survey study concerned to investigate the cultural. On the other hand, the strategy proposed by Mahnkopf would seem to be particularly well-suited to studying the internal homogeneity of the working class. By definition, a survey study cannot set out from the methodological assumption that culture is local or restricted to a certain social group, nor can it concentrate on the group-specific processes of experience-moulding. In these two important respects, a survey study cannot represent a genuine cultural study. There are, however, some important lessons it can learn of this understanding of studies on culture and consciousness: above all, it can learn a new method of studying the formation and mediation of class determinants and other structural determinants (gender, generation, age groups, educational and ideological identification, etc.) related to the practices of civil society. This will draw attention to the connection between the structuration of class location and other 'boundary lines' within civil society. On the other hand, this understanding of cultural studies can also instruct a survey on worker consciousness to emphasize the *connections between experience and action, or the relevance of the former to the latter*. As well as analysing the 'images of society' embedded in worker consciousness, we must also concern ourselves with such questions as collectivity, solidarity, willingness to take action and organization.

Finally, there have been some warnings that social scientists may have an 'overly integrative' conception of worker experience and consciousness. Insofar as worker experience and (moral) consciousness do not appear in a systematically articulated form but rather as a confused feeling of injustice, it may prove difficult for the social scientist to grasp the meaning and implications of this resistance (Honneth 1981; cf. Moore 1978). This argument is consistent with the position of many cultural researchers; it emphasizes the need to take into account the *specific form of existence* of worker consciousness and experience, and to beware of the risk of postulating a satisfied worker on insufficient evidence.

To sum up, we have seen that the representative samples required in an extensive international comparison of classes and class groups can only be collected by using the survey method. This applies to all levels of class analysis, although additional material can of course also be gathered as appropriate. The secondary sources that we have used in the present study include historical statistics, the results of earlier empirical research and an experiment of our own based on qualitative interviews. In the context of class research, the limitations caused by the tendency of the survey method to 'objectivate' its subjects are particularly problematic in the analysis of consciousness; therefore our analysis at this level is perhaps more exploratory than at any other level. Of course, it would have been possible to utilize other methods and sources, especially qualitative ones, to a much greater extent than we have now — but only at the cost of representativity.

40

2 The Finnish class structure: Empirical and theoretical comparisons

Since the dawn of capitalism and the capitalist mode of production, the class structures of advanced industrial societies have been in a continuous state of flux. The two main trends have been the increase in numbers engaged in wage employment and the decrease in the number of entrepreneurs, particularly farmers. These developments, of course, reflect the major changes that have taken place over the past few decades in the structure of production within capitalist society.

In this chapter we shall first examine the class structure of contemporary Finnish society through a comparison with two other advanced capitalist societies, namely Sweden and the United States. We then move on to discuss the class criteria of occupation, authority and autonomy. Following these empirical examinations, we proceed to compare the theories of Poulantzas and PKA and their power in explaining the Finnish class structure. Finally, we recapitulate the lessons learned from these comparisons.

2.1. The class structures of Finland, Sweden and the USA

Finland has been an agrarian society for the best part of the present century. After World War II, almost half of the country's labour force still earned their living from agriculture, which has traditionally been carried on by peasant farmers rather than capitalist entrepreneurs. From the mid-1940s onwards, however, the Finnish industrial structure began to change very rapidly. This is evident in a comparison with certain other European countries (Table 2.1.).

Table 2.1.

Employment in forestry/agriculture and industry/ construction in seven European countries from 1910 to 1960: per cent of gainfully employed population

	1910	1920	1930	1940	1950	1960
Forestry and agriculture						
Britain	9('11)	7('21)	6('31)	-	5('51)	4('61)
Netherlands	28	24	21	-	19	11
Sweden	46	41	36	-	20	14
Norway	40	37	35	-	26	20
Finland	70	70	66	60	46	35
Portugal	57('11)	-	51	49	48	43
Greece	-	50	54('28)	-	48('51)	55('61)
Industry and construction						
	1910	1920	1930	1940	1950	1960
Britain	52('11)	48('21)	46('31)	-	49('51)	51('61)
Netherlands	33('09)	36	36	-	37	42
Sweden	26	31	32	-	41	45
Norway	26	29	27	-	36	37
Finland	10	12	13	16	28	32
Portugal	22('11)	-	17	21	25	27
Greece	-	16	16('28)	-	19('51)	20('61)

These statistics suggest that capitalism arrived in Finland at a much later stage than in many other European countries. On this basis it would seem legitimate to classify Finland in the same category as those countries of eastern and southern Europe which are considered to represent an economic periphery of the European continent. This conclusion is supported not only by the late development of the country's industrial structure, but also by certain features in its economic development: for example, large numbers have emigrated from Finland to more industrialized countries in search of a job. On the other hand, there are certain economic indicators which clearly contradict the idea of backwardness; statistics on national product per capita for 1960 are a good example.

Table 2.2.

National product per capita in seven European countries in 1960 (USD)

Sweden	1678
Britain	1262
Norway	1093
Finland	1001
Netherlands	890
Greece	410
Portugal	260

This contradiction between what clearly represents a backward industrial structure and a fairly high level of economic development has its background in the special features of the Finnish case of capitalist development. A central role in this process has been played by the country's forest industry, which traditionally accounts for a major part of total Finnish exports. The agrarian population has depended on the forest industry for a large part of its income. Up until the 1960s large numbers of farmers and other workers in the rural areas were employed on a part-time basis, especially during the winter months, by the leading export companies in the seasonal work of timber acquisition. Therefore official statistics on the size of the industrial population do not tell whole truth: the substratum of industrial labour power and the basis for the valorization process has been much broader than is suggested by a purely statistical analysis. What is more, a large part of the forest land has actually been owned by peasant farmers who have earned considerable extra income by the sale of timber. It is clear then that the Finnish agricultural population of the twentieth century is not directly comparable to the corresponding categories of other European peripheries. Finland's political position within the international community was also altered rather dramatically after World War II, when it became the first capitalist country to pursue a policy of friendship and mutual cooperation in its relations with the Soviet Union. At the same time, the heavy war reparations that were imposed on Finland led to significant structural changes in the country's international trade. Up until World War II the growth of the Finnish national economy had been essentially based on exports of paper and pulp, but now the country was forced to concentrate on building up a metal and engineering industry to meet the indemnity schedules. This of course diversified the country's industrial capacity, but nonetheless the total number of products exported and particularly their degree of conversion has traditionally been lower than in other small European countries. Today, the Finnish economy is as dependent on its exports as ever.

In international comparison, the structural changes that took place in Finland were indeed extremely violent. Statistics for the period 1960-1977 show that the size of the agricultural population declined in Finland by 23.5 % as compared with an average 11 % in all OECD countries. On the other hand, while the figure describing numbers employed in services and capital circulation increased by 20.5 % in Finland, the average for all OECD countries was 12 % (Alestalo 1980, 15). When we further take into account the simultaneous growth in public and private services, we may conclude that, over the past few decades, wage workers have represented the fastest-growing category in the Finnish class structure.[1]

As we just noted, almost half of Finland's labour force earned their living from agriculture as late as 1950. In fact the numbers employed in agriculture and forestry continued to grow until the early 1960s, although in relative terms the proportion of the agricultural population was already declining. Thus the label of 'industrial society' is not really applicable to Finland until the 1960s and 1970s. And since then, the movement towards a service society has been extremely rapid.

The rapid development of the production forces has adversely affected the economic position of farmers. At the same time, state agricultural policy has aimed to solve the problem of overproduction by means of rationalization, which has meant a sharp decline in the number of small farms since the 1960s and a minor increase in the number of larger units. Nonetheless, at the beginning of the 1980s small holdings were still in the majority.

These changes in the economic structure have also caused certain changes in the social structure. In the context of class theory, the question of social mobility is particularly important when we are concerned with historical developments. In the Nordic countries the typical pattern of mobility shows that the children of farmers have first become blue-collar workers, and the children of blue-collar workers have then become white-collar workers. In Finland, people with an agrarian background have often moved upwards directly to white-collar positions. On the whole social mobility among the age groups born during the twentieth century has been extremely rapid in Finland (Table 2.3).

Only 13 % of our respondents had not experienced any form of inter- or intragenerational mobility. Within the remaining majority, we can distinguish

Table 2.3.
Social mobility in Finland in the twentieth century (based on Wright's class criteria)

Unchanged	13 %
Intergenerational mobility	33 %
Career mobility	12 %
Intergenerational mobility + up 1 social class	30 %
Intergenerational mobility + up 2 social classes	12 %
Total	100 %

between two dominant patterns of social mobility. First, there is the traditional type of intergenerational mobility where the individual moves up in relation to the position of his or her parents; in the Finnish case this has typically meant moving up from an agrarian position to a white-collar position. In the second main type of mobility, the individual moves an additional step upwards in relation to his or her former social position. The typical case in Finland is the person of agrarian origins who has first moved to a blue-collar position and later, during his or her working life, to a white-collar position.

The high rate of social mobility in Finland also means that, with the exception of the peasantry, the social groupings of today have been recruited from many different classes. In the social group of peasants more than 90 % have an agrarian background, whereas among industrial workers, for instance, the rate of self-recruitment is only 30 %; among managerial wage earners it is 22 %; and among workers in the service sector 5 %.

By the early 1980s, it would seem that these violent changes that have been going on for the past 20 years or so have now come to an end. The young people who are now entering the labour market represent second-generation wage workers, in the real sense of the word.

Table 2.4. shows the distribution of the Finnish economically active population into different class groups on the basis of data collected in 1981.[2] The largest group is the working class, representing 46—62 %. The former figure is based on the 'narrow' working class concept, the latter also includes semi-autonomous employees and supervisors. The bourgeoisie accounts for 3—13 % of the gainfully employed population. Here, the former figure includes top managers, while the latter also includes all managers and small employers. Finally, it may be noted that wage workers occupying contradictory locations represent 16—32 %. The lower percentage includes all class groups located between the bourgeoisie and the proletariat with the exception of foreman positions, the latter also covers supervisors and semi-autonomous employees.

The comparison presented in Table 2.5. shows that there are significant differences between the Finnish, Swedish and US class structures.[3] In Finland the petty bourgeoisie (farmers) is a much larger class group than in Sweden and the USA. The proportion of managerial and supervisory positions, in turn, is significantly higher in the USA than in Finland and Sweden. Third, because of the large number of women employed in the state reproduction sector, Sweden has by far the highest proportion of semi-autonomous employees. Sweden also has

Table 2.4.
Finnish class structure according to Wright's typology (%)

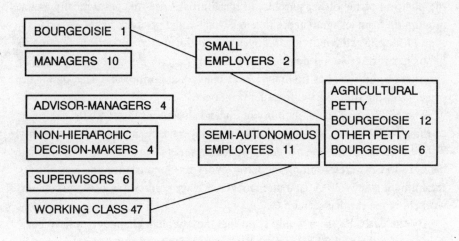

BOURGEOISIE: more than 10 hired employees and control over the company's investments, physical capital and labour power

MANAGERS: wage earners with decision-making authority in matters concerning the
whole organization (including authority to suggest approval of matters)

ADVISOR-MANAGERS: authority to give advice in matters concerning the whole organization

NON-HIERARCHIC DECISION-MAKERS: decision-making authority in matters concerning the whole organization but no control over other people's labour

SUPERVISORS: no decision-making authority but influence on the pay of other workers,
promotions, and discipline

WORKING CLASS: excluded from control over investments, use of physical capital, and
other people's labour power

SEMI-AUTONOMOUS EMPLOYEES: as above, but have control over their own work
process

SMALL EMPLOYERS: 2-10 hired employees and control over investments, use of
physical capital, and other people's labour power

PETTY BOURGEOISIE: max. one hired employee, control over (minor) investments and
physical capital, but not over other people's labour

Table 2.5.
Class structures of the USA, Sweden, and Finland by gender (%)

Class groups	USA Men	Women	Sweden Men	Women	Finland Men	Women
Managers	16	9	16	5	14	6
Advisor-managers	5	4	4	2	8	7
Supervisors	15	12	8	6	5	5
Total Managers	36	25	28	13	27	18
Semi-autonomous employees	8	9	14	20	10	11
Working class	39	55	43	62	39	54
Petty bourgeoisie	7	7	7	3	19	17
Small employers	8	5	7	2	4	1
Bourgeoisie	3	1	1	0	1	0
Total Self-employed	17	13	15	5	24	19
Total	101	101	100	100	100	101
N	820	675	total	1070	511	491

the highest figures for wage workers classified as working class.

In all three countries — and particularly in Sweden and the USA — the clear majority of managerial and supervisory positions are occupied by men. However, within the group of managers proper the proportion of women is clearly highest in the United States. In Finland and the USA men and women are more or less equally represented in the group of semi-autonomous employees, but in Sweden women are clearly overrepresented. In all countries women represent the majority of the working class. The Swedish petty bourgeoisie is dominated by men, while in Finland and the USA there are no considerable gender differences. Small employers and the bourgeoisie are male-dominated in all three countries.

On the whole we can see a very clear duality in the gender compositions of these class groups: white-collar positions are predominantly occupied by men and blue-collar positions by women. In certain respects there are significant differences here between the three countries: notice especially the high proportion of women in the group of semi-autonomous employees in Sweden and the relatively high proportion of women among the self-employed in the USA.

2.2. Occupations, autonomy and authority

Ahrne and Wright (1983) explain in their comparative study the differences between the Swedish and American class structures by relating these to the respective occupational structures. Noting that there are 9 % more managers and supervisors in the USA than in Sweden and that the proportion of semi-autonomous employees is 8 % higher in the Swedish class structure than in the USA, the conclusion they draw is that the class structures of different industries and occupational groups are different. Ahrne and Wright also suggest that the high number of semi-autonomous employees in Sweden is related to the size of the state sector.

These results clearly point to differences in work organization. In particular, within the corporate hierarchy in the United States there is a tendency to delegate the control of labour power to 'ordinary worker occupations' (ibid., 22-26). For example, craftsmen and workers in skilled services have far more authority in the US than in Sweden. On the other hand, Sweden has a greater number of workers who are autonomous on the job but who have no authority. On the whole then, there is a greater degree of differentiation among wage workers in the United States than in Sweden.

Comparing these results with the situation in Finland, Table 2.6. shows the extent to which Finland differs from Sweden and the US in terms of autonomy and authority in different occupational groups. Positive values indicate that the respective occupational groups in Finland have more autonomy or authority and negative values that they have less autonomy or authority.

In the light of this comparison *Finland comes much closer to Sweden than to the United States*. There are several worker groups in the United States who have more control over other people's labour power and over conditions of work than in Finland and Sweden. On the dimension of authority, there are three occupational groups in which differences between the US and Finland are particularly clear:

-       workers in skilled services (40 % more authority in the US than in Finland);
-       craftsmen (28 % more authority in the US);
-       technicians (22 % more authority in the US).

In the category of skilled services, there are far more (20 %) workers in Finland who have 'only autonomy' than in Sweden and the US. In craftsmen the difference

Table 2.6.
Autonomy and authority of occupational groups in Finland
as compared with Sweden and the US (%)

Occupational groups	only autonomy		only authority		autonomy and authority	
	Sweden	US	Sweden	US	Sweden	US
Professionals	12	11	- 1	- 9	- 6	0
Teachers	-11	- 2	0	- 2	14	9
Technicians	- 3	7	-11	- 8	7	-14
Managers and officials	- 4	2	- 9	- 8	12	5
Clerical	- 1	3	- 1	-11	- 2	- 5
Sales and marketing	- 8	-15	- 4	- 3	- 4	2
Foremen	0	7	- 9	-14	18	5
Craftsmen	8	9	- 4	-22	2	- 6
Operatives and transport workers	- 4	0	- 2	-13	- 1	1
Labourers	-15	- 2	- 1	- 9	- 5	3
Skilled services	19	21	- 6	-29	0	-11
Unskilled services	-15	- 1	- 2	-15	2	- 2

in favour of Finland is almost 10 %. In the group of technicians, there are more (+ 7 %) 'only autonomy' workers in Finland than in the United States but less (- 3 %) than in Sweden.

In the following four occupational groups Finnish wage workers have more authority (i.e., authority without autonomy on the job) than their American colleagues:

-       office workers (16 % more authority in Finland);
-       operatives and transport workers (12 % more authority in Finland);
-       professionals (9 % more authority in Finland);
-       foremen (9 % more authority in Finland).

Considering all three countries, there are rather clear differences in the group of foremen: Swedish foremen have less authority (76 %) than their Finnish (85 %) and American (94 %) colleagues. The percentage of foremen who have 'only autonomy' is 7 % higher in Finland than in the USA; a comparison between Finland and Sweden shows that there are no differences here. In Sweden, there a more foremen who have both authority and autonomy on the job than in Finland, and less foremen who have 'only authority'.

The most significant difference between Sweden and Finland is found in the authority of teachers (14 % more authority in Finland); a similar finding is made in comparison with the United States. Swedish teachers tend to fall in the category 'only autonomy' more often than in Finland.

Two opposite interpretations may be offered to the finding that there is a higher level of authority in worker occupations in the USA than in Finland and Sweden. The first is that within the category of wage workers (working class + other wage earners) the power and control hierarchy is less steeply graded; the second possible explanation is that the employer camp has successfully pursued a strategy of *divide et impera*. If the former interpretation were valid, then wage earners should represent a relatively homogenous group and have the backing of a powerful labour movement; in other words a high level of authority within worker occupations would indicate that the working class is a powerful social force. On the other hand, if the latter interpretation were valid and the high level of authority in certain elite (political, ethnic or racial) groups were the result of a conscious employer policy to undermine the strength of the working class, then we should see a high degree of internal differentiation among wage workers, clear labour market segmentation and a weak labour movement. Earlier analyses of the capital accumulation process, the homogeneity of the labour power and labour market segmentation in the USA (e.g. Gordon et al. 1982) suggest that, at least in the case of the United States, the latter interpretation is true.

Ahrne and Wright also argue that the differences between Sweden and the United States in the mode of work organization can at least partly be explained by conscious employer policies (Ahrne and Wright 1983, 22-26). According to this interpretation the high degree of wage worker differentiation by authority positions in the US would have a political background. On the other hand, as Littler (1982) has pointed out, there are also significant historical differences between the USA, Britain and Japan, for example, in the development of the capitalist work organization. In the United States foremen were effectively integrated into the new organization from the very outset, while in Britain shopfloor resistance was much more persistent.

2.3. The theories of Poulantzas and PKA

In a comparison of different class theories, there are two sets of complicating factors: First, there are many different approaches even to the most basic questions of social theory. And second, class theories are not only descriptions of class structure, but also of class consciousness and class organization. All these dimensions must be taken into account in a relevant comparison.

Looking at the basic structure of class theories, we can see differences at least in (1) their scope of analysis (which may range from a mere description of class structure to all levels of class analysis); (2) the emphasis given to mediating syntheses in proceeding from the economic basis of classes to class organization, political action and class consciousness; and (3) the extent to which theoretical solutions are empirically tested.

Our intention is to compare the class theories of Poulantzas and PKA. We shall also compare the empirical results of these theories in order to test which of them is 'better'; our point of reference is the class theory of E.O Wright. Poulantzas represents the Anglo-Saxon tradition of class theory, PKA is perhaps the major representative of the West German debate. As was discussed earlier, there has been no critical dialogue between these two traditions.

In his theoretical work Nicos *Poulantzas* was primarily concerned with the reproduction of class hegemony and with the relationship between classes and the state. His main contribution was therefore not in the development of concepts required for the analysis of class structure (the theoretical development of Poulantzas is discussed in detail in Jessop 1985). However, for the present purposes we must of course restrict ourselves to Poulantzas's theory of class structure.

Poulantzas argues that class boundaries cannot be determined solely on the basis of economic criteria; in addition, we have to consider *political and ideological criteria*. From these premises, he goes on to propose a broad definition of the petty bourgeoisie and a rather narrow definition of the working class. These two main characteristics of his theory are closely intertwined, in that he places certain wage worker groups in the petty bourgeoisie (or excludes them from the proletariat) on the basis of their expert position: unlike the proletariat, these groups (engineers, technicians, foremen, civil servants) are capable of organizing the production process. In other words: they are not working-class because their position in the social division of labour is a consequence of the political and ideological subordination of the working class to capital. Other factors that according to Poulantzas lie behind class differentiation include social status and obstacles to class mobility.

There are three main lines of criticism against Poulantzas's theory. Firstly, several writers have questioned Poulantzas's distinction between productive and unproductive labour, i.e. his 'economic criteria' (e.g. Wright 1980, 348-349). Surely, the critics point out, productive and unproductive workers have basically similar reproduction interests; and surely the economic interests of the traditional petty bourgeoisie differ considerably from those of productive workers. Furthermore, many critics are doubtful about Poulantzas's argument that these different economic positions produce the same effects at the ideological level: can the meaning of careerism, for instance, really be the same to the old petty bourgeoisie and to unproductive workers?

Secondly, it has been pointed out that Poulantzas has no analysis of the concrete work process in his class theory. He also fails to consider the consequences of the fact that different work processes are subordinated to capital in different ways and through different mechanisms. The latter question is particularly significant in the analysis of wage-worker consciousness and organization. It should be clear that it is far from unimportant to the individual worker what kind of work process he is engaged in; quite the contrary, this is a central element in the formation of wage-worker subjectivity. In a critique of Poulantzas, Thorbek (1980) says that the extent to which the concrete work process is subordinated to capital is in fact an essential criterion in defining the boundaries of the working class: 'I would like suggest that those workers who are employed by capital, who are exploited by capital, and whose work process is subordinated to capital in the sense that machines or other industrial forms of production play a decisive role in this subordination, be included [in the working class], regardless of whether they work with material objects or symbols.'

Third and finally, Poulantzas takes too many short cuts in his class analysis. In particular, he fails to provide a detailed account of the structuration of class situation, forms of consciousness, and forms of organization before proceeding to a discussion of class consciousness, class organization and politico-ideological relations.

What are the empirical results of Poulantzas's theory? In Table 2.7., which describes the Finnish class structure on the basis of Poulantzas's criteria, we see that both the bourgeoisie and the petty bourgeoisie are extremely large in

Table 2.7.
The Finnish class structure according to Poulantzas (%)

Bourgeoisie	21.8
Old petty bourgeoisie	17.5
New petty bourgeoisie	36.7
Working class	24.0
Total	100.0
	(998)

BOURGEOISIE: all self-employed with two or more hired workers and upper leading employers

OLD PETTY BOURGEOISIE: self-employed with 0-1 wage workers

WORKING CLASS: workers within manufacturing industry, construction and transportation in non-leading positions (direct question) *or* workers whose job does not involve mental work (estimated according to the code of occupational structure)

NEW PETTY BOURGEOISIE: wage employees not included in the classes mentioned above

comparison with the working class, which represents only 24 % of the gainfully employed population. Statistical analyses in different countries have produced rather similar results, with the working class reduced to 15—40 % of the economically active population (Wright 1978 and Thorbek 1980).

The main differences between the class theories of Poulantzas and E.O. Wright can be summarized in three points: (1) Wright's working class is more than twice as large as Poulantzas's; (2) Poulantzas's bourgeoisie is considerably larger than Wright's, including Wright's bourgeoisie proper plus the majority of the (managerial) contradictory class locations between the working class and the bourgeoisie; and (3) Poulantzas's new petty bourgeoisie includes part of Wright's working class and, in addition, the majority of supervisors and semi-autonomous workers.

Apart from these quantitative differences, there are also certain other factors which distinguish the class theories of Wright and Poulantzas. The contradictory wage-worker locations described by Wright are also bearers of contradictory economic and social interests. Poulantzas, on the other hand, slots part of these locations directly into the bourgeoisie and part of them (supervisors), together with about one third of the workers who according to Wright are working-class, into positions where the ideological effect leads to the development of a petty-bourgeois consciousness and interests.

The theory of *Projekt Klassenanalyse* (PKA) is basically concerned with the relationship between class structure and worker consciousness. PKA represents the 'capital logic' type of economic reductionism: it attempts to develop criteria for the definition of social classes and form determinants of social consciousness strictly on the basis of Marx's critique of political economy. The starting-point of PKA's theory of class structure lies in the *circulation of capital*, in which capital assumes different forms corresponding to different relations to work and to non-equivalent appropriation. The following discussion is restricted to this part of PKA's work: we shall deal neither with its theory of class consciousness nor with its contributions to the theory of ideology.

PKA includes in its definition of the bourgeoisie both the owners of the means of production (entrepreneurs with more than three hired employees) and 'active capitalists', i.e. top managers. Its petty bourgeoisie ('non-capitalist commodity producers', the 'traditional middle classes'), then, comprises the owners of the means of production who have less than three employees; three because this is assumed to be the minimum number of employees required so that one can be freed from the immediate labour process.

PKA's analysis of the internal differentiation of wage workers is no doubt the most significant contribution of the project to class theory. In this analysis it focuses on the comparatively small number of wage workers engaged in non-capitalist commodity production and circulation (services) and, particularly, on wage workers engaged in capitalist commodity production and state employees. The project works on the assumption that the main criterion for class divisions must be derived form the economic structure of the capitalist social formation: that criterion is the *form of income*. On the one hand, there are wage workers whose salaries are 'primary income', i.e. workers who sell their labour power to capital and who themselves produce the reserves out of which their salaries are paid; PKA also calls this group 'wage workers in the strict sense'. On the other hand, there are middle-class wage workers (such as state employees) whose salaries are 'derived income', i.e. which come directly out of taxes.

Within the former category, PKA makes a further distinction between 'productive' and 'unproductive' workers; and further, it divides productive workers into 'machine workers' and 'aggregated personnel'. These distinctions are based on the idea that there are significant differences between these groups in how they experience the repression of capital, in the sense of uncertainty caused by the cyclical movement of capital, in degrees of job autonomy and, consequently, in the preconditions for the development of class consciousness. In its distinctions within the category of state employees, PKA attempts to demonstrate that state employees have an essentially different relationship to the process of capital reproduction and to the *Herrschaft* of capital in society.

PKA's criteria for class divisions are presented in Table 2.8., which describes the internal differentiation of the Finnish working population on the basis of these criteria.

According to PKA's criteria, the bourgeoisie represents 2.6 % and the petty bourgeoisie, or non-capitalist commodity producers, 19 % of the Finnish economically active population. In addition, 1 % of the workers are engaged in non-capitalist commodity production.

Wage workers of capital represent the largest single wage-worker group: it is more than twice as large as the middle class. In addition to this group, PKA includes in its definition of working class those workers who are engaged in non-capitalist commodity production, as well as the unemployed. Using these criteria, the working class represents 56 % of the economically active population, which is 10 % less than the figure for the West German working class calculated on the basis of official statistics in 1978.

In the category of wage workers of capital, there are far more productive workers than unproductive workers. The majority of productive workers fall in the category of machine workers.

PKA's middle class consists more or less exclusively of state employees; workers of organizations represent merely 1 %. The middle class represents about one quarter of the Finnish working population, which is some 5 % more than in West Germany. Of those classified as state employees, about two thirds are engaged in labour power reproduction; one in six works with the state's repressive apparatus; and one in six in the production of general material conditions of production.

How does the description of the Finnish class structure that is based on PKA's criteria compare with the picture we get with Wright's criteria. In short, there are both major differences and striking similarities.

Most of the contradictory managerial locations between the working class and the bourgeoisie are wage workers of capital (51—64 %). Productive and unproductive workers are more or less equally represented in these groups. As might

Table 2.8.
Internal differentiation of Finnish wage earners according to PKA (%)

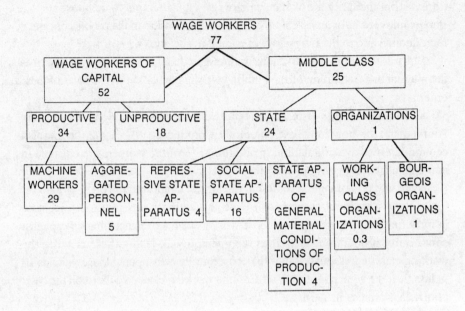

WAGE WORKERS: wage workers within the capitalist sector of the economy (including the state); petty bourgeoisie = entrepreneurs with 0-3 hired employees; bourgeoisie = entrepreneurs with more than 3 hired employees and "active capitalists", i.e. top managers

WAGE WORKERS OF CAPITAL: all workers who sell their labour power to capital and whose wages are "primary income"

PRODUCTIVE WORKERS: all wage workers who produce surplus value (part are engaged in circulation, including tasks such as packing, storage, etc.)

UNPRODUCTIVE WORKERS: workers engaged in circulation (do not produce surplus value)

MACHINE WORKERS: wage workers whose pace of work is determined by production machinery

AGGREGATED PERSONNEL: other productive wage workers engaged in supervision, planning, service and maintenance, or process control

MIDDLE CLASS: workers who do not sell their labour power to capital and whose salaries are "derived income"; state employees, workers of organizations and pensioners represent the most important groups

WORKERS IN THE STATE'S REPRESSIVE APPARATUS: army, judicial system, public administration

SOCIAL STATE APPARATUS: tasks related to labour power reproduction, e.g. education, social security, health care

GENERAL MATERIAL CONDITIONS OF PRODUCTION: tasks related to the development of regional infrastructure, energy supply, etc.

be expected, the majority of the productive workers who correspond to Wright's managerial positions fall in the category of aggregated personnel (with the exception of supervisors, half of whom are classified as machine workers).

Semi-autonomous employees are more or less evenly divided between PKA's middle class (usually state employees) and wage workers of capital. The majority of the semi-autonomous employees who fall in the latter group are productive workers (32 %), and most of these are aggregated personnel (28 %). Most of the semi-autonomous employees who in PKA's scheme are classified as state employees are engaged in labour power reproduction. About three quarters of Wright's working class are wage workers of capital and one quarter middle-class. About half of Wright's working class consists of PKA's productive workers (all of whom are machine workers). Unproductive workers represent about one fifth of Wright's working class. The majority of state employees who fall in Wright's working class are engaged in labour power reproduction.

PKA's middle class seems to be rather heterogeneous. Almost half belong to Wright's working class (narrow definition); using the broad definition (including semi-autonomous employees and supervisors), the figure is as high as 74 %. The most proletarianized state employee group in PKA's class structure — from the point of view of Wright's criteria — is that engaged in the production of general material conditions of production (65 %); the least proletarianized state employees are those engaged in labour power reproduction (39 %). The latter group includes by far the highest proportion of semi-autonomous employees (27 %), which explains its (seemingly) low degree of proletarianization.

On the whole, the majority (48 %) of PKA's state employees fall under Wright's working class; 21 % are semi-autonomous employees; and about one third are in various managerial locations (17 % managers proper).

The highest concentration of managerial locations is found within the state's repressive apparatus and in labour power reproduction. Supervisors, in turn, are overrepresented in the state's repressive apparatus, which has the most rigid hierarchic structure. Most of the so-called non-hierarchic decision-makers are engaged in labour power reproduction.

2.4. What did we learn from our comparisons?

In the foregoing we have compared the empirical consequences of three different theories of class structure: Wright, Poulantzas and Projekt Klassenanalyse. Below, we shall sum up our findings and move on to consider the theoretical foundations of these constructs in greater detail. Our aim is to bring the class theory of Erik Wright into sharper focus.

A very fundamental difference between the theories of Poulantzas and Wright is immediately clear when we examine the composition of Poulantzas's new petty bourgeoisie on the basis of Wright's criteria: we find within this group the working class, supervisors (a contradictory class location between the working class and the bourgeoisie) and semi-autonomous employees (a contradictory location between the working class and the petty bourgeoisie), i.e. three qualitatively different kinds of class groups. The most striking point, of course, is that the same groups which in Poulantzas's scheme fall into the new petty bourgeoisie are in Wright's theory classified as working-class.

The obvious reason for this difference lies in the use of totally different sets of criteria: whereas Wright defines contradictory class locations on the basis of relations of domination within production, Poulantzas's political and ideological criteria are based upon relations of authority and the distinction between manual and mental labour. The thesis behind Poulantzas's decision to exclude these locations from the working class and to place them in the working class is that the class locations concerned produce a 'petty bourgeois' ideological effect. This reasoning leads Poulantzas to conclude that the consciousness and interests of these groups differ significantly from those of the working class; they come much closer to those of the old petty bourgeoisie. Wright, however, argues that those petty bourgeois workers that in his definition are working-class carry a fundamental interest in socialism; and those whom he calls supervisors and semi-autonomous employees have contradictory (but nevertheless socialism-oriented) interests.

Of the class groups identified in PKA's scheme, those that come closest to Wright's working class are, in this order, machine workers, productive workers, unproductive workers and state employees. Machine workers and productive workers have no authority on the job, and they also have a low level of job autonomy. In the group of unproductive workers, the number of managerial locations and non-hierarchic expert positions is twice as high as among productive workers. Finally, in the group of state employees there is a high concentration of managerial locations and semi-autonomous employees.

PKA's middle class, then, consists primarily of workers who according to Wright represent the working class or adjacent groups. Apparently the use of derived income as a criterion for inclusion in the middle class means that worker groups who are actually subjected to the conditions of reproduction of the normal wage worker become included.

We now move on to summarize the main characteristics and problems of the three theories concerned, starting with Wright's class theory (which we have already criticized at considerable length earlier). Wright's criteria for determining class boundaries are based on the relations of appropriation prevailing in production, which at the same time are relations of domination. This is the most distinctive and also the most problematic part of Wright's analysis. There is no empirical evidence in support of the theory that these two elements coexist, and the criteria he actually applies in his analyses are the relations of authority and control prevailing within production. Furthermore, he identifies these criteria as being qualitatively equal in different organizations. This is problematic in two respects. Firstly, capitalism is a social construct where *Gesellschaftlichkeit* mediated by exchange-value prevails. From the point of view of carriers of different structural positions, this means that their subordination to the living conditions of a certain class not only fixes them to a specific position in production; it also implies the unity of the process of labour power reproduction and position in production. Secondly, by restricting his attention to the organizational level, Wright ignores the fundamental differences between the various structures of capitalist society, particularly the structural differentiation of economic and political reproduction (economy and the state).

Wright's concept of semi-autonomous employees, which he defines on the basis of the nature of work rather than structural relations of subordination, is also problematic. In a sense the category of semi-autonomous employees is a mirror image of PKA's machine workers: whereas semi-autonomous employees have considerable latitude in planning their work process, machine workers have only very little freedom in this respect. It is important to note, however, that Wright and PKA have different notions of autonomy: Wright attaches special importance to planning and conceptualization, PKA is mainly concerned with the restrictions imposed by the industrial production machinery.

Poulantzas, then, clearly fails in his class theory to present a systematic analysis of the objective position of wage employees; this shortcoming is intimately bound up with his use of productive labour as a class criterion. He does, however, moderate his argumentation by pointing out certain groups of the new petty bourgeoisie whose position approximates that of the working class: workers on the lowest levels of commodity circulation, certain workers within the service sector, state employees in performance-level tasks, and technicians and engineers engaged in productive work.

As discussed earlier, Poulantzas explains his decision to place the new petty bourgeoisie under the petty bourgeoisie by reference to the ideological effect of this position. The methodological problem with this solution is that it merely postulates a connection between an objective position and an 'ideological level', without any serious analysis of the structural mediations involved. Indeed, there is reason to believe that many of the ideological similarities between the new and old petty bourgeoisie (e.g. the emphasis of autonomy) and the similarities in their structural functions (and the way in which they are subordinated to capital accumulation) are not founded on reality. In the light of Wright's class criteria, too, there are very fundamental differences between these segments of the petty bourgeoisie. So what remains as the hard core of Poulantzas's theory is his description of the mediation of political and ideological reproduction within the sphere of production, with a large part of wage workers performing the functions of this reproduction and therefore adopting petty-bourgeois ideologies.

Our main objection against PKA's class theory — which we repeat in spite of the fact that the project has persistently defended its theoretical premises (see Bischoff et al. 1982) — concerns its economic reductionism. The crucial question is: to what extent do its form-determinant criteria for class distinctions (primary vs. secondary income and productive vs. unproductive labour) uncover the essential differences between the reproduction conditions of different class groups; or, from a Wrightian perspective, to what extent are the differences between class groups that are based on form determinants at the same time differences between positions of domination. At several points PKA's class analysis leads to rather serious mistakes in drawing class boundaries, as we saw in the previous section. Indeed, it is highly questionable to use the criteria just mentioned for outlining a coherent category of state employees, a middle-class category which differs essentially from the working class (wage workers of capital) in terms of reproduction conditions. Similarly, the inclusion of pensioners in the middle class is a very strange solution. PKA's theory leans heavily on the idea that there are major differences in forms of consciousness (class conscious-ness) between different class groups, but their own empirical study fails to support this hypothesis.

In the recent debate there have emerged a number of interesting alternatives to the more traditional approaches to class theory. Mention must of course first be made of Carchedi (1977), who identifies the working class on the basis of the distinction between the global functions of capital vs. the functions of the collective worker, and who also deals with the question of the 'new middle class'. Other theorists have adopted *the way in which the labour process is subordinated to capital* as a central criterion for defining the working class; others still (e.g. IMSF) have used as a criterion the *differences in reproduction positions,* as reflected in the unfolding of the commodity nature of labour power. These kinds of alternatives seem to open interesting perspectives. In particular, it is important to note the idea — which in fact is inherent in the logic of the concept of class — that there is a kind of universal subordination to certain reproduction conditions which derive from the inherent laws of capital, in that the structures of reproduc-tion and activity of the carriers of these conditions tend to be qualitatively similar. This would mean that all the class criteria that do not reflect *the universality of structural subordination to certain conditions of living* are inadequate. IMSF takes this important consideration into account in its starting-points, although it fails to develop sufficiently systematic criteria on this basis.

According to IMSF, the most important criteria for inclusion in the working class are the non-ownership of the means of production, the lack of privileges in the sale of labour power and in keeping one's job and the lack of special qualifications. The theory emphasizes the increasing capital subsumption of different social spheres with the development of the capital relation, which narrows down differences between different wage-worker groups (e.g. between white-collar and blue-collar workers). On this basis, IMSF also argues that produc-tive labour has become less and less important as a class criterion. All spheres of life become potential targets for capital investments, and therefore the reproduc-tion conditions of other wage worker groups begin to approximate those of productive workers. To a certain extent IMSF's reasoning follows the same lines as Thorbek's. IMSF believes that an industrial type of division of labour will gradually take over in most kinds of white-collar work.

In conclusion then, it seems obvious that *class analysis must proceed along a path which leads from objective position in production through the reproduction of labour power to the structuration of class situation — and back again. This is the only approach which can guarantee an adequate class theory: a theory which clearly distinguishes between classes and class groups which are subjected to the same structural conditions of living.*

3 The internal differentiation of wage workers

3.1. The problem

There are two main questions which have commanded the attention of class theorists concerned with the internal differentiation of wage workers: how homogenous (or how fragmented) is the category of wage workers, and how should the working class be demarcated? In addition to these two basic issues, at least the following are relevant to the problem concerned:

(1) How does one fix the boundary line between the working class and the middle class? What is the role of such criteria as employment in productive work, white-collar position, relations of authority and domination, ideological and political criteria, and cultural factors?

(2) How does one fix the boundary line between the middle class and the bourgeoisie? In addition to the questions listed above, we must also consider the criteria of ownership and domination.

(3) How homogenous is the working class; how homogenous is the middle class? The working class may be fragmented on many different dimensions. Marxist class research, particularly its 'capital logic' tradition, has been mainly concerned with the position of different worker groups in the reproduction of capital: hence the distinction between industrial workers, workers of money and commodity capital (circulation) and workers in public or private services. Other influential lines of theorizing have emphasized the distinctions between the 'core' and 'periphery' of the working class, or the role played by different worker groups in integrating the working class into capitalism (labour aristocracy and

bureaucracy). In recent years analyses of labour market segmentation have also become increasingly important. Finally, all these differences may be further intertwined with such factors as gender, age, ethnic and racial background, etc. (see Table 3.1. below).

From the outset it is important to stress one unifying factor which is common to all wage earners: their engagement in *wage employment*. The 'character mask' of wage earners imposes certain coercions upon them which restrict their freedom of action (such as the requirement to sell and reproduce their labour power). In addition, in industrial society the institution of wage employment is also significant in that it is a cultural characteristic of that society.

A major concern of recent studies dealing with the middle class question has been to make a distinction between white-collar and blue-collar workers; between higher and lower white-collar groups; and to identify a separate 'service class' amongst middle-class wage earners. Furthermore, many analysts have examined the similarities and differences between the 'new middle class' (or classes) and the old middle class (entrepreneurs). On the whole there seems to be fairly widespread agreement among modern class theorists that rather than one coherent middle 'class', there are in fact a number intermediate groups between labour and capital.

Together with the historical changes occurring in the position of different wage earner groups and the problems related to their proletarianization or embourgeoisement, the questions outlined above are among the most important problems of class research and class theory. The main difficulty in producing an adequate analysis of these issues lies in the fact that we may find very different theoretical approaches (e.g. Marxian or Weberian) behind similar conceptions of class structure. Therefore it is important to not only to describe the differentiation of wage workers between different class groups, but also to examine *the foundations and nature of this process*.

The middle class started to emerge as a significant social force at different times in different capitalist societies: in the United States, Germany and Britain it began to gain in strength at the beginning of the century; in France after World War II (Kadritzke 1982); and in Finland around the 1950s and 1960s. The problems that were created in these countries were therefore very different, as can be seen in the diversity of concepts employed in theoretical analyses: 'the new working class', 'the new petty bourgeoisie', 'the new middle class', 'wage-working middle strata', 'the third person rubric' and 'service class' describe different sets of problems and mediate different kinds of theoretical conceptions. The most significant differences are reflected at least in (1) whether is it possible to identify a coherent middle class comparable to the working class or the bourgeoisie; (2) how narrow or broad a concept is adopted of the middle class/the working class; and in (3) whether the main trend of development is towards increasing homogeneity or fragmentation, or towards increasing proletarianization or embourgeoisement.

The first writers to translate the new social phenomenon into a theoretical problem were German socialists, who referred to the growth of what they called 'neuer Middelstand' (see Burris 1986). White-collar workers were viewed as a functional substitute for the old 'middle estate', and it was widely expected that they would form a buffer stratum between the working class and the bourgeoisie and in this position effectively lessen social conflicts.[1]

In the English-speaking world, the late 1950s and the 1960s saw the beginning of a debate on the embourgeoisement of the working class, in which it was argued that the economic, social and cultural differences between the middle class and the working class were being eroded. However, the embourgeoisement thesis was soon refuted by the famous study by Goldthorpe and his colleagues (Goldthorpe et al. 1969), who went on to assume that the traditional solidary worker type and his group commitment had given way to a new instrumentally oriented worker.

More recently, the sociology of work and qualification studies have given a major impetus to the ongoing debate on the middle classes. In particular, mention must be made of Braverman's controversial argument that with the declining skill and qualification levels of office workers and workers in services, there can be seen in these occupational groups a tendency towards proletarianization. Although these and other discourses on the internal differentiation of wage workers have unfolded in a certain chronological order, there nevertheless remain contradictory assumptions both about the main trends in development and about the most significant differences between the working class and the middle class. The following Table summarizes some of the main assumptions of recent theorizing on the internal differentiation of wage workers.

Table 3.1.

Internal differentiation of wage workers: a summary of recent theories

Conception of class structure	Main trends in wage workers' position and internal homogeneity
WRIGHT Working class (about half of the economically active population), contradictory class locations between the bourgeoisie and the working class, and semi-autonomous employees. Groups between the bourgeoisie and the working class which have different degrees of authority. Semi-autonomous employees have become differentiated from the working class due to the nature of their work.	A homogeneous working class and a number of contradictory class locations which have become increasingly fragmented with the development of capitalism.
POULANTZAS A narrow working class concept, large new petty bourgeoisie. A large proportion of high-ranking wage earners classified under the bourgeoisie. Clear difference between the working class and the new petty bourgeoisie (partly because of political and ideological factors).	Wage workers internally differentiated: authority related to position (political reproduction) and mental work (ideological reproduction) important distinguishing factors. The new petty bourgeoisie is not affected by the process of proletarianization, although in certain groups there are such tendencies.
PROJEKT KLASSENANALYSE Wage workers of capital (divided into productive and unproductive workers and representing about half of the economically active population) and the middle class, divided into state employees and workers of organizations (and the former further divided into groups according to tasks in the state apparatus).	Development of the position of different wage worker groups bound up with the accumulation of capital; a crisis may lead to increasingly homogenous wage worker consciousness.
BRAVERMAN[a] Industrial workers and workers in trade and services, office workers (no separate concept apparatus for class groups).	Dequalification in monopoly capitalism leads to increasing proletarianization in white-collar groups; may ultimately lead to large homogenous working class.

KADRITZKE[b]

(Concerned with the development of white-collar positions).

The position of white-collar employees approaching that of blue-collar workers. Recent crises and rationalization have led to 1) increasing uncertainty among white-collar employees over their chances of reproduction; 2) lesser chances of upward social mobility; and 3) increasing emphasis on performance and output.

ARMANSKI ET AL.[c]

(Concerned with the development of the position of the intelligentsia).

Functional connection between the intelligentsia and bourgeois domination becoming weaker; with the emergence of a 'mass intelligentsia' domination no longer represents the hard core of the consciousness of the intelligentsia.

CARCHEDI[d]

Managers, the new middle class, and the working class.
The new middle class differs from the working class in that it carries the functions of both the collective worker and global capital.

The new middle class becomes increasingly proletarianized in monopoly capitalism when the value of its labour power declines and it begins to carry the global functions of capital to a lesser and lesser extent. The loss of value is due to the decreasing value of consumer goods (with the increase in productivity) and above all to dequalification.

ABERCROMBIE & URRY[e]

Service class, lower white-collar middle class and working class.
The service class differs from the rest of the middle class through its involvement in conceptualization, control and reproduction (and, unlike the lower middle class, there is a compatibility between its functions and class position). The service class comes close to the bourgeoisie. Small capitalists form a parallel class group. The lower middle class differs from the working class in its functions (has certain tasks in conceptualization, control and reproduction), but in terms of position it comes rather close to the working class.

The lower white-collar middle class is becoming increasingly proletarianized (in terms of its position at work and on the market). The service class is not affected by the proletarianization process, and its power resources for furthering its interests are increasing.

67

GIDDENS[f]

Large middle class, a relatively small working class engaged in physical labour. Middle class highly fragmented (mainly because of differences in market capacity).

Managerial control based on technical division of labour increasing; consequently the majority of wage earners losing control over the work process.

NICOLAUS[g]

Large unproductive middle class, small working class.

Wage workers are not becoming proletarianized; the new unproductive middle class ('surplus class') is growing. The latter trend is due to the increasing productivity of work and the consequent problems of excessive accumulation of capital and underconsumption. The new unproductive middle will solve these problems.

IMSF[h]

Working class, wage-working middle strata (and intelligentsia) and capitalist managers.

Working class is growing and becoming increasingly homogenous; these trends are related to extended reproduction of capital (and since 1960 to the intensive expansion of reproduction) and to the increasing number of spheres of social life subordinated to capital. The work situation and social status of lower ('working-class') white-collar workers are approaching those of the working class. Differentiation and polarization of middle white-collar groups gathering momentum.

a.   Labor and Monopoly Capital, New York 1974.
b.   Angestellte als Lohnarbeiter, Kölner Zeitschrift für Soziologie und Sozialpsychologie 24/1982.
c.   Vom Bourgeoisideologen zum Massenintellektuellen. Beiträge zur Marxschen Theorie 7, Frankfurt 1976.
d.   On the Economic Identification of Social Classes, London 1977.
e.   Capital, Labour and the Middle Classes, London 1983.
f.   The Class Structure of the Advanced Societies, London 1973. Giddens's conclusions on current trends are based upon Braverman's idea, see Klassenspaltung, Klassenkonflikt und Bürgerrechte. Gesellschaft im Europa der achtziger Jahre, Soziale Welt, Sonderband 2, Soziale Ungleichheiten, 1983, and Power, Dialectics of Control and Class Structuration; in Social Class and the Division of Labour, Essays in Honour of Ilya Neustadt, Cambridge 1982.
g.   Proletariat and the Middle Class in Marx: Hegelian Choreography and the Capitalist Dialectic, Studies on the Left 7, 22—49.
h.   Klassen und Sozialstruktur der BRD 1950—1970, I—III, Frankfurt 1973/74, esp. part II Erster Halbband, 192—197, 269—272 and 341—345.

Our table serves two main purposes: first, it highlights the differences between the theories considered; and second, it proves our point that the internal differentiation of wage workers is relevant both to the analysis of the working class and to investigations of the middle classes and the intelligentsia. Many of the positions described in the table can actually be regarded as representative of entire theoretical schools rather than individual works of individual theorists. For instance, Crompton and Gubbay are on very similar lines as Wright and Carchedi; Goldthorpe and Renner come rather close to Abercrombie and Urry; and Fritsch and Kolbe et al. have many points in common with the theory the IMSF.[2] In addition, there is a separate school in class research which assigns greater significance to the tendencies of fragmentation and marginalization among wage earners in general and within the middle strata in particular.

A major difficulty in describing the tendencies towards homogenization or proletarianization among wage earners arises from the failure of most theories to explain the mechanism behind these trends and the relationship of this mechanism to the changes in the preconditions for capital valorization and accumulation. Of course, the fact that different theories of class structure have differing views on the strength of these processes in different wage-earner groups causes extra difficulty.

It is generally agreed that the tendencies towards proletarianization are due in the first place to the underlying processes of dequalification and polarization; additionally, as Carchedi has emphatically pointed out, in several wage-worker groups there is in evidence a tendential loss of the functions of global capital. Furthermore, the differentiation of mental and physical labour is another significant factor behind increasing proletarianization; this argument is supported by the 'service class' theory (see Abercrombie and Urry 1983).

Empirical studies on the internal differentiation of the middle classes clearly point to the heterogeneity of these strata[3] and to the proletarianization of lower white-collar strata (in fact in our table above, both Kadritzke's results in Germany and the studies of Abercrombie and Urry in Britain support the proletarianization thesis). Most analysts are also agreed that in further studies the emphasis should be on (1) international comparisons and (2) such factors as age structure, gender and the increasing participation of women in wage labour.

The approach to class analysis and the conception of class theory we have adopted in the present work differs in certain important methodological respects from those of the studies described above. Our basic strategy is to start from an analysis of class positions, then move on to the structuration of work and reproduction situation, to the structuration and organization of consciousness, and finally to social forces and hegemony. There are two significant assumptions behind this strategy:

(1) We cannot proceed from one level of analysis to another without first producing what we call a 'mediating synthesis' of all prior levels of analysis.

(2) We cannot produce a relevant class theory by concentrating on the position of classes on different dimensions; we must also look into various *modes of structuration*. Thus in our empirical analyses we are concerned, for example, with the role of job autonomy, managerial strategies and forms of labour control in the structuration of work situation; or with the relative weight of experience and consciousness in different class groups. Similarly, in the analysis of white-collar workers our dual aim is to demystify the concept itself and to take into account the blue-collar/white-collar distinction, particularly its role in maintaining cultural differences and in producing social segregation.

In Chapter 2 we compared Wright's theory of class structure with Poulantzas's and Projekt Klassenanalyse's in the light of the empirical consequences of these theories. This comparison revealed that Wright's theory provides us neither with the conceptual tools required for an analysis of the internal differentiation of the working class (and apparently for this reason gives an overly optimistic picture of its homogeneity), nor with concepts we need in studying the internal differentiation of state employees. In addition, as was pointed out earlier, Wright's concept of semi-autonomous employees is also rather problematic.

In conclusion then, analysis of the internal differentiation of the working class requires several different kinds of mediations between theory and empiria. In the search for these mediations, we must pay special attention to the differences between class groups in the structuration of their work situation, consciousness, etc; short cuts à la Poulantzas (political and ideological criteria) or Wright (fundamental interest in socialism) will lead to a distorted description of the class structure.

3.2. Fragmentations within the working class

In Marxian class theory the working class is traditionally pictured as a relatively homogenous, coherent class group, strictly separated from other social classes. An example is provided by Semjenow's (1972, 91-92) description of the structure of the working class, which has been influenced by Engels and Lenin. He identifies two horizontal categories, i.e. the urban and the rural proletariat and five vertical categories, i.e. the labour aristocracy and bureaucracy, the industrial proletariat, other industrial workers and the unemployed. The labour aristocracy and bureaucracy are the two main social sources of opportunism. The former consists of wage earners who have secured their position through their skills and qualifications, the latter refers to workers who represent working-class organizations in bourgeois democracy and who thus occupy a higher position than the rest of the working class. However, with the advance of capitalism and rising educational levels, the distinction between the labour aristocracy and the labour bureaucracy tends to become eroded. (Kolbe et al. 1976, 231-232; Semjenow 1972, 194.)

In advanced capitalist society we can identify a number of processes which have rendered this description completely obsolete: the accumulation and centralization of capital, increasing capitalization, the specialization of different types of capital, the division of labour, increased state interventions and the women's engagement in wage labour. According to Fritsch (1981), the two main tendencies in the changing class structure of this society are (1) the increasing polarization of classes and (2) the internal differentiation of classes.

Polarization means we have a growing working class; this is chiefly due to the proletarianization of white-collar workers and the declining number of peasants and petty-bourgeois positions. Accordingly, the most problematic group in an attempt to describe the class structure is represented by those wage earners who are not directly engaged in material production but who nevertheless meet the criteria for membership of the working class: they do not own the means of production, they are forced to sell their labour power, and they are engaged in shopfloor jobs.

That different theories have different views on the boundaries and internal fragmentations of the working class is, in the last instance, due to the fact that they search for what they consider to be the most important determinants at different levels of abstraction. At the highest level of abstraction we have the structure of capitalist economy, where there are no determined factors.[4] The next

71

level is the circulation of capital and the socio-economic level. Finally, at the micro-level, we have the worker's position in the work organization and the nature of the concrete work process. At this surface level, social stratification can be examined from two different points of view: social composition (age, gender, generations) and labour market position (educational level, income level). The closer we get to this level, the more complicated the underlying determinations.

Theories that determine the working class on the basis of criteria derived from the highest levels of abstraction lead to a rather narrow definition. Examples of these strict criteria are the distinction between productive and unproductive labour (Poulantzas 1975) and form of income (PKA 1973/74, II). It is obvious that estimates of the size of the working class depend ultimately on the criteria adopted. Fritsch (1981) has compared the results of different West German studies, according to which the working class represents anything between 42 % (Kuczynski) and 75 % (IMSF) of the economically active population.

IMSF (1972) reached this extremely high figure by using determinants from all levels of abstraction. The project (ibid., 99-113) argues that the hard core of the modern working class is to be found in industry and in large-scale industries in particular; this, IMSF says, is where the 'commodity nature' of labour power is at its purest and also where fragmentations within the working class begin. Around the core there are various intermediate strata, whose relative positions are determined by the branch of industry, concrete form of capital, organizational level and life situation: of these, the lower groups whose labour power has the same kind of commodity character as industrial workers, are classified as working-class.

Wright (1978) includes in the working class those workers who do not own the means of production, who are forced to sell their labour power and who are subjected to control at the workplace; in other words, those who own neither physical nor money capital and who have no decision-making authority over other people's labour. The working class, for Wright, is a residual category. He does not analyse the internal differentiation of the working class in any systematic fashion.

Our analysis below of the internal differentiation of the working class starts from a division in which we distinguish between workers of industrial capital, commodity circulation, money circulation and services. These distinctions are based on the *social division of labour*, which in turn is based upon the different stages in the reproduction of capital and upon the different relationships of the various types of capital emerging in this process to the production of surplus value. Additionally, we are working on the assumption that changes in the industrial structure have their basis in the reproduction of capital. According to PKA (1978, 112-118), the different forms assumed by capital at the different stages of the circulation process have their counterparts in different relationships to work and in different strategies of appropriating unpaid work.

It is necessary to bear in mind, of course, that the distinctions we propose between production, circulation and services are analytical tools which we are using at a high level of abstraction; they do not necessarily have any direct bearing on the individual worker's wages, status or consciousness. In the analysis of concrete societies, the relationship between general form-determinants and empirical phenomena represents one special problem of research. Although the question of class is essentially an empirical problem (Söderfeldt 1980), the main concern of empirical class research cannot be with substantiating the theory.

Ever since Braverman published his *Labor and Monopoly Capital* in 1974, class theorists have been engaged in a debate on the causes and consequences of changes in the organization of the capitalist labour process. Braverman argued that technological development and the growth of scientific management within monopoly capitalism is leading to the proletarianization of the majority of white-collar workers and therefore to the polarization of the class structure. However, Littler (1982) and many other critics of the proletarianization thesis object to the view of Braverman that there is a straightforward deterministic relationship between the logic of capital and changes in the labour process; the reality of capitalism, they say, is far more complicated than that. In between the purchase and utilization of labour power there is a sphere of motivation, consciousness and resistance, which allows the adoption of various control strategies; it is a sphere of continuous vacillation between conflict and consensus. In introducing these control strategies, capital must take into account the existing level of wage-worker consciousness and resistance. This means that the composition of the working class and changes in this composition become a central question, for the existing class structure is the main precondition for deskilling, the reduction of the price of labour power, and labour market segmentation (ibid., 18-19).

Moving on to examine the internal differentiation of the Finnish working class on the basis of our empirical materials and the distinctions introduced above, we find that in industry almost 70 % of all workers are working-class. In circulation (merchant capital and money capital) the figure is 60 % and in services only 46 %. According to Wright's criteria, a total of 59 % of all Finnish wage earners are working-class.

Table 3.2. describes the internal differentiation of the Finnish working class by main sectors of the economy. The majority, 54 %, are employed in industry or material production. Almost 30 % are in services — and the figure is probably still rising with the ongoing structural changes in society — while only 17 % of the workers are engaged in circulation. Almost half of the working class are therefore engaged in jobs that do not count as material production. We can also see a clear trend towards 'feminization', as almost 60 % of the Finnish working class are now women. In industry women represent a surprisingly high 42 % of the labour force, and in circulation and services more than 80 %.

Table 3.2.
Differentiation of the working class by sector (%)

		Women	Men	Total	N
Industry	54	42	58	100	249
Merchant capital	12	76	24	100	54
Circulation	5	79	21	100	24
Services	29	76	24	10	131
Total	100	58	42	10	458

On the whole the Finnish working class would seem to be fairly hetero-geneous. The traditional hard core of the working class has shrank rather consid-erably and now represents only 4—15 %. On the other hand, there have emerged around this core new significant groups, particularly female workers engaged in collective services and industrial white-collar workers.

3.3. Labour market segmentation

Theories of labour market segmentation represent an interesting new approach to the internal differentiation of the working class and wage earners in general. Rejecting the starting-points of the neo-classical tradition, segmentation theorists start from the assumption that the stigmatization of certain worker groups on the labour market cannot be examined as a local phenomenon on the basis of ad hoc assumptions; the focus must be on the general social preconditions. By labour market segmentation, this school means those *historical processes in which political and economic forces divide the labour market into separate segments.*

The roots of segmentation theory can be traced back to neo-institutionalist labour market theories (see e.g. Loveridge and Mok 1979; Edwards et al. 1975). The first of the pioneers was Clark Kerr (1954), who introduced the idea of the 'Balkanization' of the labour market. His work was followed up in the 1960s by several scholars, notably David Gordon and Michael Piore, who found that the Blacks and other underprivileged groups in big cities were recruited to different labour markets than white male workers. This finding was later crystallized in the *dual labour market* thesis (e.g. Doeringer and Piore 1971). In the seventies there developed a slightly different approach to segmentation in the Federal Republic of Germany. Rather than concentrating on the demand for labour power, German theorists focussed on the supply side (e.g. Lutz and Sengenberger 1977). The following summary describes the main points and assumptions behind the different theories that may be placed under the generic term 'segmentation theory':

(1) Labour markets are not made up of a linear sequence of workplaces, but of a series of separate segments. There is very little mobility between these segments. The original dual market thesis has recently been elaborated by theorists who make a distinction within the primary sector (which offers stable employment) between the segment of firm labour power and external labour power, or between workers engaged in routine tasks and workers in more independent types of work.

(2) Position in the labour market is determined not only by wages and professional skills, but also by stability of employment, career prospects, autonomy, etc.

(3) Educational level or qualifications are not the main criterion in the employer's decision to hire new workers. There is empirical evidence that education is a far more significant asset for workers in the primary sector than for those in the secondary sector. Edwards (1979) has emphasized the significance of control as a decisive criterion in hiring workers: 'Labor markets are segmented because they express a historical segmentation of the labor process; specifically, a distinct system of control inside the firm underlies each of the three market segments. The secondary labor market is the market expression of workplaces

organized according to simple control. The subordinate primary market contains those workplaces (workers and jobs) under the 'mixed' system of technical control and unions. And the independent primary market reflects bureaucratically controlled labour processes.'

(4) Many theorists hold that labour market segmentation is based upon the division of the economy into two segments, viz. the monopolistic and the competitive.

(5) Segmentation theories do not necessarily assume a simple duality but allow for the idea that the division of the labour market segments does not coincide with the differences in the stratification of genders and races (Blackburn and Mann 1979).[5] This is to say that the bourgeoisie has access to several alternative methods in reinforcing divisions between the working class, keeping its wages down and in preventing effective political mobilization.

(6) European labour market studies have also paid attention the occupational segmentation of the labour market. The occupational markets are characterized by the following features: the demand for labour power varies considerably between individual firms; the worker identifies himself with his or her profession, i.e. his or her own skills; the individual's work career continues throughout his or her life.

Our operationalization of the capitalist labour markets distinguishes between five segments and the respective types of labour market position:

1. Firm labour power (internal labour market of the primary sector)
   - 28 %
   - no changes of occupation
   - one employer
2. Skill-based labour power (occupational labour market)
   - 5 %
   - no changes of occupation
   - several employers
3. Labour power of primary sector (external labour market)
   - 35 %
   - changes of occupation
   - stable jobs (over 2 years)
   - unemployed not more than once
4. Labour power of secondary sector
   - 17 %
   - changes of occupation

-   unstable jobs (under 2 years), or unemployed more than twice
5.   Newcomers
-   13 %
-   less than two years in the labour market

By labour market segments, skilled workers represent only 5 % of the total Finnish labour force. The highest figure is found for the labour power of the primary sector (35 %). Firm labour power represents 28 % and secondary labour power 17 % of the economically active population.

Edwards (1979, 164) has pointed out that while secondary labour power was previously thought to represent only a very small part of the labour force, more recent studies suggest that the upper section and the lower section of the primary labour market as well as the secondary labour power each constitute a section of one third or one quarter of the labour market. Against the background of this argument our results are certainly rather surprising, but it is well to remember that Edwards has not taken into account the occupational labour market. Also, the situation in Finland is apparently changing in this respect.

A major theoretical problem that deserves to be mentioned at this point is the relationship between labour market segmentation and social classes. There are several theorists who believe these are fully interchangeable. Piore (1975), for example, holds that the division into upper, middle and lower classes exactly corresponds to the division of the labour market into the primary segment (two sectors) and the secondary segment. Others, such as Kreckel (1980, 525-550), deal with the problem of social inequality not in the context of classes, but by relating the power mechanisms involved to labour market strategies. Kreckel's key concept is Weber's idea of 'social closure'.

However, it is important to note that both Kreckel and Piore are abstracting from those social processes which for Wright constitute the very basis of class theory. We would argue that the most essential task is to analyse both theoretically and historically the links of the labour market's power mechanisms to the development of managerial hierarchies and job autonomy.

To the best of our knowledge there do not exist any historical analyses of the relationship between labour market segmentation and other dimensions of the internal differentiation of wage earners. Gordon, Reich and Edwards (1982) do take some steps in this direction, but they do not extend their analysis to a consideration of class differences among wage earners. They conclude that segmentation represents the third stage in the development of the internal structure of the American working class, a stage which is seriously undermining its homogeneity.

However in international comparisons we find that there are significant differences in how the development of forms of labour control are affected by labour market segmentation. It is obvious that the special characteristics of the American case — the exclusion of unskilled workers from trade unions, racial discrimination, etc. — mean that we cannot generalize the trends of segmentation discovered in the American labour market to other countries, even though there is evidence of increasing segmentation in many places (cf. Wilkinson 1982).

In the present study, segmentation is defined as *the level which mediates between class position and class situation (work and reproduction situation)*. Additionally, we are concerned with the question of how wage-worker consciousness is affected by segmentation.

Table 3.3. describes the breakdown of Finnish wage earners by labour market segments, and clearly highlights the fact that contradictory wage worker locations are indeed contradictory. The proportion of managers proper who fall in the secondary segment is much lower than in the other groups, but in lower class locations and among women in particular there is a very high proportion of workers whose privileged class position is adversely affected by their unstable position in the secondary labour market. This is especially true of women non-hierarchic decision-makers, supervisors and semi-autonomous employees. As regards men, we can see that semi-autonomous employees differ rather clearly from other contradictory locations. Men with a high degree of authority on the job are more likely to have a secure position in the labour market than others.

Looking at these statistics from a different angle (Table 3.4.), we find that in every segment there is higher and a lower section. Of all wage earners, some 60 % belong to the working class and 40 % occupy contradictory locations; the ratio is more or less the same in all segments. The necessary exception to the rule is represented by firm labour power, where there are slightly more contradictory class locations.

About one fifth of the working class is firm labour power, which means that for these workers (especially male workers in trade and services) good career prospects in the internal labour market give some compensation for their poor class position. A high proportion of workers in services are secondary labour power. In the working class, men are employed in the secondary segment more often than women, who in turn tend to belong to the external labour power of the

78

Table 3.3.
Labour market segmentation by class group and gender

	Skill-based labour power			Firm labour power			Secondary sector			Primary sector			New-comers			Total		
	All	M	W	All	M	W	All	M	W	All	M	W	All	M	W	All	M	W
Managers	7	9	4	32	29	39	7	11	0	43	47	43	7	4	14	99	100	100
Advisor-managers	13	17	8	29	17	46	10	11	8	35	39	31	13	17	8	100	101	101
Non-hierarchic decision-makers	6	7	5	34	47	25	20	13	25	31	27	3	9	57	10	100	101	100
Supervisors	0	0	0	38	36	42	17	14	21	34	36	32	11	14	5	100	100	100
Semi-autonomous employees	3	3	2	35	38	31	23	22	24	25	22	27	15	14	16	101	99	100
Workers in agriculture and forestry	9	11	0	36	44	0	27	22	50	27	22	50	0	0	0	99	99	100
Industrial workers	5	5	5	23	24	21	19	22	15	39	30	52	14	19	7	100	100	100
Workers in trade	6	0	7	26	38	22	13	15	12	35	31	37	20	15	22	100	99	100
Workers in money circulation	4	20	0	21	20	22	13	40	6	47	20	56	17	0	17	102	100	101
Workers in services	5	0	6	27	33	25	17	33	12	39	23	43	12	10	13	100	99	99
Total	5	6	5	28	30	27	17	20	14	37	32	42	13	13	12	100	101	100

Table 3.4.
Breakdown of segments by class location (%)

	Skill-based labour power	Firm labour power	Secondary sector	Primary sector	New-comers	Total
Contradictory wage worker locations	42	49	39	39	36	42
Working class	58	51	61	61	64	58
Total	100	100	100	100	100	100
N	(40)	(223)	(131)	(287)	(99)	(780)

primary segment.

On the whole, it would seem that the Finnish evidence contradicts the popular assumption that women's labour markets are characteristically secondary labour markets. In fact, the only segment where women are overrepresented in comparison with men is the external labour market of the primary segment.

3.4. White-collar workers and the class structure

It is sometimes argued that the growth of white-collar occupations is leading to the growth of a new coherent middle class between the working class and the bourgeoisie. At the same time, this same trend is assumed to be leading to the erosion of traditional class boundaries. In the context of class research, however, we have to bear in mind that the term 'white-collar worker' is first and foremost a *statistical* category: within it you will find wage earners employed in the private and the public sector; corporate managers and typists; medical doctors and translators. The term *does not* in itself imply anything about class location.

The distinction which is routinely made in social-scientific literature between white-collar and blue-collar workers is often understood as a crude division between the middle class and the working class. A closer analysis of the position and consciousness of white-collar will soon make it clear, however, that there are various fragmentations within this category and that a growing number of white-collar workers live under exactly the same kind of conditions as the traditional working class.

The number of white-collar workers has indeed been growing at an accelerating rate over the two past decades, in all advanced capitalist countries. The increase is basically due to the structural changes that have taken place in the capitalist economy: the numbers engaged in the circulation of capital and in social services have increased dramatically in comparison with the number of workers employed in industry and construction. It is important to note, however, that there are significant differences between different branches of industry. Today the majority of white-collar workers are engaged in the circulation of capital and in various jobs in the state sector; the role of industry is far less significant. By branches of industry, the highest numbers of white-collar workers are found in public services and in trade.

In the Nordic countries, statistical analyses usually categorize white-collar workers into two groups, 'upper' and 'lower' white-collar workers. This distinction is based on certain characteristics of their occupations and job tasks. The majority of white-collar workers are women: the number of white-collar women is 1.5 times higher than the number of white-collar men. Women are clearly overrepresented in the category of lower white-collar workers, whereas men represent 60 % of the higher group.

White-collar employees are traditionally engaged in tasks which require technical expertise in industry, in tasks related to capital circulation and in various tasks within the state sector. If we further divide these groups according to whether the workers concerned have decision-making tasks of private capital or the bourgeois state, we may draw the following picture of the internal differentiation of white-collar workers in Finland.

The majority of Finnish white-collar workers are in non-managerial positions; this is especially true of white-collar workers in capital circulation and in the state sector, the two most important fields of white-collar employment. Women represent 39 % of managerial and 79 % of non-managerial white-collar workers. As regards their formal position, the majority of white-collar workers are employed in routine tasks. Only 18 % occupy managerial or expert positions. Every fifth white-collar worker has more than five subordinates, and 64 % of all white-collar workers have no subordinates. Only one third of the white-collar workers have

Table 3.5.
Internal differentiation of white-collar workers (%)

Technical white-collar workers in managerial positions	10
Lower technical white-collar workers	5
Managerial white-collar workers in circulation	14
Lower white-collar workers in circulation	22
State white-collar workers in managerial positions	16
Lower state white-collar workers	26
Other white-collar workers in managerial positions	3
Other lower white-collar workers	3
N = 417	99

some decision-making function on the basis of their position, and only one in seven can independently make a decision concerning the whole organization.

We have already noted that a large part of white-collar workers are employed in the state sector. Within this sector, the majority is occupied in state services related to labour power reproduction: 86 % of the upper and 54 % of the lower white-collar workers are engaged in these tasks. Around 15 % of the Finnish white-collar workers are employed in the repressive state apparatus. Government-owned business enterprises and industries employ only one fifth of the white-collar workers, almost all of which are lower white-collar workers.

There are significant differences between white-collar worker groups and genders in income and educational levels. Managerial white-collar workers earn between 10 to 18 % more than non-managerial workers. Male white-collar workers have a far higher educational level than female white-collar workers, both in terms of the total number of schooling years and in vocational training. This would suggest that the income differentials between men and women are also related to differences in qualifications and in the value of their labour power.

The position of white-collar and blue-collar workers in the class structure also differs rather clearly between different groups. The majority of both blue-collar and lower white-collar workers fall into the working class (narrow definition); the figure among upper white-collar workers is only 8 %. The majority of upper white-collar workers are in management positions, but on the other hand one third of them are semi-autonomous employees.

The statistical categories of 'upper white-collar workers' and 'lower white-collar workers' are clearly too crude for purposes of examining the extent to which different white-collar groups bear the functions of global capital. The majority of lower white-collar workers belong to the working class, and three quarters of them are in wage worker locations close to the working class. Is it possible, then, that behind this seemingly 'neutral' statistical category there is in fact concealed an ideological project aiming to accentuate the significance of the internal differentiation of wage earners.

We can also distinguish between different fragments within the group of white-collar workers according to the nature of their work and their consciousness. There are clear differences even between the two crude statistical categories of upper and lower white-collar workers in levels of job autonomy, the strenuousness of work and the content of work. On these dimensions there are particularly significant differences between managerial and non-managerial white-collar

Table 3.6.

Class position of white-collar and blue-collar workers (%)

	Higher white-collar	Lower white-collar	Industrial workers	Other workers	Total
Managers	39	13	3	1	12
Advisor-managers	16	11	4	4	9
Supervisors	5	10	5	1	6
Semi-autonomous employees	32	13	13	5	14
Working class	8	53	75	89	59
N = 790	100	100	100	100	100

workers: more than 60 % of managerial workers and only 20 % of non-managerial white-collar workers have a high level of job autonomy (following Wright's criteria). 46 % of managerial white-collar workers have the opportunity to develop their skills at work, whereas the figure for non-managerial white-collar workers is only about 25 %.

In conclusion, we may note that the majority of Finnish white-collar workers are employed within the state sector and in tasks related to capital circulation. Most of them are in non-managerial positions. Only less than 10 % have decision-making authority in matters concerning the whole organization. A further 10 % have lower managerial tasks. The majority of white-collar workers are women, most of whom are in lower positions; men are clearly overrepresented in managerial positions.

White-collar workers do not represent a new middle class, but are internally differentiated in many different ways. The vast majority of white-collar workers have routine jobs with no authority and no real influence at the workplace level. Rather than representing a class group proper, we propose that these workers form several cultural groupings within working life.

3.5. State employees

The striking growth in the numbers of civil servants and the growth of bureaucracy in general has given rise to a lively debate in Finland in which there are two rival camps: those in favour of developing the public sector and those who argue that the social state should be dismantled. The questions involved in this debate directly concern wage earners who are in the employ of the state, municipal authorities and government-owned business enterprises. These 'state employees', as we shall call them here, have one important feature in common: their salaries come directly out of taxes rather than from the profits of capitalists.

In this section we are concerned with the position of state employees within the class relations of modern capitalism. The civil servant question in general has received a great deal of attention in sociology and other adjacent disciplines, and in recent years it has also become a focal issue of many Marxian analyses. Among Marxists, however, there are many different emphases and views on the position, tasks and consciousness of state employees, and also different interpretations of the critique of political economy.

PKA (1978, 274), for instance, holds that state employees represent the middle class capital because their salaries come directly out of taxes. Poulantzas (1975, 188), then, classifies state employees under the bourgeoisie or the new petty bourgeoisie, depending on their specific position and tasks.

In Wright's classification state employees represent a group whose position is not directly determined by production relations; other such groups are housewives, students, pensioners and the unemployed. State employees do not constitute a separate category, but they are classified under *employees in political and ideological apparatuses* (1978, 95-96). According to Wright, different positions within the bureaucratic structures of the political and ideological apparatuses of capitalist society have different relationships to bourgeois and proletarian class interests. He identifies three functional categories:

(1) Bourgeois positions, i.e. state employees with control over the creation of state policies and the production of ideology in ideological apparatuses.

(2) Contradictory locations, i.e. state employees with functions related to the execution of state policies and dissemination of ideology.

(3) Proletarian positions, i.e. state employees who are excluded from the creation and execution of state policies and ideology.

Wright argues that these three levels can be operationalized in the same way

84

as in the case of private capital, which means that he applies the same principles in analysing both these groups. However, this approach involves certain serious problems. In the first place Wright omits to specify the role of the state as an employer and therefore ignores the form of income aspect. Secondly, he fails to make any distinction between different state sectors, in which the positions of state employees may differ significantly. Finally, the decision-making procedure in the state apparatus differs in certain important respects from that in private firms. The Comparative Project on Class Structure and Class Consciousness has itself produced many critical comments on this aspect of Wright's work (see e.g. Ahrne and Leiulfsrud 1984; Hoff 1985).

In Finnish capitalism, the state has always played an extremely important role. It was particularly active in building up the country's industrial infrastructure after the Second World War, and even today it represents a major political and economic influence in society. On the other hand, the state accounts only for a rather small share of total GNP: the main objective of state economic policy has been to secure the international competitiveness of the country's major export industries.

In comparison with many other OECD countries, Finland has a rather small public sector. At the end of 1985 it employed a total over 650,000 workers, or almost 30 % of the economically active population and about 40 % of all wage workers. The distribution of Finnish state employees by branch of industry is shown in Table 3.7.

The data in Table 3.7. also show the main differences between the state and the rest of the public sector. In Finland the state is responsible for organizing public administration and national defence, and also for a large part of public transportation. Most collective services such as health care and education are primarily organized by municipal authorities.

Below we move on to discuss certain aspects of decision-making authority and control functions in different state employee groups. The majority of Finnish state employees are engaged in performance-level jobs, or in various expert positions. 73 % have no subordinates; 10 % have less than five subordinates; and 17 % have more than five. Supervisory tasks therefore seem to be highly concentrated as well.

About 60 % of the state employees are women. Without going into the gender differences in any detail, it is useful to note that women have far less decision-making authority than men; that they occupy supervisory positions less often than

85

Table 3.7.
Breakdown of state employees by branch of industry (%)

	State	Public sector (state and local government)
Agriculture and forestry	1	1
Industry	7	5
Construction	13	13
Transportation	31	14
Trade and commerce	1	1
Public administration and defence	36	18
Education	9	17
Health care	1	19
Other services	1	13
	100	101

Source: STV 1979, Table 285

men; and that they have poorer opportunities for career advancement.

One important advantage of Wright's theory is that it makes possible an analysis of quantitative developments in various class groups occupying contradictory locations. Table 3.8 below describes the position of Finnish state employees in the class structure on the basis of Wright's typology. We notice that 34 % of our state employees are engaged in various managerial and supervisory tasks, 46 % belong to the working class and 20 % are semi-autonomous employees. Wright classifies most members of the intelligentsia under semi-autonomous employees; in the case of state employees, these include teachers and health care personnel.

Examined by gender, these statistics indicate that three quarters of women state employees are excluded from all types of control on the job; the figure for men is less than 50 %. The proportion of men who are managers proper (27 %) is more than twice as high as the proportion in women (12 %). Women belong to the category of semi-autonomous employees slightly more often than men, and they are engaged in performance-level jobs with no decision-making authority far more often: 66 % of all state employees occupied in such positions are women. Finally, 69 % of semi-autonomous and 40 % of managerial state employees are women.

86

Table 3.8.

Class position of state employees by gender (%)

	Women	Men	Total
Managers	12	27	17
Advisor-managers	7	16	10
Supervisors	4	9	6
Semi-autonomous employees	22	17	20
Working class	54	31	46
Total	100	100	100
N	(172)	(118)	(290)

PKA's theory has a definite advantage over Wright's in that it allows us to differentiate between various state employee groups by type of function within the state apparatus. Table 3.9. shows that a clear majority of state employees are engaged in various tasks related to labour power reproduction. Only 16 % of all Finnish state employees are engaged in public administration.

As we pointed out earlier, different class theories have differing views on the class position and consciousness of state employees; the obvious reason lies in the different interpretations they offer of the critique of political economy and of its relationship to historical materialism. However, in the context of class analysis our main concern should not be to pigeonhole state employees into this or that stratum or class, but to identify the underlying factors that determine the position and consciousness of state employees, and also to examine the relationship of state employees to the state and social classes.

There are two basic points which must not be ignored in the analysis of state employees: first, the structural distinction between the state and civil society and second, the economic and political dependence of the state on the process of capital accumulation. Although state employees reproduce their labour power in exactly the same way as other wage-earner groups through the wages they receive, there are significant differences in the actual wage-forms: the wages of state employees are behind various political mediations.

There is a high degree of internal differentiation within the category of state employees: over 80 % of Finnish state employees are engaged in performance-level tasks. Half of them occupy positions which are comparable to working-class positions and one third occupy managerial positions; this is about 5 % more than among all wage earners. In the category of state employees there are also more

Table 3.9.

Internal differentiation of state employees according to PKA

A. Employees in state's repressive apparatus		
1. Internal administration	8	
2. Economic administration	3	
3. Defence forces	3	
4. Public security	2	
5. Judicial system	-	16 %
B. Employees in social state apparatus		
6. Education	12	
7. Science and culture	8	
8. Health care	22	
9. Social welfare	17	
10. Radio and TV	1	
11. Other	1	61 %
C. Employees in state apparatus for production infrastructure		
12. Community services	5	
13. Economic enterprises	13	
14. Other	6	24 %
N = 290		101 %

semi-autonomous employees than in other sectors of the economy.

Further, it is important to note that the work of state employees is organized on completely different principles than within the technical mode of production. There are of course various tasks in the state apparatus which exactly correspond to ordinary office work and which are therefore subjected to the same kind of rationalization process as in the private sector, but on the whole we may safely argue that state employees have greater autonomy on the job than industrial workers, for example. State employees also have better chances to decide on matters related to their work process than most other wage earners.

In recent years there has been a clear tendency in all advanced capitalist societies for the state to play an increasingly active role in social life. At the same time, we have seen the growth of such marginal groups who are excluded from the economically active population; in a sense, students, pensioners and the unemployed are in the same position as state employees, in that their income is paid directly out of taxes. Likewise, the bourgeoisie, the petty bourgeoisie and the peasantry are also dependent on the state through various types of subsidies and loans.

3.6. Managers and the differentiation of managerial functions

Who are managers, what do managers do? How much power do managers have? Who are today's companies and organizations actually run by? During the past 20 years or so company management and managerial strategies have been discussed in a number of sociological studies (see e.g. Edwards 1979; Friedman 1977; Hill 1981; Scott 1979). Most of these have been primarily concerned with organizational control and with the development and differentiation of forms of control.

In early capitalism the functions of management and ownership were not separated in the same way as they are today, but were personified in one and the same owner-manager: the capitalist who owned the factory was also responsible for its management. In the biggest factories he would have a few hired foremen to take care of supervision on the shopfloor, or alternatively an independent contractor who would be responsible for certain parts of the production process and at the same time for the supervision of these workers. These contractor arrangements represented a kind of 'system of co-exploitation'. There were very few hired managers (Hill 1981, 17-23).

Inside the factory, the workers were kept under strict control by means of both economic and non-economic sanctions. However, there were considerable differences in how different worker groups were treated: skilled workers and craftsmen were usually in a much better position than unskilled labourers.

The expansion of production and technological development meant that the capitalist had to make certain organizational and administrative changes. In addition, the bourgeois state became an influential actor in labour relations, as legislation on employment relations began to increase in the early nineteenth century. There were a number of revolutionary technological innovations such as the conveyer belt, which was first introduced in the textile industry in the mid-nineteenth century, and these had a significant impact on the size of factory units. One single factory could have a payroll of several thousand workers. These changes meant that the owner-manager was no longer capable of running the factory on his own. He needed hired managers who took over part of his tasks.

Table 3.10.
Distribution of different manager types into Wright's class groups (%)

	Top managers	Middle managers	Lower managers	All
Managers	96	62	10	44
Advisor-managers	-	-	30	14
Non-hierarchic decision-makers	4	38	7	16
Supervisors	-	-	12	6
Semi-autonomous employees	-	-	24	11
Working class	-	-	17	9
%	100	100	100	100
N	45	71	105	221

Consequently, company organizations became far more complicated. (For an important analysis of the development of management and managerial structures, see Chandler 1977; comparisons of strategies in different countries can be found in Chandler and Daems 1980.)

In a comparison of the class structures of Finland, Sweden and the USA, the clearest differences are found in the proportions of managers and the petty bourgeoisie. Finland has by far the largest petty bourgeoisie, which is of course due to its larger agricultural population. In the USA there are more managers than in Finland and Sweden: the proportion of managers proper is 12 %, that of advisor-managers 4.5 %, and that of supervisors 13 % (Wright 1982, 32). The latter figure in particular differs significantly from the numbers in Finland and Sweden: in Finland, supervisors represents a mere 3.5 % of the economically active population. The reason for these differences lies in the fact that both industrial production and public administration are organized on a different basis in the two countries, in that direct control is more common in Finland. In comparison with Sweden, the number of managers and advisor-managers is roughly the same in both countries, but the proportion of supervisors is higher in Sweden (Ahrne 1982, 25).

Categorized according to Wright's class scheme, less than half of Finnish managers belong to the class group of managers, and 80 % occupy managerial positions. One fifth of the managers are semi-autonomous employees or working-class, i.e. they are excluded from control over investments, the means of production, or the use of other people's labour power.

In the group of top managers, 96 % fall under the class group of managers and the remaining 4 % under non-hierarchic decision-makers. Middle managers are divided between managers proper (62 %) and non-hierarchic decision-makers (38 %). Lower managers (supervisors and foremen) are divided more evenly between the various class groups.

In the following analysis managers are divided into three different types on the basis of Wright's class typology. The main criterion in this classification is involvement in the company's or organization's decision-making process:

Top managers: take part in decision-making concerning number of workforce, products/services produced, amount of work to be done and budgeting. Decides alone or as a member of a group on at least three issues.

Middle managers: takes part in decision-making concerning number of workforce, products/services produced, amount of work to be done and budgeting. Decides alone or as a member of a group on at most two issues.

Lower managers: take part in decision-making concerning number of workforce, products/services produced, or amount of work to be done. Decides alone or as a member of a group on at most one issue.

Table 3.11.
Managers by manager types (%)

	%
Top managers	23.9
Middle managers	33.8
Lower managers	42.3

The majority of the managers included in our material do not have decision-making authority in any matters concerning the whole organization; these lower managers represent almost half of the total managerial sample. One fourth of them are top managers and about one third are middle managers. A significant part of the managers are also excluded from real organizational control: their position within the managerial hierarchy is based more on the social division of labour than on real power in the organization. It would therefore seem that the question of managerial hierarchies is more intimately bound up with class relations than we have previously assumed.

There are rather clear differences between the Nordic countries and Northern America in the internal differentiation of managers. Nordic countries have far more top managers than the USA and Canada, where the proportion of lower managers is accordingly higher. At the level of the class structure, these differences are reflected e.g. in the lower proportion of supervisors in the Nordic countries. In their comparison of the class structures of Sweden and the USA, Erik Wright and Göran Ahrne argued that this difference is at least partly due to the conscious efforts of American capitalism to undermine the strength of the working class by endowing proletarian positions with a certain measure of formal power (Ahrne and Wright 1984).

The Finnish managers we studied were surprisingly young: 47 % of them were under 35 years of age, and only 7 % were 55 or over. Top managers were older than the other manager types. These figures indicate a dramatic change in the age structure of managers: according to the results of a Finnish study carried out in 1962 (Laaksonen 1962, 88), only 3 % of the managers were under 35 years and 42 % were over 55. In comparison with Sweden, Finnish managers are slightly younger. In the material investigated by the Swedish class project, 31 % were under 35 and 15 % were over 50; the figures for supervisors were 35 % and 25 %, respectively (Ahrne 1982, 22).

Women have traditionally been excluded from managerial and supervisory tasks. However, with the expansion of female employment and the improvement of their social position in general, this would now seem to be changing, albeit slowly: men still occupy the clear majority of managerial positions. 60 % of our managers — 64 % of top managers, 62 % of middle managers and 59 % of lower managers — are men.

Table 3.12.
Internal differentiation of managerial groups

	USA	Canada	Norway	Sweden	Finland	TOTAL
Top managers	13.2	12.2	23.8	16.7	23.9	17.2
Middle managers	17.2	25.6	33.6	24.9	33.8	26.4
Lower managers	69.6	62.2	42.5	58.4	42.3	56.4
Total	100	100	100	100	100	100
N	402	405	386	245	213	1696

Finnish managers are rather well-educated. About half of all the managers included in our sample had a university degree. The figure was highest in the category of top managers (60 %), which was significantly higher than the average for all wage earners (approx 25 %). Within the category of managers, lower managers had much less schooling than the other two groups: less than half of them had a university degree and 21 % had no secondary schooling. The results of a study carried out in northern Finland show that 45 % of the workers employed in the local companies have matriculated and only 5 % have a university degree (Tainio 1982, 32).

Finnish managers are employed slightly more often in the private sector than in the public sector: 51 % work for private capital and 49 % are in the employ of the state. Managers of government-owned companies were here classified as workers of the private sector. Comparing the distribution of managers by economic sector in the Nordic countries and the United States (Table 3.13.), we see that the proportion of managers employed in private companies is significantly higher in the US. In the Nordic countries the proportion of managers working in the public sector is twice as high as in the United States.

By sectors of the economy, the vast majority of Finnish managers are employed in the service sector. Industry is the second most important employer for middle and lower managers, whereas top managers work slightly more often in trade and commerce. The fact that most managers are employed in the service sector is primarily due to the recent expansion of both public and private services.

The position of managers in the social division of labour can also be examined on the basis of the size of the companies they work for. In the private sector, the category which holds the highest proportion of managers is represented by companies with 10-49 employees: 13 % of all managers are employed in such companies. However, in all managerial categories more than one third are employed in public administration. Middle managers are in the employ of the state more often than the other manager types. Top managers are rather evenly distributed between private companies of different sizes (7-9 %), but are most often employed by the state (31 %) and cooperatives (15 %).

In firms with less than 19 employees, lower managers represent 60 %, middle managers 25 % and top managers 15 % of all managers. The relative share of top managers is highest in cooperatives, in government-owned companies and in companies with 500—1000 employees (58 %, 30 % and 33 % of all managers). Middle managers represent the relative majority in companies with 10—100

Table 3.13.
Distribution of managers by economic sector

	USA	Canada	Norway	Sweden	Finland
private	64.6	-	52.1	48.6	51.4
public	23.8	-	44.0	45.3	46.6
other	11.8	-	3.9	6.2	1.9
Top managers in public sector	25	-	35	39	29

employees and in companies with 500—1000 employees (45 % and 44 % of all managers).

Looking at the position of managers in the social division of labour according to the complexity of the organization, we may note that almost 75 % of the organizations included in our analysis had a maximum of three grades or levels of supervisory positions. Lower managers were in relative terms the largest group in organizations with fewer grades, while middle managers are typically employed in organizations with only one level of supervision. Top managers, then, usually work in organizations with three levels of supervision.

As was discussed earlier, one of the main objectives of scientific management is to concentrate all information concerning the company and all decision-making authority into the hands of the managers. In Finland it seems that capitalists and company-owners have succeeded extremely well in this policy. Almost three quarters of all Finnish wage earners have no say in questions relevant to their own work organization, and only 6 % have control over investments, the means of production and other people's labour. In all, one fifth of the wage earners have decision-making authority on at least one of these dimensions. One tenth have no decision-making authority but some measure of supervisory authority.

About four fifths of Finnish wage workers are excluded from control over the use of money capital. Every tenth may suggest approval of a matter or provide advice on it. Only 9 % can decide alone or are members of a group making the decision. Decision-making authority in questions related to the use of the means of production is less centralized than control over money capital: 74 % have no decision-making authority, 14 % may give advice and 12 % are directly involved in decision-making. The distribution of control over the use of other people's labour power is more or less the same as in the case of control over the means of production. This would seem to suggest that the more important the matter or resource, the smaller the number of workers who have the authority to make final decisions. In other words, the most important strategic decisions that affect the whole organization are clearly made by a small, select elite. There is still a long way to go to true industrial democracy.

In a discussion of the concentration of power it must of course be borne in mind that the control embodied in capitalist owners is based upon their legal rights; these provide the general framework for the power of managers. Hirszowic (1981, 127) says that in large companies there are three main power centres: the shareholders, the board of directors and the managers. The power exercised by managers is subordinate to the power of the owners of the company and their representatives.

In matters related to workers' everyday activities, managers have considerable supervisory authority, but there are major differences here between different types of managers. Top managers are much more often responsible for what their subordinates do or fail to do, while lower managers have far less supervisory authority than other manager types. Our empirical material seems to suggest that supervisory tasks are also organized on a relatively centralized basis. Lower managers do not have very much individual decision-making authority over their subordinates' work; the final decisions are usually made by top managers. The centralization of decision-making authority is also evident in the numbers of subordinates: top managers have an average 21 subordinates and lower managers only 5 subordinates.

Table 3.14.
Supervisory responsibility and decision-making authority of managers (%)

	Top managers	Middle managers	Lower managers
Delegates tasks to subordinates	87	57	43
Decides on subordinates' working methods	73	52	44
Decides on pay rises	56	23	27
Gives notice	51	24	21

N = 221

Table 3.15.
Trade union membership in managerial groups (%)

	USA	Canada	Norway	Sweden	Finland
Top managers	9	16	57	66	51
Middle managers	7	28	64	67	79
Lower managers	14	32	67	80	80
Non-managerial	19	36	62	81	81

It is generally believed that different wage worker groups tend to have very different kinds of daily routines; that managers and other groups occupying supervisory positions enjoy far greater freedom at work than performance-level workers; and that blue-collar workers must observe stricter rules and regulations on the job than white-collar workers. Our empirical analysis supports all these assumptions.

Of all Finnish wage workers, 63 % have a job in which they can design central aspects of the work process, or in which they can use their initiative in carrying out their tasks. Among managers the figure is 92 %. The clear difference between managers and other wage earner groups is also evident in other aspects of work, such as the possibility to decide on one's working hours, taking days off, determining the pace of one's work, etc. Only one out of five wage workers can decide independently on working hours as compared with 41 % of managers. One fifth of the wage workers but every other manager can have a day off without loss of pay. Managers also differ from other wage worker groups in terms of job autonomy, and there are significant differences even between different manager types: top managers have much greater freedom in arranging their daily work than others.

In terms of unionization levels among managers, there are some very clear differences between the Nordic and North American countries. In the United States, where unionization levels in general are rather low (with approx. 20 % of all wage earners registered as union members), only very few managers belong to the union. In the Nordic countries, where unionization levels are extremely high by any standards (with more than 80 % of all wage earners in Sweden and Finland registered as union members), unionization levels are also higher among managers. It would seem that in the Nordic countries managers have fundamental common interests which they are trying to promote via unionization (see Melin 1990).

3.7. Semi-autonomous employees

Semi-autonomous employees are those workers who occupy a contradictory location between the petty bourgeoisie and the working class. Wright explains the position of this group by reference to the historical process of proletarianization of the petty bourgeoisie, in which the central motive force was the need of capital to increase its control over the labour process (Wright 1978, 80-83).

Wright points out that this process is constantly being re-enacted; it was not completed at the beginning of this century:

> Today there are still categories of employees who have a certain degree of control over their own immediate conditions of work, over their immediate labour process. In such instances, the labour process has not been completely proletarianized. Thus, even though such employees work for the self-expansion of capital and even though they have lost the legal status of being self-employed, they can still be viewed as occupying residual islands of petty-bourgeois relations of production within the capitalist mode of production itself. In their immediate work environment, they maintain the work process of the independent artisan while still being employed by capital as wage labourers. They control *how* they do their work, and have at least some control over *what* they produce. (ibid., 80-81)

Wright defines autonomy as control over one's work process; this is the main criterion he uses in defining positions as occupying the contradictory class location between the working class and the petty bourgeoisie. There are, however, certain difficulties in this line of reasoning. Wright starts from the requirement that autonomy must be directly visible in the nature and conditions of the immediate labour process. Unlike most sociologists of work, Wright does not develop indicators of autonomy on the basis of different dimensions of control over the labour process (pace, tasks, planning, schedule, etc.); his central criterion is the ability of people to realize their own ideas at work, to plan and design certain aspects of the product or service they are producing. The minimum criterion for semi-autonomy is that such positions must involve at least some control both over what is produced (minimal economic ownership) and over how it is produced (minimal possession). This definition, Wright argues, captures the petty-bourgeois character of semi-autonomy, as the petty bourgeoisie is characterized by the unity of mental and manual labour.

Wright links up his discussion with Poulantzas's analysis of mental labour. Poulantzas defines mental labour as labour which involves 'secret knowledge' of the production process. He argues that experts of various sorts help to legitimize the subordination of labour to capital, by making it appear natural that workers are incapable of organizing production themselves.

Mental labour can therefore not be defined as 'brain work' and manual labour as 'hand work', but the division must be regarded as an aspect of the social division of labour — as concerning the organization and coordination of the total labour process — and the related 'secret knowledge'. Wright argues that semi-autonomous employees have this kind of knowledge and also the possibility to use it at work. This is what he means by minimal control over what is produced and how it is produced.

Wright's description contains elements both of the general theory of mode of production and of the separation of mental and manual labour. At this point it is useful to single out three major theoretical problems in Wright's argumentation:

(1) There is an obvious mismatch between the theoretical derivation and the empirical scope of Wright's concept. He derives autonomy from simple commodity production yet includes in it phenomena which originate in different historical processes.

In order to solve this problem, we must transcend Wright's research setting. First of all, it is necessary to specify the role of autonomy in the structuration of work situation in greater detail.[6] For this purpose the Finnish class project has introduced a typology of different subtypes of autonomy, which are represented by the following positions:

- traditional occupations of the intelligentsia (professional autonomy);
- occupations retaining features of petty-bourgeois autonomy and control over the whole labour process (craftsman's autonomy);
- occupations related to the new cognitive and motivational requirements of work (scientific-technical autonomy);
- occupations in the field of caring and reproduction (autonomy of caring and reproduction);
- occupations in office work where the division of labour is not highly differentiated (office work autonomy);
- occupations in small enterprises where the division of labour re-mains more or less undifferentiated (autonomy of small enterprises);
- autonomy of employees required by the valorization of capital (capital-adequate autonomy).

Even this crude characterization of our typology knocks the bottom out of certain important tenets of Wright's theory. Firstly, it is obvious that autonomy is not restricted to the petty-bourgeois labour process. As Wright himself points out, autonomy is intimately bound up with the strategies adopted by the bourgeoisie for purposes of controlling the labour process, and these change with history.[7] The important difference, however, is that these strategies are determined by the class conflicts and power relations prevailing at each moment in time. It is therefore highly questionable whether autonomy can be derived from the theory of mode of production in the first place. In addition, if autonomy is a result of ideologically mediated processes, then is it justified to regard it as a determinant of class structure; at what level can such a theory of autonomy be systematized?[8] If, as it seems, there exist a number of different types of autonomy and mental labour, then obviously these should be taken into account in developing our class criteria. This would lead us to the discovery that there does not exist any privileged type of mental labour, and that autonomy is not necessarily a residual criterion in the determination of managerial positions.

Bearing in mind these problems and contradictions in Wright's theory, we shall attempt below to produce a rough picture of the class group which according to Wright's criteria represent semi-autonomous contradictory class locations. Our aim is to describe the position of semi-autonomous employees in the social division of labour and the paths along which people seem to end up in these locations in Finland.

On the whole Finnish semi-autonomous employees have a comparatively high level of education. One third of them have passed the matriculation examination, which is far more than in the working class (less than one in seven) and in supervisors (one in five). In addition, the proportion of those who have some vocational training is higher among semi-autonomous employees (65 %) than in any other class group. Those who have a university degree represent 46 % of semi-autonomous employees, while the figure for all Finnish wage workers is only 22 %. By contrast, on-the-job training is less common in the group of semi-autonomous employees than in supervisors and managers.

On the basis of our typology of subtypes of autonomy, we can compare the empirical characteristics of semi-autonomous employees with Wright's conceptualizations.

About half of the autonomy occurring in this class group is of the type that provides the basis for Wright's definition of this class group: *professional* (28 %) and *craftsman's autonomy* (21 %). Half is not perhaps a very accurate estimate, but this 'original' autonomy is nevertheless highly concentrated in the group of semi-autonomous employees; there is no other wage earner group with higher proportions of these types of autonomy. Looking at our statistics from the opposite direction, we note that over half (52 %) of professional autonomy and over one third (36 %) of craftsman's autonomy is situated in the group of semi-autonomous employees. The other half of autonomy in this group is evenly divided between different types: scientific-technical (14 %), caring and reproduction (14 %) and autonomy typical of small enterprises (11 %). The share of capital-adequate autonomy is relatively low (9 %).

There are clear gender differences in the prevalence of types of autonomy. In women, a large number have professional autonomy (42 %) and caring and reproduction autonomy (29 %); in men the most common types of autonomy are craftsman's autonomy (37 %) and scientific-technical autonomy (21 %). In other words, both genders have succeeded in gaining new types of autonomy and in maintaining traditional types, and even the 'new' type corresponds to the traditional gender roles and the gender division of labour. From the prevalence of the 'old' type of autonomy, we might conclude that women require a more solid basis on which they can fight to maintain their autonomy on the job.

By object of work, the tasks of semi-autonomous employees are clearly differentiated along the gender lines; see Table 3.16.

Semi-autonomous employees are almost completely excluded from work whose object is money or which concerns the whole organization; in this sense we may argue that they do not bear important functions of capital. The most common object of work in semi-autonomous employees is represented by information. Women are more often engaged in tasks related to information processing and in tasks whose objects are other people; men tend to work more often on the

Table 3.16.
Object of work of semi-autonomous employees by gender (%)

Object of work	Women	Men
Human being	33	2
Material product	15	28
Infrastructure	-	26
Human action	2	7
Information	49	33
Money	2	3
	101	101
(N)	(55)	(58)

material side, in the production of goods and infrastructures. This means that the majority of women in semi-autonomous locations have tasks which can be described as extensive (93 %) and non-routine (80 %); the same applies to men, although the figures are much lower (69 % and 60 %).

In conclusion, semi-autonomous employees seem to represent an extremely heterogeneous class group, which is typically entered via educational and occupational socialization. The heterogeneity of this group is further enhanced by the marked differences between men and women. However, there is no evidence in support of Wright's theory that these people should be slotted in a class group somewhere between the petty bourgeoisie and the working class, or that its autonomy is a remnant of labour processes characteristic of the petty bourgeoisie. Semi-autonomous employees do of course differ from the working class in that they have greater autonomy on the job and also a higher level of education and a more stable position in the labour market; but it is not justified to regard these characteristics as remnants of 'petty-bourgeois production relations'.

4 The structuration of class situation at work

4.1. Class theory and the labour process

In this chapter our main concern is with the problem as to how work situation is structured by class location. At this level of analysis it is necessary to start with a discussion of the labour process; more specifically, with a discussion of the subsumption of labour under capital, strategies of labour process control, and job autonomy.

In *Capital* Marx conceptualized the relationship between the labour process and the valuation process by proposing a distinction between formal and real subsumption of labour under capital (Marx 1976). Although he links up the production of absolute and relative surplus value with formal and real subsumption, the latter are not only logical and analytical concepts but also important tools in describing the historical development of the capitalist mode of production. The concepts of formal and real subsumption have therefore served as a theoretical basis not only for historical and conceptual analyses of the labour process, but also for elaborations of the critique of political economy.

The concept of real subsumption forms the basis of Jürgen Mendner's (1973) detailed theory of the labour process. There is one particular argument in Mendner's theory that deserves special attention: he says that there exists an adequate form of capitalist labour process which is concretized in the Taylorist work organization. Under Taylorism, the fragmentation and systematic organization of work lead to the intensification of work and at the same time to a process of labour dequalification, which make it an ideal form of labour process organization both from the point of view of capital reproduction and from the point of view of the reproduction of the capital relation. Mendner does not deny that crises may emerge within this pure form, but as he points out these are based on the conflict between labour and capital. Any new forms of work organization that might appear are merely propaganda or transient phenomena bound up with technological development; ultimately they will all fall victim to the process of real subsumption (ibid., 129-154, 169-182).

Mendner's views are almost identical with Braverman's theory of the capitalist labour process,[1] but nevertheless there are certain differences in emphasis. Braverman holds that the processes of Taylorization and degradation of work are fundamentally determined by the conscious effort on the part of the capitalist to subject the worker to ever stricter control, but Mendner emphasizes the preconditions for the *production of surplus value*. Indeed, a major deficiency in Braverman's concept relates to his failure to take into account the direct and indirect costs that are caused to capital by the mechanisms of control.

However, attempts to develop the theoretical legacy of the critique of political economy on the basis of the concept of real subsumption have opened other, broader perspectives as well. A consideration of the capitalist form-determination of the labour process leads us to new questions: Does the technology that is materialized in the production machinery have a specifically capitalist nature? And what about use values?

An accurate description of form adequacy can be derived from the first categorical imperative of capital:

> Form-adequate is whatever makes possible the production of surplus value; in concrete terms, form-adequate is whatever makes possible the maximization of profits. Although the hierarchic organization of the labour process, for example, is and will always be a permanent characteristic of the capitalist work organization, capitalism does not fix itself to certain concrete forms of use value, but flexibly changes the use value quality so as to ensure optimal valorization. (Hartikainen 1979, 101)

According to this interpretation, crises of real subsumption (i.e. valorization) are caused not only by worker resistance and class conflicts, but also by all those historical changes which undermine the concrete preconditions for capital reproduction. Resistance merely represents one of many potential counterforces: the international division of labour within capitalism, technological change, natural crises such as environmental pollution, changes in the needs of wage-worker subjects, etc.

Erik Wright bases his theory on the assumption that job autonomy, the level of control exerted by the worker over the labour process, is the result of the development of class relations (Wright 1978, 64-67). In the course of capitalist development, there is a progressive loss of worker autonomy; the only group which has retained something of the full autonomy of the artisan is represented by semi-autonomous employees. But even Wright admits that autonomy has not just disappeared; it has been dispossessed through the subsumption of labour under capital. On the reverse side of the coin, we have various forms of external control over the labour process. Through a study of these processes, we can obtain a cross-sectional picture of levels of autonomy in different class positions and on this basis distinguish semi-autonomous employees from the working class.

As we pointed out, the progressive loss of autonomy and control over the labour process is basically due to the real subsumption of labour under capital. If this process followed a given historical course, we could justifiably use the present 'stage' of development at each moment in time as a criterion of class position. However, we do not believe that this is the case. We start from the hypothesis that real subsumption is a historical process which is determined by the internal contradictions of the capital relation and which can only be unravelled by empirical research. That is, real subsumption is not a predetermined, straightforward process. It is a process that recurs in ever-changing forms.

Friedman (1977) makes a distinction between two basic forms of organizational control in modern capitalism: (1) direct control (technical control) that is based on Taylorist principles, and (2) responsible autonomy, where workers are integrated to the organization's goals by allowing them some degree of freedom (autonomy) and by encouraging them to adapt to possible changes in work and in the work organization. The means used to this end include rewarding, offering status and sharing responsibility. The choice of strategy is in the last instance determined by the strength of worker resistance: if it is well-organized, the tendency is to use responsible autonomy; when the workers are more divided, the employer will opt for the method of direct control. In a later context Friedman (1986, 113) has pointed out that one should not confuse any particular managerial technique (such as Taylorism) with a definition of direct control; a strict conceptual distinction must be made between strategies and techniques.

Edwards (1979) has suggested that the predominant mode of labour control in modern capitalism is represented by bureaucratic control, the main instruments of which include strict regulations (e.g. promotion ladders), discipline, wage scales, determination of responsibility and so on. Bureaucratic control institutionalizes the hierarchic use of power in enterprises and other organizations. It aims

104

above all at eliminating the influence of the trade union movement, integrating the workers to the goals of the enterprise and at getting the trade union movement involved in the control of workers.

Although Friedman and Edwards make an important contribution to our understanding of labour power control under modern capitalism, it is obviously incorrect to give too much prominence to one particular form of control because most capitalist enterprises, for most of the time, pursue a number of different control strategies at the same time. The kind of pure types they propose do simply not exist in reality. Additionally, both Friedman and Edwards omit to consider the most fundamental economic coercion of capitalism: the need to sell one's labour power in order to reproduce it. This of course represents a highly efficient means of labour power control, particularly in times of economic crisis and unemployment. Furthermore, the strength of the working class varies from one country to another depending on its political organization and the stage of development of political forces. The studies by Littler (1982) and Burawoy (1983) on the Taylorization of the labour process and the development of forms of control clearly point to the importance of national differences and the mediating role of the state. Burawoy (1985) has also pointed out that forms of control are always part of a wider structure of social and political relations in production, a 'regime'.

One of the main deficiencies Erik Olin Wright's theory is that it does not elaborate in detail the development of real subsumption and the processes which create and dispossess workers of job autonomy. The same applies more generally to his concept of autonomy.

Wright's argument that the progressive loss of worker control over the labour process represents a basic process of class relations exactly corresponds to the reasoning of Braverman. Braverman identifies two parallel tendencies in the loss of control exercised by skilled workers: first, the Taylorization of production and supervision and second, the development of machinery which results from technological and scientific progress. Wright summarizes: 'The close supervision of the labour process is much easier when tasks are simple and routinized and their pace is determined by machinery rather than the worker. Thus, capitalists look for innovations which tend to reduce skill levels and reduce the autonomy of workers on the job.' (Wright 1976, 65)

There are, however, a number of problems with Braverman's arguments (cf. e.g. Burawoy 1978; Stark 1980; Elger 1982). In the first place he draws a rather idealistic picture of precapitalist relations of production: throughout his discussion

105

of deskilling and loss of autonomy, he uses an ideal type of artisan as a yardstick. Braverman also fails to consider the possibility of alternative managerial strategies and working class resistance. If monopoly capital resorts to the strategy of responsible autonomy in the subordination of labour, this can hardly be related in conceptual terms to simple commodity production.

4.2. The structuration of work and reproduction situation

The main concern of class theory is not to demonstrate that some people are rich and others poor. Nonetheless it is reasonable to argue that the distribution of wealth in society is largely determined by relations of domination and appropriation.

Figure 4.1. shows the annual income and standard of living of Finnish households by class group. The latter figures are based on the respondents' estimates of how much disposable income the family has available and should therefore be interpreted with caution: the answers obviously reflect both the respondents' financial situation and their consumption habits. However, our aim here is not to describe in detail the living conditions of Finnish households, but merely to give a preliminary answer to the question as to whether class structure plays any role in the reproduction situation.

Employers and hired representatives of employers are clearly better off than other wage-earner categories in Finland. The reproduction situation of semi-autonomous and supervisory wage workers is also relatively good, although their position on the labour market is less secure. Workers in money circulation lead a more secure life in this respect, but they have more difficulties in making ends meet. In the reproduction situation of wage workers engaged in commodity circulation, services and above all in industry, insecurity represents a greater threat than financial difficulties; industrial workers have the additional problem of poor working conditions. The small agrarian proletariat lives more or less at subsistence level and is also in the worst position in terms of both security and qualifications required on the labour market.

In the petty bourgeois category, the reproduction situation of farmers depends more or less directly on how much personal property they have. If the agricultural petty bourgeoisie had to go out and do wage work to earn a living, their reproduction situation would be extremely difficult because they lack all the skills and qualifications required on the labour market. Small entrepreneurs represent an extremely heterogeneous non-agricultural group which comprises both

106

Figure 4.1.
Income levels and standard of living of Finnish households in 1980 by class groups

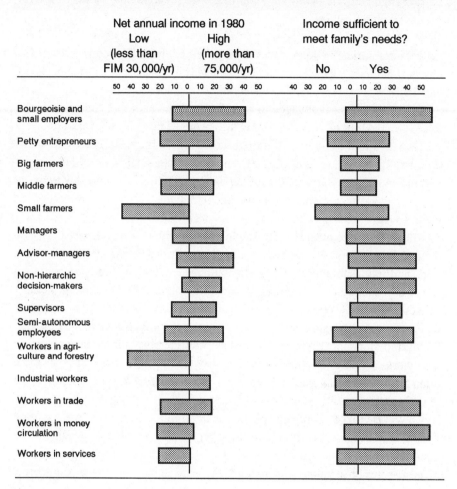

affluent and poor people, people with good and poor resources for economic survival and even various marginal groups.

Almost one third of the Finnish economically active population have been unemployed at least once during their work career. Experiences of unemployment are also reported by members of the bourgeoisie and managerial groups. Among industrial workers, over 40 % have been unemployed, often more than once; the figure for other working-class groups is about 30 %; and for small entrepreneurs 25 %. Wage workers occupying contradictory locations have rarely been unemployed more than once.

Work consumes labour power and in so doing it also maintains the worker's skills and abilities, in some cases even develops them. Therefore it should be obvious that individual jobs cannot be evaluated on the single dimension of 'good' and 'bad'; as a rule they tend to have both good sides and bad.

In class groups not engaged in wage labour, the factor that contributes most to the wearing out of labour power is the absolute length of the working day. If we also take into account the time of day at which the work is done, then the element of wearing out is also significant among industrial workers and workers in trade and services. Irregular working hours, sometimes combined with forced overtime working, are rather common in contradictory wage worker locations as well.

All class groups outside wage employment are more or less free to decide on their working hours. Working-class groups in general and workers in services and trade and industrial workers in particular have less latitude in this respect than workers in contradictory locations. Given the additional fact that a large number of workers in these class groups are engaged in shiftwork or regular evening or nightwork, time structure is quite obviously a factor which adds to wearing out. In contradictory locations, managers have considerable latitude in deciding on their working hours but at the same time they tend to work irregular hours more often than others. Supervisors, then, have less independence here, and one third of them are engaged in other than daywork.

In wage-worker groups, experiences of strenuousness are most common among workers in agriculture and forestry, factory workers, supervisors and non-hierarchic decision-makers. In the whole economically active population, the highest scores of strenuousness are found for small employers and the bourgeoisie.

However, it is important to bear in mind the differences in the type of strenuousness between class groups. The bourgeoisie and workers occupying contradictory locations rarely complain that their work is physically strenuous, but they often point to mental strain. On the other hand, agricultural work tends to be physically but not mentally strenuous. In the working class, there are no systematic differences on this dimension.

Experiences of strenuousness are clearly revealed in workers' expectations as to whether they believe they will be able to continue in their present work until

108

retirement. One third of all economically active Finns say they 'doubt it'; among workers in trade and industry the figure is as high as 50 %.

In terms of job aspects which allow wage earners to learn from their work and to develop their skills and capacities in its prosecution, we may note that the bourgeoisie, different managerial groups and small employers are typically engaged in jobs which are most developing. The same applies with some qualifications to contradictory wage earner locations. On the other hand, working-class groups, especially industrial workers and workers in agriculture and forestry, very rarely can learn new things in their job. Typical jobs in circulation and services allow for some degree of skill development.

The skill development aspect is intimately bound up with task-range and with degree of routinization. On the latter dimension, contradictory locations are clearly distinguished from the working class: the former are almost always engaged in jobs that may be classified as non-routine, whereas the majority of working-class wage earners have highly routinized job tasks. In the case of task-range, the differences are less pronounced and in fact quite the opposite: almost all wage earners in contradictory locations have a job with a wide range of tasks, while in working class groups both wide and narrow types seem to be represented. The necessary exception to the rule is provided by industrial workers, whose jobs are all characterized by a narrow task-range.

There are major differences on the above-mentioned dimensions also between the bourgeoisie, whose job tasks are rarely routine but on the other hand rather wide in scope, and the petty bourgeoisie, who are typically engaged in jobs which are rather routine in spite of their wide scope.

The bourgeoisie as well as all farmers enjoy considerable discretion in arranging their work. Interestingly enough, this does not seem to be the case in the group of small entrepreneurs: the explanation probably lies in the high proportion in this category of personal services (e.g. taxi drivers, hairdressers), in which the pace of work is often determined by the customer's deadlines.

The self-employed and other bourgeois groups are least affected by external control. There are also very few external restrictions in the jobs typically held by contradictory wage worker locations, although here supervisors represent a clear exception. Not surprisingly, working class groups are subjected to external control and various other restrictions more often than other wage earner groups.

Autonomy is of course by definition a key criterion in characterizing the

Table 4.1.

Discretion in use of time in different class groups by gender (%)

	Working hours		Day off at will		Self-paced work		Freedom to decide what to do	
	W	M	W	M	W	M	W	M
Bourgeoisie (1+6)	(100)	(100)	(100)	(83)	(100)	(67)	(100)	(100)
Small employers (7+18)	(100)	72	(71)	50	(43)	50	(71)	89
Petty bourgeoisie (19+36)	68	89	22	50	39	51	84	72
Large farmers (11+12)	91	92	45	92	73	83	100	92
Middle farmers (25+27)	96	93	60	52	92	85	92	100
Small farmers (27+11)	78	100	41	73	74	73	89	100
Managers (29+69)	41	51	34	59	69	88	63	82
Advisor-managers (13+19)	23	53	29	47	69	74	73	65
Non-hierarchic decision-makers (20+16)	15	69	50	56	79	88	71	82
Supervisors (19+28)	11	25	26	21	72	64	65	60
Semi-autonomous employees (54+59)	19	29	16	26	57	64	52	60
Workers in agriculture and forestry (2+10)	(-)	60	(50)	30	(50)	30	(-)	50
Industrial workers (99+139)	9	11	13	6	43	42	17	17
Workers in trade (41+13)	5	15	15	31	60	42	39	20
Workers in money circulation (18+5)	22	(-)	33	(20)	44	(80)	14	(60)
Workers in services (100+32)	4	9	8	13	59	53	30	11

(Frequencies listed in parentheses after class group)

Table 4.2.

Wearing out of labour power by class group (%)

	Hard pace of work	More work than one is able to do	Physically strenuous work	Mentally strenuous work	Tired after work	Out-of-work time used for necessary reproduction	Cannot hold on till retirement
Bourgeoisie	85	71	14	72	43	71	57
Small employers	80	60	24	80	64	88	36
Petty bourgeoisie	53	31	34	42	34	79	31
Large farmers	32	67	67	-	29	46	26
Middle farmers	55	43	70	23	45	42	25
Small farmers	39	33	70	10	54	41	28
Managers	68	50	13	49	22	21	19
Advisor-managers	50	38	16	53	12	22	28
Non-hierarchic decision-makers	50	44	14	58	28	31	33
Supervisors	60	42	18	57	27	25	30
Semi-autonomous employees	53	44	18	42	27	31	31
Workers in agriculture and forestry	67	42	67	16	39	41	25
Industrial workers	55	29	35	31	33	33	46
Workers in trade	62	36	32	24	26	35	54
Workers in money circulation	48	22	22	39	21	22	4
Workers in services	49	23	32	27	24	24	30

Column one lists answers "often" or "almost always", columns 2-6 answers "always" or "almost always", and column 6 answers "no".

Table 4.3.

Opportunities for skill-development by class group (%)

Percent of respondents in each class group who think that they can use their skills and capacities at work, learn new things in its prosecution, and develop their skills to a great or very great extent

	Can use skills and capacities at work	Needs to learn new things	Chances to develop skills	N
Bourgeoisie	86	57	57	7
Small employers	80	76	60	25
Entrepreneurial petty bourgeoisie	77	51	44	55
Large farmers	77	48	33	23
Middle farmers	60	49	24	53
Small farmers	49	28	18	39
Managers	88	72	50	98
Advisor-managers	78	62	44	32
Non-hierarchic decision-makers	67	72	33	36
Supervisors	62	66	34	47
Semi-autonomous employees	71	58	44	114
Workers in agriculture and forestry	25	25	8	12
Industrial workers	23	25	13	239
Workers in trade	44	32	26	54
Workers in money circulation	52	48	30	23
Workers in services	37	43	23	132

position of the working class and semi-autonomous employees: in working class locations there is little or no autonomy, in semi-autonomous locations there is a high degree of autonomy. Class groups not directly involved in wage labour and managers proper have a high level of autonomy on the job. However, almost every other supervisor has below-average autonomy.

Looking more closely at the different dimensions of autonomy, we find that working class groups enjoy at least some freedom in designing certain aspects of their immediate work process. Workers in money circulation and industry have the lowest autonomy scores on all dimensions, and workers in services have more autonomy than other working class groups.

The bourgeoisie enjoys a high degree of autonomy on all dimensions. On the other hand, the work of small employers and entrepreneurs involves a surprisingly high number of tasks which do not require problem-solving or designing new products. In these class groups the concrete work processes may also be highly specialized and thought out in advance: examples are provided by the job of a subcontractor or certain services which are strictly bound up to given schedules.

Considering Finnish wage earners as a whole, all dimensions of autonomy tend to be concentrated in the groups of managers and semi-autonomous employees. Among contradictory wage worker locations, supervisors have least autonomy. Semi-autonomous employees differ from the working class only in terms of their greater autonomy. Therefore in this respect supervisors come closer to the working class than to other contradictory wage worker locations.

In conclusion, we shall attempt to sketch a general picture of how work situation, i.e. the individual worker's position in the concrete labour process, is structured by class location: what are the most outstanding negative and positive aspects of work in different class groups.

In class groups that are not directly engaged in wage labour — farmers, the bourgeoisie proper, small employers and small entrepreneurs — the main draw-back is presented by long working hours. However, the *bourgeoisie* can use their skills at work, they enjoy considerable self-direction, and are rarely tired after the working day, even though there is a high mental stress factor. *Small employers and entrepreneurs* have more difficulties: they often feel pressed for time and work long hours. Although they can use and develop their skills and enjoy high autonomy, there is also a lot of mental stress involved: recovering seems to take up most of their out-of-work time.

Farmers too usually work long hours. In addition, their work is physically very demanding. On *big farms* there tends to be greater freedom and better chances to use one's skills and knowledge at work. *Middle farmers*, by contrast, are free to design their work but they rarely have the opportunity to learn new things. Finally, the work of *small farmers* is also free, but they are not able to develop their skills. On small holdings women in particular do very heavy physical work.

Among wage labourers, there are marked differences between contradictory locations and working class locations: in the former, the positive sides of work tend to be accentuated, in the latter the negative sides.

Managers have good jobs, even though they typically have long and irregular working hours, which often means taking their work home. On the other hand

113

they are able to use and develop their skills and capacities and they rarely complain that their work is tiring. They are even left with time for themselves and their family. In other managerial groups, too, positive aspects tend to outweigh the negative ones, and their work is also less strenuous than that of managers proper. *Advisor-managers* and *non-hierarchic decision-makers* have relatively free jobs, they can use their skills, but not develop them as often as managers proper. The work of non-hierarchic decision-makers involves quite a lot of mental stress, and they seem to spend more time and effort than other managerial groups in the reproduction of their labour power.

In the work of *supervisors* there are far less positive aspects. They have little or no say in deciding on their working hours. They are able to use their skills but not develop them and they often work under strict external control. All this causes considerable mental stress. The work of *semi-autonomous employees* is to a certain extent tied to the clock, but on the other hand they have control over the immediate work process. They are able to use their skills and a certain degree of creativeness is required.

In the working class, the situation of *agricultural workers* closely resembles that of farmers in that their work is physically rather strenuous. However, their income depends to a far greater extent on the amount of work they do and on their pace of work. Also, there are no chances of skill-development. *Industrial workers* have inconvenient working hours, no or little discretion, they work under strict external control, and they have no chances of developing their skills. On the other hand, because of their comparatively short working hours, they have a lot of leisure time (although this applies mainly to men). The negative sides are less pronounced among *workers in trade*, but nonetheless they too are subjected to external control and have no chances to develop their skills. They have inconvenient but not very long working hours, which means they are rarely tired at the end of the day. *Workers in money circulation* have a number of positive aspects in their work: although they are subjected to external control, they are not required to do very much work. To a certain extent they can even develop their skills in the course of work. The main complaint of *workers in services* is that they have inconvenient working hours, no freedom, and that they are subjected to strict external control. In terms of skill development there are certain contradicting features in their work: although it does not allow workers to develop their skills, it nevertheless involves problem-solving and designing certain aspects of the work process. However, short working hours mean that the majority regard their work

114

as not particulary strenuous.

4.3. The proletarianization of white-collar workers

Gugliemo Carchedi (1977) proposes in his class theory a distinction between positions which perform 'the function of the collective worker' and those which perform the 'global functions of capital'; the former represent the working class and the latter the bourgeoisie. This fundamental distinction provides the basis for Carchedi's definition of the new middle class, which, without real ownership of the means of production, performs both functions. The top strata in the NMC mainly perform global functions of capital, whereas the lower strata usually perform the functions of the collective worker. Since NMC positions are typically involved in both kinds of functions, they occupy contradictory locations in class relations.

These are the general starting-points from which Carchedi sets out to discuss phenomena which he considers symptomatic of proletarianization: declining standard of living, dequalification, the threat of unemployment, etc. (ibid., 97-103). He defines proletarianization as a process in which the labour power of the NMC is devalued; i.e., through the removal of global functions from the worker's task-range, the value of his labour power is tendentially reduced to the average. Carchedi argues that bearers of the global function of capital enjoy various privileges both in the work process and in their reproduction situation. Proletarianization implies that the worker is deprived of these functions and consequently of the privileges involved.[2]

Carchedi identifies three stages in the proletarianization process (ibid., 188-193). In the first stage there is a real subordination of labour to capital, the second stage unfolds with the development of monopoly capitalism, and the third stage begins after World War II. In the first stage, the functions of capital are performed by the individual entrepreneur. The white-collar worker is at this point merely an 'extension' of the entrepreneur, in that he will substitute for the entrepreneur in his absence, for example. However, the functions involved at this stage are not yet those of *global capital*, because labour control and supervision are not yet organized within a hierarchic structure. On the other hand, the white-collar worker also performs many functions of the collective worker (e.g. book-keeping). For the white-collar worker, this situation has various consequences:

115

(1) Since the number of entrepreneurs is rather low in comparison with the industrial working population, there are also relatively few white-collar workers.

(2) The white-collar worker interacts directly with the entrepreneur, with no mediating links.

(3) Since he performs certain functions of capital, the white-collar worker enjoys certain privileges and also a better pay than other workers.

(4) The position of the white-collar worker within the capitalist production process requires a certain level of legal and financial expertise. Given the elitistic nature of the educational system, this means that the white-collar worker will usually have a petty bourgeois or bourgeois background.

For these reasons, Carchedi argues that, at this stage of capitalist development, the white-collar worker represents the petty bourgeoisie both in political and in ideological terms.

At the second stage, with the growth of the bureaucratic and hierarchic organization, a more comprehensive or global approach develops to performing the functions of capital. The white-collar worker is no longer in direct personal contact with the entrepreneur. The hierarchic structures of control and the increasing complexity of the production process lead to a substantial increase in the number of white-collar workers.

In spite of this quantitative increase, white-collar workers are not yet fully proletarianized; they continue to enjoy many of their privileges:

> He does not work in unhealthy environments; he has a certain degree of autonomy in performing his functions (even though the first forms of specialization, leading to a reduction of that autonomy, already start appearing); he has a degree of freedom to determine when he should be at the office (because his presence is not strictly checked by the entrepreneur or managers); he still requires a broad culture for the performance of his function (a fact which makes his replacement difficult); he has a higher salary and has the possibility, individually speaking, of making career. (ibid. 189-190)

In the third stage of the proletarianization process, there is an increase not only in the absolute number of white-collar workers but also in relation to the industrial population as a whole. At the same time, the skills and capacities required of white-collar workers begin to lose importance, since their tasks become increasingly fragmented, specialized and repetitive. With the growth of typically female occupational groups such as typists, secretaries, keypunch operators, etc., there is also a significant change in the social composition of white-collar occupations.

116

The distinction between the blue-collar and white-collar worker begins to narrow down:

- global functions are removed from the white-collar workers' task-range and the value of their labour power is tendentially reduced to the average; this means their wages tend to decline in comparison with those of skilled workers;
- the white-collar worker has progressively less autonomy on the job;
- on the whole the status of the white-collar worker tends to decline, which is followed by increasing alienation (ibid., 191).

We now move on to test Carchedi's relevant assumptions and discuss the proletarianization of Finnish white-collar workers on the basis of our empirical evidence. We make a basic distinction between *upper* and *lower* white-collar workers, and compare their working conditions with those of industrial workers engaged in *immediate production*, which here represents purely proletarian working conditions. The aim is to determine the extent to which white-collar workers have retained their privileges in the work process. In addition, to determine the significance of higher education, we shall include the *intelligentsia* in our comparisons, i.e. workers with a college or university degree. Finally, the working-class group of *workers in money circulation* is included.

Table 4.4. describes the proletarianization and privileges of Finnish white-collar workers. Generally speaking it would seem that the dynamics of the proletarianization process can largely be explained by reference to Carchedi's idea that there is a close connection between the functions of global capital and the value of labour power. The salary of lower white-collar workers does not seem to differ from the wage levels in immediate production, whereas upper white-collar workers earn about 50 % more.

On all dimensions of working conditions the situation of upper white-collar workers differs considerably from that of the working class; they are also in a far better position than lower white-collar workers. The only exceptions to this general trend are represented by the high level of mental stress and irregular working hours. Physical stress is a more striking feature among industrial workers, whereas mental stress is a typical feature of the work of upper white-collar workers and the intelligentsia. These findings support the earlier conclusion that the real subsumption of labour to capital may assume very different forms in different wage earner groups. Nonetheless it is clear that among upper white-collar workers there are no signs of proletarianization.

The situation of lower white-collar workers is more complicated. They can be

Table 4.4.
Proletarianization and privileges of white-collar workers

	Workers in immediate production	Managerial white-collar	Non-managerial white-collar	Intelligentsia	Workers in money cir-culation
Autonomy (%) (at least medium)	19	82	32	73	9
Narrow scope of tasks (%)	66	2	19	15	9
Routine tasks (%)	98	17	65	35	100
Monthly salary (%)	13	94	89	89	91
Physical stress (%) (always & often)	45	19	26	17	25
Mental stress (%) (always & often)	33	49	35	41	34
Chances of skill-development[3] ($\bar{x}$)	2.5	5.6	4.2	5.1	4.1
Cannot hold on till retirement (%)	56	23	29	30	34
Shiftwork (%)	36	6	13	9	5
Irregular working hours (%)	3	11	7	9	4
Income (FIM 1000/month)	3.1	4.6	3.1	4.1	2.5
Machine/supervision/ regulations do impose restrictions[4] (%)	13	82	35	61	22

regarded as fully proletarianized as far as the value of their labour power is concerned, but on the different dimensions of working conditions the proletarianization thesis applies to varying degrees. On the one hand, their jobs are highly routinized and they have only little autonomy on the job: two thirds of the lower white-collar employees have routine tasks and only one third have at least average autonomy. On the other hand, only less than one fifth of the lower white-collar workers have a narrow task-range, and they also seem to be able to develop their skills far more often than industrial workers. In addition, they continue to enjoy the privilege of receiving a monthly salary and of convenient

Table 4.5.
Work orientation of white-collar workers (%)

	Workers in immediate production	Managerial white-collar	Non-managerial white-collar	Intelligentsia	Workers in money cir-culation
Instrumentality	33	7	11	11	4
Identification with concrete work content	21	72	51	61	39
Prevented instrumentality	4	3	10	7	0
Prevented identification	39	17	28	17	43

working hours.

There are no significant differences between the intelligentsia and upper white-collar workers in terms of proletarianization. A college or university degree guarantees not only a better salary but also various privileges in the work process.

The most proletarianized group of those included in this comparison is represented by workers in money circulation, who by definition have a low level of job autonomy. Less than one tenth in this category have marginal average autonomy. Their tasks are highly routinized and they are under strict external control. The high degree of proletarianization among these workers is also evident in the lack of opportunities for skill development. Nevertheless even money workers have retained some of their privileges: some of them have a fairly wide task-range, they are paid on a monthly basis, their work is not physically strenuous, and they rarely have to do shiftwork.

Judged by their monthly income, workers in money circulation are in fact even worse off than the core groups of the proletariat. The contradiction implied by Carchedi's theory is also clearly visible: the proportion of workers in money circulation who say that their pay is sufficient for a decent living is almost equally high as among the bourgeoisie and advisor-managers.

The work orientation of lower white-collar workers and workers in money circulation differs clearly from that of the core proletariat. However, the share of prevented identification tends to increase in the more proletarianized white-collar worker groups. On the other hand, a higher degree of proletarianization does not

119

seem to lead to increased instrumentality.

We may conclude that there are significant differences between the working conditions of upper and lower white-collar workers. On virtually all dimensions, upper white-collar workers differ in important respects from the core groups of the proletariat, and their position is far better than that of lower white-collar workers. In fact, the latter are proletarianized to a significant extent, particularly in terms of their wages and work content: two thirds of them have highly routinized jobs and have no autonomy on the job. However, lower white-collar workers have better chances than industrial workers to develop their skills and capacities at work, and they have also retained the privileges of receiving a monthly salary and of not having to work shifts.

4.4. Types of autonomy

Erik Olin Wright argues that autonomy is a characteristic feature of the labour process of simple commodity production. Following Braverman, he points out that increasing capital accumulation entails intensified control of the labour process, and this continuously threatens to restrict the autonomy of wage earners. As far as we can see this is an overly simplistic theory. Therefore, in the following, we propose a more elaborate analysis of different types or sources of autonomy.

In developing our typology we start from the assumption that behind different types of autonomy there are various more or less general and contingent processes. These processes cannot be reduced to the simple explanation offered by Friedman (1977), who argues that employers apply the strategy of responsible autonomy in relation to worker groups which have the greatest potential for resistance. What is it that creates this resistance potential? Rather than defining resistance simply as the outer limit to the expansion of capital, it is pertinent to ask how far the real subsumption of labour can be taken within the bounds of the internal logic of the concrete labour process itself. What we are actually looking for are those preconditions in the material basis of labour which are alien to the system of valorization and which the Frankfurt sociologists describe as real contradictions in the subsumption of labour (Benz-Overhage et al. 1982, 88). It may be also assumed that in an empirical analysis of cross-sectional data we will discover stages in the development of capital where the processes of real subsumption are still not 'complete'; this is because every individual capital has its own real history.

However, all structures of labour subsumption also contain, by logical necessity, the subordinators and their concrete work: the pole where the bearing of the functions of capital maintains autonomy. The more evenly the functions of global capital are divided across the control hierarchy, the more inevitable is the clash of control and autonomy in the concrete labour process.

These ideas provided the theoretical framework for our typology, which was then worked out on the basis of empirical analyses, but including in it only those workers who had (at least medium) autonomy on the job. We worked on the basis of the respondents' descriptions of their jobs. The fact that we focussed on the nature of work obviously means that only those types appeared in which the conditions of the labour process itself are central. In other words, this typology cannot help us to uncover types of autonomy achieved through organized resistance, or autonomy organized to prevent such resistance. The following typology was suggested:

- craftsman's autonomy
- professional autonomy
- capital-adequate autonomy
- scientific-technical autonomy
- autonomy of caring and reproduction
- autonomy of office work
- autonomy of small enterprises

In addition, there is a 'miscellaneous' category which includes various types of individual cases, as well as the interesting group of workers who deny autonomy.

A couple of these types of autonomy can also be derived from Wright's theory.[5] The type which most closely corresponds to Wright's ideas is traditional *craftsman's autonomy*: most of the examples he cites are workers who move from simple commodity production to wage labour (Wright 1978, 81). Although there is a clear trend in this direction, the process is nonetheless very slow, and there remain significant numbers representing this type of autonomy. It may be assumed that workers with this type of autonomy have retained the possibility to choose to work either in wage employment or as independent entrepreneurs (carpenters, bricklayers, etc.). In other words, 'craftsman's autonomy' would be threatened by the movement of the boundary line between capitalism and simple commodity production, but as long as the same kind of work is done on both sides of the boundary, certain occupational groups will maintain a relatively autonomous position even in wage employment.[6]

Professional autonomy is traditionally found in the kind of jobs typically occupied by the intelligentsia; this is another example that Wright uses (ibid., 81-82).[7] These formerly 'free' professions have now been incorporated in bureaucratic organizations. In this process they have lost their independent position in society but managed to retain their autonomy in the immediate work process. Professional autonomy may also be an endangered species in the long run, but at least for the time being it seems to be a very strong feature of these positions. We assume that this type of autonomy will be kept alive by the process of professionalization: a process of professional socialization which creates the necessary cognitive and motivational capacities and which helps to promote the social organization and influential position of the profession.

Those workers who occupy contradictory locations between the bourgeoisie and the working class have control over other people's labour. However, in the case of these locations Wright does not consider it relevant to speak of autonomy, because semi-autonomous employees are excluded from the definition.[8] It is nevertheless relatively easy to derive from Wright's theory the type of *managerial-supervisory (or capital-adequate) autonomy*. It should be clear that workers who have control over other people's labour are also free to control their own work. This does not, however, follow by any logical necessity; but it is adequate for the function of capital — insofar as the primary imperative of capital is to produce surplus value. Although the structural and technical rationalization of retail trade, for instance, has deprived and continues to deprive workers of control over their own labour process, selling and marketing still requires a certain extent of *capital-adequate autonomy*, a certain degree of freedom which helps to motivate the worker and which allows him to take the customer's needs into account. Of course, other types of autonomy may also be adequate in the production or circulation of capital, but these do not originate in the logic of capital.

In an historical perspective, capitalism itself also creates new types of autonomy: scientific and technological progress creates new occupations, in which extensive conceptual knowledge is required of the workers. Typically, this kind of work is carried out in large organizations because the practical realization of scientific achievements usually requires heavy capital investments. The *scientific-technical* type of autonomy may in fact even be gaining ground. On the other hand, it is also possible that while the new scientific and technical work processes are becoming more autonomous, they are at the same time being subjected to increasingly minute control.

People engaged in caring work cannot adequately perform their tasks unless they enjoy a certain degree of autonomy in their work process. It is certainly possible to restrict the *autonomy of caring and reproduction* to a certain extent (as in hospitals by fragmenting the division of labour), but it can never be taken away altogether.[9] Without autonomy, it is impossible to look after children in day care; in this case the object of work requires considerable flexibility and continuous problem-solving. The idea that robots could feed, condition and teach children is, at least for the time being, a distant (dys)utopia.

In office work the division of labour is typically less differentiated than in industrial production, and clerical workers continue to enjoy some autonomy on the job (although usually less than medium). It is of course possible that this represents a peripheral phenomenon of modern capitalism which will eventually disappear with office automation and rationalization. Nevertheless in the *'autonomy of office work'* there may also be certain deep-rooted elements, such as the holistic approach required in the handling of information.

The size of the workplace is a key factor in considering how far certain tasks can be differentiated and accordingly how much autonomy can be taken away from workers in performance-level jobs. The *'autonomy of small enterprises'* may of course disappear from any organization. The historical record would seem to suggest that the process of capital concentration is to an increasing extent bringing small companies under centralized control. Bureaucratic structures of control have recently appeared in the field of social services, for example. However, it would be unrealistic to assume that all small units will disappear: new small enterprises and subcontractors will certainly continue to grow up, which means that this type of autonomy is bound to survive.

In the course of studying our empirical materials, we also found a few cases where the respondent said he or she definitely had no autonomy at all, even though his or her tasks closely resembled those of several other workers who said that they had at least medium autonomy. The degree of autonomy was not determined by the researchers, but always by the respondent. If the respondent's and the researcher's views (which were based on studies of other cases) were clearly at variance, then the respondent was classified under the category *'denial of autonomy'*. From an empirical point of view this finding is at best annoying, but in theoretical terms it is interesting indeed: what are the factors behind this phenomenon? We attempted to answer this question by examining the respondent's situation more comprehensively, looking into all the data produced by the respective questionnaire. We produced an intuitive and preliminary typology, which opens up rather interesting perspectives on conflicts of experience and consciousness.

The phenomenon concerned may be a reaction elicited by a sense of overwhelming control; in certain cases it also had clear ideological overtones. Although most of these respondents probably had at least some degree of autonomy and sometimes even managerial authority, it seems that they were in some way expressing their consciousness of class society, bureaucracy, or modern, impersonal technology (nuclear power plant). The tone of 'denial' was often negative, frustrated, but in some cases also affirmative: it is right to be dutiful to the large machinery. It is also possible that some of these responses reflected strong instrumentality, an active denial of attachment to the content of work.

The most common type of autonomy among Finnish wage earners is represented by capital-adequate autonomy, which is found in one form or another in one out of five wage earners. One out of seven have what we call craftsman's autonomy, and slightly less have professional autonomy. In about half of all cases, the type of autonomy corresponds more or less directly to the types presented by Wright (although capital-adequate autonomy partly falls outside Wright's presentation). Is this a good achievement or not? In any event we may again conclude that class theories tend to be biased in favour of male workers: 60 % of the male wage workers included in our sample can be fitted into Wright's types of autonomy in comparison with 40 % the women.

Among workers who occupy a position within the control hierarchy, the sources of autonomy tend to be rather different than in the case of the working class and semi-autonomous employees. Capital-adequate autonomy is the most common type, whereas traditional craftsman's autonomy is a (masculine) phenomenon which is excluded from the tasks of capital; the corresponding phenomenon in the semi-autonomous locations occupied by women is professional autonomy. In general, women's autonomy is typically related to the special requirements of caring and reproduction work; this applies both to the working class and to contradictory locations. In small companies, the undifferentiated division of labour means that especially those workers who occupy non-hierarchic contradictory locations have autonomy.

Upon closer inspection, we find that those who deny their autonomy are typically working-class men. As we have already seen, the working conditions of

124

supervisors are structured in largely the same way as those of the working class; the denial of autonomy is apparently symptomatic of a type of consciousness which is common in locations subjected to strict external control.

All types of autonomy described in the foregoing are essentially individual types. However, the labour process may also be based upon collective autonomy. In recent years industrial employers have been experimenting with various new methods of work organization (production cells, self-directed groups, quality-control circles, etc.) (Kauppinen-Toropainen and Hänninen 1981) — and in principle there may even be something left of the more traditional collective autonomy. However our questionnaire did not contain any questions concerning collective autonomy, and therefore our estimates are based on the respondents' spontaneous entries. Only 5 % of those who had autonomy on the job referred to collective autonomy. It would seem to be commonest among workers in services (15 %) and non-hierarchic decision-makers, i.e. in the field of social reproduction. These findings suggest that the majority of Finnish wage earners work within communities where freedoms and responsibilities are individual rather than collective. — More recent studies of technological changes in work organization have discovered a new trend which is not yet visible in our empirical analyses: that is, it is perfectly adequate for capital to increase the autonomy of certain key groups on the shopfloor (Kern and Schumann 1984; Kortteinen, Lehto and Ylöstalo 1986).

The informal work organization is also a relevant factor from the control point of view (Lilja 1983), in that it may serve either as a basis for resistance or as an obstacle to the application of new ideas. Most of these questions fall beyond the scope of our study, but it is useful to note that very few of our respondents felt their colleagues or workmates restricted their autonomy. In the theoretical debate it is commonly argued that the workplace organization represents the workers' most important asset in their struggle to maintain their autonomy. Our empirical material also sheds some light on trade unionism among Finnish wage workers: in our interviews we asked them whether they saw any tradition of common action which would reflect their resistance potential. According to our results, there is little variation in the (low) autonomy of working class locations; and that low level of autonomy is so regardless of whether workers present their resistance collectively, through their representatives, or individually. Total lack of autonomy is nonetheless more common among those who rely on their representatives or their individual action (64 %) than among those who work collectively to achieve

Table 4.6.

Types of autonomy by class group and gender (at least medium autonomy) (%)

Type of autonomy	Managers		Advisor-managers		Non-hierarchic decision-makers		Supervisors		Semi-autonomous employees		Working class		Total	
	W	M	W	M	W	M	W	M	W	M	W	M	W	M
Craftsman's	7	7	-	11	6	6	6	16	4	38	11	35	6	22
Professional	14	13	25	17	6	31	6	12	42	14	-	-	18	12
Capital-adequate	25	50	17	28	24	13	38	28	4	14	7	9	14	25
Scientific-technical	4	15	-	17	-	13	-	24	7	21	4	12	4	17
Reproduction	32	-	17	-	24	6	19	-	29	-	30	-	28	-
Office	18	7	17	5	6	-	13	-	2	2	24	-	13	3
Small enterprise	-	3	17	11	29	25	6	-	11	11	13	14	11	9
(Miscellaneous)	-	-	-	5	-	-	-	4	2	-	2	7	1	3
Denial	-	4	8	5	6	6	13	16	-	-	9	23	5	9
Total	100	99	101	99	101	100	101	100	101	100	100	101	100	100
N	28	68	12	18	17	16	16	25	55	56	46	57	174	240

126

their common goals (52 %). So even at this level, our results lend some support to the resistance hypothesis.

4.5. The control of work

Various dimensions of control represent central criteria of class location in Erik Wright's theory of class structure. Control over other people's labour may be exerted either directly or indirectly, by laying down the conditions under which the labour process is carried out. This means that the work situation of the individual wage earner is structured not only on the basis of a number of separate dimensions; the relationship between the exercise of control authority and the position as an object of control is also a significant aspect. In the analysis of labour control the survey method again imposes its own restrictions, because we have to deal with each respondent in isolation from the relevant organizational context. An adequate study of the mechanisms of control of the development of labour processes needs to be based on an analysis of entire organizations, their internal relations and structures.[10]

For the present purposes we conceptualize the control to which the working class is subjected, the degradation of work through fragmentation and standardization, as a manifestation of real subordination. Although the logic of capital is present in all spheres of societal labour, it is reasonable to argue that real subordination occurs in its most repressive form in those fields where capital is most powerful. The stricter the subordination of labour to capital (and the separation of conception and execution), the greater the degree of polarization within the division of labour. In other words, we may assume that there are greater differences between contradictory locations and working class locations in those fields where capital is most powerful (in terms of accumulation and concentration). To put this assumption to the test, we divide employers into different categories by the type of capital they represent: the competitive and monopoly sectors of private capital, government offices and social services (see Table 4.7.).

The results on the form of wage payment clearly support this assumption. In fact in small companies within the competitive sector the difference between contradictory and working class locations is hardly noticeable. In both groups the pay that workers receive depends essentially on their performance and (presumably) on the market situation. On the other hand, in fields where capital has a stronger

127

Table 4.7.
Control of work in contradictory (CTR) and working-class (WCL)
locations by employer category (%)

	Small companies in competitive sector (less than 10 workers)		Small companies in competitive sector (10 workers or more)		Monopolies		Government offices		Social services	
	CTR	WCL	CTR	WCL	CTR	WCL	CTR	WCL	CTR	WCL
Monthly salary	63	58	71	46	79	24	92	91	87	76
Relatively free from time restrictions	69	32	68	25	62	20	81	27	50	21
Machine/supervision/ regulations do not impose restrictions	75	16	72	12	83	17	62	-	75	13
Wide scope of tasks	81	58	76	52	62	35	81	59	88	63
Narrow scope of tasks	19	32	24	48	38	65	19	41	12	37
No routine tasks	38	11	63	0	76	3	85	0	85	10
Routine tasks	62	89	37	100	24	97	15	100	15	90
High autonomy	25	-	45	-	52	-	50	-	67	-
No autonomy	-	47	-	61	-	67	-	55	-	54
Prevailing type of autonomy	[1]	[1]	[2]/[6]	[6]	[2]	[—]	[4]	[—]	[3]/[5]	[5]

[1]autonomy of small enterprise
[2]capital-adequate
[3]professional
[4]scientific-technical
[5]caring and reproduction
[6] craftsman's autonomy

hold there is greater autonomy in contradictory locations, but at the same time working class locations come under stricter control. Also, both groups have less freedom to decide on working hours, although wage workers in contradictory locations retain more of their freedom than the working class.

In working class locations there are considerable restrictions within the labour process regardless of the strength of capital, but monopoly capitalism gives more freedom to wage earners in contradictory locations than does capital in competitive sectors. The degradation of work appears as a specific function of capital: in sectors where capital is more powerful, the proportion of jobs with a narrow task-range tends to increase in working class locations, and the proportion of jobs with a wide scope of tasks tends to decrease in contradictory locations. On the other hand, our results also suggest that specialized tasks tend to become more demanding and less routine-like in contradictory locations. In small companies operating within the competitive sector, there is a high proportion of routine tasks; there are only minor differences between contradictory and working class locations. As capital gains in strength, this difference becomes much bigger. Similarly, autonomy tends to increase in contradictory locations and to decline in working class locations. On the whole, the subordination of labour is clearly characterized by highly repressive and polarized forms.

However, a similar polarization also appears in the public sector, where the employer applies slightly different strategies of control. The vast majority of state employees receive a monthly salary. There is a marked difference in freedom from time restrictions between contradictory and working class locations, but in social services even those wage earners who occupy contradictory locations have less freedom in this respect than their colleagues working for private capital. In public administration there are various direct restrictions (rules and regulations): in contradictory locations these are more common than in the private sector, but nevertheless the general trend is that working class locations differ in significant respects from contradictory locations. Workers occupying contradictory locations have a wide scope of tasks and they are rarely engaged in routine types of work; they also tend to have a higher degree of autonomy than their colleagues working for private capital. In the public sector working-class tasks are more routine-like but wider in scope than in the private sector.

A study of the prevailing types of autonomy in the different employer categories reveals certain interesting differences. In small companies operating within the competitive sector, the dominant type of autonomy is what we call autonomy of small enterprises. In bigger companies, craftsman's autonomy is the predominant type, although in contradictory locations there also appears capital-adequate autonomy. Among wage earners occupying contradictory locations in monopolies, capital-adequate autonomy is the predominant type; in working class locations there is no autonomy. In government offices, the most typical type of autonomy in contradictory locations is scientific-technical autonomy; again, working class locations have no autonomy. Finally, in the field of social services caring and reproduction autonomy is dominant, but in contradictory locations there are also elements of professional autonomy.

Let us now revert to the question of how authority and control are intertwined. As we have seen, the labour process of the working class is controlled by wage earners occupying contradictory locations. On the other hand, at least supervisors are themselves subjected to external control, whereas semi-autonomous employees continue to enjoy some autonomy on the job.

Although dimensions of control have a major part to play in analysing the concrete class structure, they nevertheless tend to leave important aspects of the source of control completely untouched. That is, we know very little about the dynamics which structures the situation of managers, about the position from which they exert control over the labour of other people. Because managers are wage earners, the main reason they work is to ensure the preconditions for their own (and their family's) reproduction. But how is this human aspect taken into account? Class theories which slot managers under the bourgeoisie usually start from the assumption that managers are first and foremost wage workers of capital who enjoy various privileges and a salary which exceeds the value of their labour power. However, this can be hardly the whole truth. At least this explanation is in conflict with the fact that the working class tends to have a more instrumental orientation to work than wage earners in contradictory locations, who are inclined to orientate themselves according to content. Or should we just accept the simplistic assumption that positions of control are reserved for people who have a lust for power? Below, we move on to study in closer detail the ways in which the hierarchic structure of control is reproduced.

The reproduction of class locations is a process which takes place at the level of society as a whole. However, the immediate reproduction of the relevant hierarchic structures takes place within the organizations of societal work in which the bearers of class locations act. This means that the reproduction process consists in the reproduction of those societal relations which come into interaction at the organizational level. As far as the individual wage earner is concerned, his situation is not determined by the sum of the positive and negative aspects of his position, but by the relationship between his own position and other positions and by the time perspective of these relations. At the organizational level, the relations

130

between different workers are largely determined on the basis of active managerial strategies.

A useful illustration of the processes through which managerial strategies create and maintain hierarchic structures which reinforce distinctions between 'good' jobs and 'bad', is provided by Tainio's (1982) study of industrial companies in northern Finland. This type of managerial strategy is a form of control. However, it is important to note that it may be both an *active* and a *passive* strategy.

The strategy is actively applied towards those jobs and worker groups which are vital to the function of the organization. The use of an active managerial strategy can be empirically ascertained by studying whether the employee receives on-the-job training, whether he or she is able to use his or her skills and capacities at work, and to what extent other workers in the same position get promoted.

Our results suggest that an active managerial strategy is more often applied in relation to workers occupying contradictory locations than those in working-class locations. However, there are certain differences even within the former category. Managers receive a considerable amount of training on the job, they often have to try their skills in several different tasks, and they are also able to use their skills and capacities at work. Advisor-managers are trained to a lesser extent, but on the other hand they have better opportunities for promotion than managers. In both managerial groups control has become a process of intensive socialization where motivation is created by structural means. Supervisors also receive a lot of training on the job. They are often moved from one task to another and they have fairly good prospects of promotion; on the other hand in terms of work content they are not in the best possible position. This particular class group is integrated in a strict hierarchic structure where control over the labour of other people does not automatically guarantee autonomy. Non-hierarchic decision-makers seem to be excluded from the control hierarchy in this respect as well. The managerial strategy applied in relation to industrial workers reflects an active neglect of the development of their labour power; the exploitation of the labour power of these workers is based on other means, notably technology, the division of labour, specialization, the degradation of work, centralization, etc. By contrast, workers in money circulation are primarily controlled by fragmenting their tasks and by the narrow scope of their tasks; at the same time, considerable attention is given to on-the-job training and to the social integration of these workers. In the core groups of the working class, the high frequency of changing tasks cannot be

Table 4.8.
Indicators of active managerial strategy in wage-earning class groups (%)

	Received on-the-job training	Can use skills and capabilities at work	Prospects of promotion	Engaged in same task throughout career
Managers	81	88	43	61
Advisor-managers	69	78	50	66
Non-hierarchic decision-makers	69	67	23	78
Supervisors	74	62	54	55
Semi-autonomous employees	65	71	45	76
Workers in agriculture and forestry	42	25	-	50
Industrial workers	26	23	27	66
Workers in trade	43	44	26	70
Workers in money circulation	57	52	32	78
Workers in services	50	37	25	78

interpreted in the same way as in the case of contradictory locations. A more plausible explanation is that the employer moves these workers around on profitability considerations, regardless of their individual skills.

All groups look forward to the future with optimism. There are, however, considerable differences between different class groups. All groups expect they will be earning more in the future; the only partial exception is represented by workers in agriculture and forestry. As regards expectations of promotion, working-class groups tend to be more pessimistic than workers occupying managerial positions; the groups which fall between capital and labour are the most optimistic with regard to their opportunities for advancement. Non-hierarchic decision-makers and semi-autonomous employees do not expect their position to improve to any significant extent, which suggests that their situation is structured differently to that of worker groups occupying positions in the control hierarchy. Of the working class groups, workers in money circulation believe in their opportunities for promotion to the same extent as managers; this finding may reflect the intensity of managerial strategies applied to them. Workers in agriculture and forestry are rarely in organizations where they could expect any specific improvement or deterioration of their position. They have two basic alternatives: either they work or they do not work. Accordingly, they do not believe their tasks will become more interesting; in fact there were quite a few who considered the opposite a more likely alternative. On the whole there was also quite a lot of pessimism among working-class groups. Managers occupying a position in the control hierarchy were the most optimistic with regard to the chances of their tasks becoming more interesting. All groups expect to see improvements in their working conditions rather than in the nature of their tasks; working class groups were the least optimistic, and managers and supervisors the most optimistic.

Considering these results as a whole, the improvements that the workers expected to see in their own position and in the nature of their tasks are perhaps most closely related to the social structure of the organizational hierarchy. It is precisely through these improvements that the individual can hope to move upwards to a higher social position — provided of course that the ladders are there within the organization. An alternative path to career advancement is to get a new job. If we additionally consider our earlier data on the rate of promotions within the corresponding position, then the difference is clearest between the working class and managerial groups. Supervisors and managerial groups have the best prospects of building themselves a career; workers in agriculture and forestry do not really have a 'career' at all.

Our workers' optimistic expectations regarding their wages and working conditions are not related merely to individual career prospects or managerial strategies: improvements in wages and working conditions are typically achieved through collective bargaining. We can also assume that the expectations of rising wages may reflect a belief in continued economic growth; and that expectations of improving working conditions reflect a belief in continued technological development.

Employers also use working conditions (working hours and form of wage payment) as a means of integrating their workers into the company organization. Although workers occupying contradictory locations are often required to work in shifts, on the whole this class group tends to be more or less restricted by the time factor. For managerial groups, inconvenient working hours usually means the same thing as irregular hours: they often do more than the regular eight hours, but on the other hand they also have greater freedom to arrange their own working day. In these groups, irregularities in the use of time may be regarded as a form of 'self-exploitation', an extra commitment to one's work and the problems of the organization. This, however, is probably a social norm and also an important precondition for career advancement.

As was discussed earlier, most wage earners in contradictory locations are paid on a monthly basis. In working class locations, workers in circulation and services usually receive a monthly salary, whereas among industrial and agricultural workers other forms of wage payment tend to be more common. In piece-work as well as in various bonus and commission systems there is a clear connection between pay and performance. Time-wages simply ties the individual's wages to the amount of time he or she spends at work. However in a sense all of these payment systems imply a link between performance and income, whether through quantity, quality, or time. On the other hand, workers with a monthly salary will usually enjoy far greater freedom than others.

But although a monthly salary implies a certain degree of freedom from immediate control within the actual labour process, it is important not to forget the other forms of control which may be involved. In large organizations, both in the private and in the public sector, there is an elaborate wage scale for monthly salaries which leaves no doubt as to the exact position of each employee within the organization's hierarchy. Monthly salaries are negotiable only in smaller private companies. From the career perspective, a monthly salary is thus related to a particular type of work orientation.

In contradictory locations the form of wage payment is in fact the single most important factor that modifies the relationship between location and work orientation. Workers who are paid on a piece-work or hourly basis clearly differ from the dominant trend in contradictory locations — identification with the content of work — and tend to fall either in the category of instrumental orientation or in that of prevented identification. In working class locations, a monthly salary or a bonus system support an orientation to the content of work.

As is clearly suggested by the evidence of many recent studies, gender is a significant factor that must not be ignored in the analysis of control structures. At the shopfloor level, employers frequently apply a strategy whereby they attempt to create animosity and conflicting interests between male and female workers. The results of these studies also show, not surprisingly, that the bulk of routine tasks are performed by women, while the skilled jobs are reserved for male craftsmen (see e.g. Nichols and Armstrong 1976; West 1982; Eckart et al. 1979; Zimbalist 1983; Game and Pringle 1983; Lown 1983).

Table 4.9.

Career development and career expectations by gender and class group (%)

| | Promotions (some & many) | | Will you still be working in your present job 5 years from now (yes) | | Career expectations ("will improve" considerably or to some extent) | | | | | | | |
| | | | | | Wages | | Position | | Content | | Working conditions | |
	W	M	W	M	W	M	W	M	W	M	W	M
Managers	34	47	82	71	64	80	25	45	32	49	61	55
Advisor-managers	46	53	77	74	69	74	46	42	46	37	62	22
Non-hierarchic decision-makers	32	13	60	81	65	69	30	38	35	19	35	19
Supervisors	42	63	78	63	58	61	37	43	16	36	42	54
Semi-autonomous employees	24	46	74	76	76	56	27	26	38	29	37	29
Workers in agriculture and forestry	(-)	-	(50)	100	(50)	44	(-)	-	(-)	-	(50)	11
Industrial workers	22	29	62	64	46	58	16	26	16	27	29	41
Workers in trade	24	33	61	62	56	77	23	62	26	46	33	50
Workers in money circulation	36	(20)	78	(40)	78	(20)	39	(40)	22	(20)	31	(20)
Workers in services	24	28	77	69	68	61	26	33	28	26	36	47

135

Gender and class location are also clearly intertwined when we examine the career expectations of men and women. In this case the gender differences are far less outstanding in the working class than in contradictory locations. Neither men nor women expect to advance in their career, and their future expectations are more or less equally optimistic (or pessimistic). However, in industry male workers are slightly more optimistic with regard to their wages and working conditions. In the field of trade and commerce, male workers differ significantly from their female colleagues; in fact it would seem that male workers are here creating a capital-adequate career for themselves. As we already noted, female semi-autonomous employees occupying contradictory locations have a wider scope of tasks and also more demanding tasks than men. Also, these women are more optimistic about their future wages, working conditions and even content of work. On the other hand, their position in the organization does not offer very good opportunities for promotion. The tasks of female and male managers are equally demanding and autonomous, but male managers tend to be more determined to advance in their career. In the group of advisor managers, the differences between men and women are rather small (except from the fact that women expect to see improvements in their working conditions more often than men). Among non-hierarchic decision-makers, men are often in a position that does not offer many prospects for promotion; therefore they are more pessimistic than women. In the case of supervisors the exact opposite is true: male supervisors are more determined to create a career, and they expect major improvements in the future.

An analysis by class groups reveals certain important aspects of the role of gender in control structures. In the working class, we find that although male workers in commodity circulation occupy the lowest rungs of the control hierarchy, they are nevertheless far more determined than women to create a personal, possibly managerial, career. Among workers in services and semi-autonomous employees engaged in the field of social services, women are typically engaged in interesting jobs, but they are rarely able to secure a position within control hierarchy. In the group of managers, gender plays a selective role: men are integrated to a great extent into the managerial structure. Not surprisingly then, two thirds of all managers are men. On these highest rungs of the control hierarchy, class location seems to be a more significant factor than gender as far as the nature of the work process is concerned, even though men are more clearly oriented towards career-building throughout the hierarchy. In other contradictory wage worker locations, the class group of immediate supervisors is particularly interesting: gender is the decisive factor with regard to the nature of tasks, the intensity of control and career expectations. The obvious conclusion is that in this contradictory class location, the authority of patriarchy is intimately bound up with the power of capital (cf. Kanter 1977). In the hierarchic control structures, gender is thus both a means of direct exercise of power and a means of social integration and of structural motivation.

4.6. How do different class theories explain working conditions?

In accordance with our theoretical strategy of advancing from one level of analysis to the next through mediating syntheses, we shall now consider the relevance of different class theories in explaining differences occurring in the structure of working conditions in different wage earner groups. We limit our comparison to the theories of Wright, Poulantzas and PKA.

Whichever theory we base our analysis on, working conditions appear to be hierarchically structured so that negative features are concentrated in one class group and positive features in another. With the exception of the mental stress involved in their work, Poulantzas's bourgeoisie and Wright's managers have the best working conditions on all dimensions. Poulantzas's new petty bourgeoisie, Wright's non-hierarchic decision-makers, supervisors and semi-autonomous employees, and PKA's aggregated personnel and middle class form an inter-mediate group. According to all theories the working class has the poorest working conditions.

On the whole the theory of Poulantzas gives a similar picture as the other two theories, but it would seem that Poulantzas's concept of the working class is too narrow. This is clearly demonstrated by the following Table, where we have divided Poulantzas's new petty bourgeoisie into wage earners who would fall into Wright's contradictory locations and working class, and then compared their working conditions.

PKA's theory of the internal differentiation of the working class is supported by a comparison of machine workers and unproductive workers. There are also marked differences in the working conditions of different groups of state workers. On the other hand, the use of primary and derived income as criteria for distinguishing the middle class and the working class is not justified.

Among productive workers, there are clear differences on all dimensions

137

between aggregated personnel and machine workers, who represent a clear majority in this category. The working conditions of machine workers are poor: their work is physically strenuous, highly routine, and they have no opportunities to develop their skills. The only dimension on which machine workers do not

Table 4.10.

Average income (FIM/month) and chances of skill development in Poulantzas's new petty bourgeoisie and Wright's contradictory locations and working class

	Income	Chances of skill development($\bar{x}$)	N
Contradictory locations	4158	5.4	120
Working class	2842	3.4	240
New petty bourgeoisie	3020	4.1	360

*) The index was formed by asking the respondents how far they were able at work to use their knowledge and skills. The set alternatives were 1 = very often, 2 = fairly often, 3 = sometimes, 4 = not very often, 5 = not at all, for which the following scores were given: 1 = +2, 2 = +1, 3 = 0, 4 = -1, 5 = -2. In addition, using the same scoring principles, the respondents were asked whether they were required at work to learn new things, and whether they had the opportunity to develop their skills.

Table 4.11.
Income level and opportunities for skill development:
a comparison of Wright's and PKA's theories

	1	2	3	4
Average monthly income (FIM)	4069	2872	4175	2784
Chances of skill development ($\bar{x}$)	5.6	2.9	5.2	3.4
N	139	331	176	122

1 wage earners occupying a middle class position (a contradictory class location) according to both PKA and Wright
2 wage earners occupying a working class position according to both PKA and Wright
3 wage earners who according to PKA belong to the working class and according to Wright to the middle class
4 wage earners who according to Wright belong to the working class and according to PKA to the middle class

come last is mental stress. By contrast, aggregated personnel have fairly good working conditions and in this regard they come closest to PKA's managers. From this point of view, it would indeed be much more appropriate to place this group in the middle class or in contradictory wage-worker locations — which in fact is where they belong according to Wright's theory. Using Wright's criteria, none of the workers classified by PKA as aggregated personnel would belong to the working class.

The obvious difficulty with PKA's theory is evident in Table 4.11 on page 138, where we compare the income and the opportunities for skill development in four different groups:

In categories 1 and 2, where PKA and Wright agree on the class location of the persons concerned, clear differences can be seen in terms of both monthly income and chances of skill development. In categories 3 and 4, there is no doubt that Wright's is the more accurate classification. The wage earners classified by PKA as working class and by Wright as occupying contradictory locations seem to be clearly middle-class, while the situation of those that Wright counts as working class and PKA as middle class comes close to the category of workers who both classify as proletarian.

In sum, it seems more pertinent to separate the working class from the middle class on the basis of the content of work (control tasks and autonomy) than on the basis of form of income.

5 Class structure, consciousness and organization

5.1. The theoretical problems

Theories of worker consciousness and organization have tended closely to reflect the historical stage of capitalist development in which they were produced. During the years of economic growth and prosperity after World War II, the main tendency was to emphasize the integration of wage workers into capitalism, the embourgeoisement of the working class and the technological determination of worker consciousness. However, with the crises that unfolded in advanced capitalist societies towards the end of the 1960s, theorists started to change their mind about the fate of the working class. Then, following the deep economic crisis of the mid-1970s, there emerged a host of new problems: mass unemployment, regressive economic policies, the closure of the political system, political apathy and alienation, the growth of alternative social movements.[1]

In the late 1950s and early 1960s there were a number of studies on workers' images of society[2] that pointed to the dual character of worker consciousness and to the growing discrepancy between consciousness, action and organization (Deppe-Lange 1970, 701-707). Towards the end of the 1960s, scholars turned their attention to the 'new worker type': the baseline assumption was that the traditional solidary worker had been replaced by a worker whose orientation to work, social life and working-class organization was essentially instrumental.[3]

Marxist research into consciousness, and particularly its German school, focused on the thesis of the contradictory determination of worker consciousness. Wage-worker consciousness was assumed to be a mixture of elements relating to the surface of capitalism (property, individualism, equality, freedom) and more critical elements evolving from experiences of subordination (e.g. PKA 1973; cf. also Diligenski 1984). Accordingly, class consciousness was defined as a process in which the true nature of capitalism was revealed to the working people, especially to productive workers, through crises and experiences of repression. It was also assumed that the class consciousness or anti-capitalist consciousness of different wage-worker groups were not necessarily analogous.

In the field of industrial sociology, research on consciousness has paid increasing attention to out-of-work time and to the cultural and ideological elements of worker consciousness. Marxist research, however, has repeatedly underlined that a purely instrumental orientation to work does not and cannot exist. Qualitative analyses have suggested that there are worker types who identify themselves with the content of work to varying degrees. They have also challenged earlier notions of the determination of wage workers' consciousness; and pointed to the importance of the 'subjective instance' (Neuendorf 1980; Hack 1977; Hack et al. 1979; and Voss 1980).

The recent debate on new social movements and their structural basis has in turn suggested that the shifts in conflict frontiers are primarily related to the dissolution of the traditional basis of reproduction and the so-called Fordist form of societalization.. This development also involves a tendency towards *Durchstaatlichung*, selective corporatism and the closure of the political system. Consequently, both the form and the actual bearers of the political alternative are changing.

In the following discussion of wage-worker consciousness and organization in social classes, we do not take for granted the common assumption that consciousness is directly related to and dependent on class location. Instead, we take it that class struggle is first and foremost a struggle concerning the formation of class subjects (Przeworski 1977, 371-373). In the neo-Gramscian debate on the 'discursive constitution of hegemony', it has been pointed out that subjects are not given at the level of production relations, and that even class subjects do not necessarily act in accordance with their class location. All social relations have their specific discursive aspect in that social practices constitute themselves only insofar as they produce meanings to actors. Different concepts — such as 'people', 'maternity', 'competition', 'equality' — have different meanings depending on how they are articulated together with other elements within a given discourse.

The neo-Gramscian and discourse-theoretical debate has been on very similar lines as the discussion on new social movements and many recent elaborations of the theory of culture and ideology. They all insist that research into consciousness, hegemony, and the formation of subjects should discard class reductionism and class apriority. This debate still has a number of problems to solve, including the formation of discourses. Nevertheless it draws our attention to an important and interesting question: Do the average social coercions included in the economic character mask of wage workers (as defined in *Capital*) provide an adequate basis for explaining wage-worker consciousness and organization?[4]

The following empirical analysis describes the connections between class structure, class consciousness and organization. We start by analysing the assumptions concerning class consciousness presented by Wright, Poulantzas and Projekt Klassenanalyse. We then describe the consciousness profiles of Finnish wage workers, using the different phenomenological levels of consciousness introduced by Kudera et al. (1979). Then, we proceed to discuss the role of those processes which structure civil society. Finally, following a brief analysis of organization, we shall discuss the relative proportions of classes in different political parties.

5.2. Class theories and consciousness

We have already compared the empirical consequences of the class theories by Wright, Poulantzas and Projekt Klassenanalyse in the case of class structure and class situation. The following assessment of these theories is restricted to the consciousness of wage workers.

Erik Olin Wright sets out from the assumption that the working class has a different kind of 'interest in socialism' (class consciousness) than contradictory class locations between the working class and the bourgeoisie. His theory is that class consciousness tends to decline as we move from the working class through supervisors to managerial positions. This is because these classes have different functions in decision-making and different degrees of authority in controlling the labour of other people.

In PKA's theory the main differences between class groups derive from the form-determinants of social labour in capitalism and from the consequent differences in forms of income. PKA's concept of class consciousness emphasizes the difference between essence and phenomenon. Class consciousness consists in the revelation of the true nature of capital to wage workers (from 'below' the illusions created by the surface-forms of capitalism). The preconditions for the formation of class consciousness are summarized in Table 5.1.

Table 5.1.
Wage-earner groups, their class position, and the determination of consciousness
(PKA)

Wage workers of capital (primary income)		Middle-class workers* (derived income)
Productive workers	Unproductive workers	State agents
- contradictory determination of consciousness - direct experience of capital despotism and the effects of conjunctures - high probability for mystification to be revealed		- contradictory determination of consciousness - indirect experience of capital despotism and the effects of conjunctures - additional effect of specific factors (patriarchal work relations, state attachment) intensifying mystification - low probability for mystification to be revealed

*) According to PKA, the middle class or what the project calls the "third rubric of persons" includes the traditional petty bourgeoisie, pensioners, workers in personal services and workers of capital and working-class organizations, as well as state employees.

Poulantzas, then, focuses on the differences between the working class and the new petty bourgeoisie and on the similarities between the new petty bourgeoisie and the old petty bourgeoisie. All wage workers with authority and control over labour power, i.e. all groups from supervisors upwards, belong to the petty bourgeoisie. Poulantzas (1975, 212) says that management and supervision are the direct reproduction of the political relations between the capitalist class and working class within the process of production itself. Additionally, on the basis of ideological criteria, the petty bourgeoisie includes all wage earners engaged in mental labour. According to Poulantzas, this category plays a significant part in legitimizing the subordination of labour to capital: experts make it appear natural that workers are incapable of organizing production themselves. Engineers, technicians, experts and supervisors do not belong to the working class, since their position in the social division of labour realizes the political and ideological subordination of the working class to capital.

Below we shall consider the validity of the assumptions presented in these three class theories of wage-worker consciousness. Our analysis is based on a typology of consciousness, willingness to take action, organization and conventional membership of working-class organizations.

The following data describe the validity of the different types of action and consciousness. *Political apathy* is lowest in 'active' types, i.e. the type which is willing to take action and which believes in its chances to influence important matters, and in the type with high organizational activity and willingness to take action; and highest in types that are only action-oriented or passive and unable to take action. — *A general critical attitude*, which represents a combination of many different factors, was most common in both consciousness-oriented ('conscious' and 'conscious+') types. — *The subjective meaning of human relations involved in organizational activity* was most important for active members of organizations and for the member + action-oriented types. — The indicator of conventional organization measures the intensity of membership of working-class organizations: membership in a leftist party rates 6 points, trade union membership rates 3 points and membership in a so-called progressive cooperative rates 1 point.

Table 5.2. describes the action and consciousness profiles of different class groups using Wright's class criteria. Conscious and action-oriented types (vs. passive and unable types) are more prevalent in the working class than in contradictory managerial locations between the bourgeoisie and the working class. As regards organizational activity, the opposite is true.

The clearest indication of this is the high proportion of those taking an active part in the work of various organizations in the group of managers proper. Two important points should be noted here. Semi-autonomous employees come closer to the working class than to managers in terms of the weight of both consciousness and willingness to take action in their profile. This result is also affected by the low proportion of the passive type and of those incapable of taking action; the profile of these types resembles that of workers in the service sector. It is also worth noting that there are major differences in the relative shares of action and consciousness types both within the working class and in managerial positions.

In the class group of managers, the type which takes an active part in organizations is predominant. The most distinctive feature of advisor-managers is their high level activity and competence, whereas non-hierarchic decision-makers are the least active and competent. The active type is virtually non-existent among advisor-managers. In comparison with other managerial groups, non-hierarchic decision-makers have a low consciousness. Supervisors also come much closer to other managerial locations than to the working class (low action

Table 5.2.
Classes, action and consciousness: Wright's theory (percentage of consciousness and action types by class group)

	act & org	org	act	comp & act	cons +	cons	pass	other	Total	org attach (x)
Managers	11	16	3	5	5	12	39	9	100	2.6
Advisor-managers	3	10	0	10	13	7	30	27	100	2.9
Non-hierarchic decision-makers	14	8	6	6	8	3	47	8	100	3.0
Supervisors	9	9	7	9	9	7	42	9	101	3.5
Semi-autonomous employees	12	8	13	8	10	16	27	6	100	3.1
Workers in agriculture and forestry	17	0	8	8	8	17	42	0	100	2.0
Industrial workers	8	5	17	6	12	19	29	4	100	3.0
Workers in trade	6	8	13	11	8	19	34	2	101	2.9
Workers in money circulation	5	0	9	5	18	23	41	0	101	2.2
Workers in services	10	10	12	8	10	15	30	5	100	3.2
Average	9	8	11	7	10	15	33	6	99	3.0

Consciousness and action typology: act&org = action-oriented and organization actives; org = organization actives; act = action-oriented; comp&act = competent and action-oriented; cons+ = conscious plus something else; cons = conscious; pass = passive and uncompetent; other = other types; org attach = conventional working-class organizational attachment

and consciousness). Although a large part of supervisors are members of conventional working-class organizations, on the whole they are not particularly active in organizations.

Before we proceed to more general conclusions, let us first take a look at the empirical validity of PKA's and Poulantzas's assumptions.

There are three main differences between the working class and the middle class. In the profile of the wage workers of capital, the shares of the active type and the passive type are higher than among the middle class, while the active type is more common in the middle class. These results do not support PKA's assumptions.

In a comparison of productive and unproductive workers, we find that the former are slightly more active and more competent, above all more willing to take action than unproductive workers. Among unproductive workers, the most common types are those who take an active part in organizations and those who are willing to take action and who believe in their chances to influence important matters.

The differences are greatest between machine workers and aggregated personnel. Machine workers are more willing to take action, more conscious, and they participate in the work of organizations more often than aggregated personnel.

As we have seen earlier, one of the main strengths of PKA's theory lies in its analysis of the internal differentiation of state employees. The present analysis lends further support to this conclusion. The dominance of conscious and active types and conscious types clearly distinguishes state employees engaged in the state reproduction sector and in the maintenance of the general conditions of production from those working within the administrative state apparatus. In addition, state employees in the reproduction sector are characterized by a relatively high willingness to take action (a feature also characteristic of state employees within the repressive state apparatus), a low proportion of the competent and action-oriented type and a low proportion of the passive type. Employees within the administrative apparatus are further distinguished from other state employees by the high proportion of the type which is active in organizations.

On the other hand, the results concerning conventional membership of working-class organizations do not support PKA's theory. True, this type of activity is more common among productive workers (and especially machine workers) than among unproductive workers, but it is also far less common among productive workers than among state employees (the middle class). Conventional membership is highest in the group of state employees within the administrative apparatus.

In short then, our empirical analysis lends support to PKA's assumptions concerning class consciousness as far as the internal differentiation of the working class (wage workers of capital) is concerned. By contrast, PKA's assumptions are not consistent with the differences we found between the working class and the

Table 5.3.

Classes, action and consciousness: PKA's theory (percentage of consciousness and action types by class group)

	act & org	org	act	comp & act	cons +	cons	pass	other	Total	org attach (x)
Wage workers of capital (503)	8	6	13	8	11	14	35	5	100	2.8
Middle class (242)	10	12	10	7	9	18	27	7	100	3.7
Average (745)	9	8	12	7	10	15	32	6	99	3.0
Productive workers (331)	10	5	15	7	11	15	33	5	101	3.0
Unproductive workers (172)	5	8	9	9	11	13	39	6	100	2.5
State employees (229)	10	12	10	7	10	18	27	7	101	3.4
Workers of organisations (13)	15	15	8	15	0	15	31	0	99	3.3
Wage workers of capital:										
Machine workers (285)	11	5	17	6	11	16	31	5	102	3.0
Aggregated personnel (46)	7	4	4	11	11	7	50	7	101	2.9
Unproductive workers (172)	8	8	9	9	11	13	39	6	100	2.5
Middle class:										
State employees										
- administrative apparatus (39)	10	18	8	10	5	10	28	10	99	3.8
- reproduction sector (152)	11	11	12	5	11	20	25	7	102	3.2
- general conditions of production (38)	8	11	3	11	11	18	32	8	102	3.4
Workers of organisations										
- working class organisations (3)	33	0	33	0	0	0	33	0	99	5.7
- bourgeois organisations (10)	10	20	0	20	0	20	30	0	100	2.6

middle class.

Our results are at sharp variance with Poulantzas's theory. Poulantzas's working class and new petty bourgeoisie have very similar action and consciousness profiles (although the active type is dominant in the working class and the organization type is more common in the petty bourgeoisie). On the other hand, there are clear differences between the new and the old petty bourgeoisie. The most important indicator of these differences is represented by the conscious types, although even this correspondence to Poulantzas's assumptions is problematic. Differences in organizational activity would be even more pronounced if its contents were taken into account.

On the whole, our results do not lend support to Poulantzas's assumptions concerning class consciousness (and class action); further, they lend only partial support to Projekt Klassenanalyse's and Wright's theories. It would seem that PKA's main proposition concerning the position of wage workers of capital and the middle class is not correct. Nevertheless, as we have pointed out, the theory is useful for purposes of analysing differences in consciousness within the working class. The major weakness of Wright's theory is that it fails to provide the necessary tools for analysing internal differences both within the working class and among state employees.

Finally, our results suggest that both Poulantzas's and Projekt Klassenanalyse's concept of the working class is too restricted. In Wright's scheme, the most pertinent boundary would seem to be the one that is drawn between

Table 5.4.

Classes, action and consciousness: Poulantzas's theory (percentage of consciousness and action types by class group)

	act & org	org	act	comp & act	cons +	cons	pass	other	Total	org attach (x)
Bourgeoisie (210)	9	12	3	8	7	10	41	11	101	2.6
Old petty bourgeoisie (167)	2	19	7	8	6	13	38	7	100	3.3
New petty bourgeoisie (355)	9	8	10	8	11	16	33	5	100	3.0
Working class (236)	9	4	19	5	11	19	29	4	100	3.0
Average (968)	8	10	10	7	9	15	35	6	100	2.9

managerial positions and the working class. According to this distinction, super-visors — although relatively 'proletarian' in terms of their membership of conventional working-class organizations, for instance — would be excluded from the working class, whereas semi-autonomous employees would be included. This crude distinction is not of course to deny the internal differentiations within the working class, which shall be discussed in more detail in the following analyses.

5.3. Consciousness profile of Finnish wage workers

The following description of the consciousness of Finnish wage workers starts from some very basic theoretical conceptualizations and generalizations concern-ing average types of consciousness. The reason why our analysis is based on such results is that we believe they are essential if our aim is to proceed to a more detailed study of cultural aspects: without these mediations, any description of the culture and way of life of Finnish wage workers would remain far too crude and simplistic.

First, however, we must make certain reservations. Since we are concerned specifically with the consciousness of wage workers, special attention needs to be given to their illusions and different types of social criticism. Here, our choice of approach is based on the conviction that Marx's theory of fetishism provides the most fruitful starting-point for a study of consciousness. In *Capital*, wage-worker consciousness appears as essentially contradictory: it involves elements which are attached to the 'surface forms' of bourgeois society (ownership, individuality, equality, freedom, etc.) and on the other hand critical elements arising from the class nature of capitalist society — its 'despotism of production'.

However, there do not exist any generally accepted guidelines for applying these starting-points in a concrete study of the forms and contents of conscious-ness. Therefore our solution should be seen as an experimental application, which may be described as follows:

(1) Our attempt to describe the different elements of worker experience and worker consciousness and their interrelations is based on the theorizing of Kudera and his co-workers (Kudera et al. 1979). Kudera presents the first systematic analysis of the illusory elements in the 'worker's situation'. Also, Kudera's distinction between the different 'phenomenological levels' of experience and

consciousness is helpful in a study of those preconditions for the formation of consciousness which are related to social contacts and conditions not occurring at the company level. Using the scheme presented by Kudera, we attempt to portray the profile of the Finnish wage workers' consciousness within the following areas: (a) the wearing out of labour power; (b) work orientations; (c) wages, entrepreneurship and income distribution; (d) work time and out-of-work time; (e) interest promotion and trade union activity at the workplace level; (f) state citizenship and the political system; and (g) understanding of society and future utopias.

Our goal is to

- describe the consciousness profile of Finnish wage workers at these phenomenological levels,
- problemize the mediations and contradictions between these levels and areas and
- determine the extent to which consciousness profiles follow class boundaries.

(2) Our baseline assumption is that the contradictions of consciousness are bound up with the fundamental determinations of wage work in capitalism. This does not mean to say that we can derive the forms assumed by these contradictions at each phenomenological level in specific historical situations and in concrete societies directly from these basic structures. Both illusions and criticalness are always historically mediated.

(3) This does not, of course, mean that a concept apparatus directly related to the basic determinants of wage employment is the only possible theoretical tool for analysing these phenomenological levels. At each level, we must separately search for the connections between the determinants of consciousness developed on the basis of the critique of political economy and conceptual apparatuses of other kinds. We have discussed the problem of transitions between different theoretical constructs earlier.

(4) The following discussion of wage-worker consciousness aims primarily at opening up new perspectives. We return to many of the central problems in later sections where these problems are discussed in greater detail. On the other hand, many explanations are necessarily excluded from a survey study; for instance, there are many aspects of consciousness which may be traced back to cultural forms.

In wage labour, the worker places his labour power at the disposal of the capitalist against payment. However, wage labour not only provides the worker with the means for satisfying his needs, but also imposes limits upon need-satisfaction in that it erodes his or her labour power. We have described the strenuousness of work in different class groups earlier.

Different class groups are subjected to different types of strenuousness. The basic distinction, of course, is between mental and physical strain. The bourgeoisie and workers occupying contradictory locations rarely complain of physical strain, but tend to point to mental stress. In agricultural work the opposite is true. Finally, among the working class there is no clear distinction between these two types of stress.

The experience of strenuousness is evident when we ask wage workers to say whether they believe they will be able to continue in their present job until retirement. In trade and industry, about half of all wage earners do not believe that they will retain their work capacity until retirement. In the entire economically active population, the proportion is about one third.

Work orientations

There are several different explanations for the processes that lead to identification with or indifference towards the content of work. In a pioneering Weberian study on work orientations, Goldthorpe et al.[5] suggested that what they called an instrumental work orientation was on the increase. This orientation has two main characteristics: first, the content of work is unimportant to the worker, and second, he or she takes a negative stand on worker collectivity. The worker's most important social relations are in the sphere of leisure and family. Finally, the worker's relation to the trade union is also instrumental: he or she is merely interested in whether there are individual benefits to be gained in trade union membership.

Goldthorpe also identified a 'bureaucratic' type of orientation, which is typical of middle class groups. Here, the main characteristics are identification with the norms of the work organization and careerism. Goldthorpe's results suggested that 'handicraft' and 'solidaristic' orientations are receding among the working class. In the former, the content of work is displayed both in personal endeavours towards self-expression and in social relations. The solidaristic orientation, then, involves a strong attachment to the worker collective and to defending common interests. It is closely related to the instrumental type in that it is primarily oriented towards wages and making ends meet rather than the content of work.

Goldthorpe explains the predominance of instrumentality by reference to post-war developments in capitalism, i.e. the dramatic increase in wage workers' incomes and consumption levels. These conclusions have been called into question by a number of Marxist analysts: what will happen, they ask, if the wage worker's standard of living ceases to rise? And can the instrumental attitude to the labour movement be explained away by reference to the characteristics of the British labour movement?

Work orientations have also, and more importantly, been thematized at the level of the general theory of capitalism. The argument here is that the workers' indifference towards their work reflects the indifference of capital. The objective indifference of capital is evident in its preoccupation with the maximization of profits: how and where it makes that profit makes no difference whatsoever. This view has been most systematically developed by PKA, which says that subjective orientations are only idealized expressions of the objective relations prevailing in society. On the 'surface' of bourgeois society the worker, the owner of the labour power commodity, is free to choose the branch to which he or she wants to sell his or her labour power, but in actual fact this individual freedom is restricted by the movement of capital. This means that in order to maintain the saleability of his or her labour power, the worker must keep it variable. As far as concrete and useful activity is concerned, this implies a tendency towards indifference. And this, in turn, gives rise to the possibility — which is then realized in connection with an economic crisis — that the illusions connected to specific vocational skills, a specific branch or individual capital are dissolved.

The wage earner who is interested only in wages is oriented towards the societal nature of his or her activity. Thus the indifference towards the specific content of work forms a basis for a consciousness of class belongingness and for the development of the workers' own solidarity or organization.

While Goldthorpe's theory implies that instrumentality leads to a reduced level of class conflict, PKA's indifference assumption implies almost the exact opposite. Indifference represents a form of consciousness where illusions disappear and where an anti-capitalist consciousness emerges. A central problem with PKA's argumentation is how to link it up with historical explanations, for it has been shown that identification with the content of work may have totally different societal contents and dynamics in different countries. For instance, the argument by Lucien Sève (1972) that a militant worker is also a good worker may reflect the special conditions of the French case.

Marxist analysts have argued that absolute instrumentalism is in fact an impossibility, and presented various types of prevented identification (cf. e.g. Kudera et al. 1979).

In the present study we have made a distinction between, on the one hand, the type that identifies him- or herself with the content of work and the type that considers wages more important — the instrumental type — and, on the other hand, the types of prevented identification and prevented instrumentalism. Our analysis is based on two questions in the interview: the first concerns the respondents present job, in the second they are asked to state what kind of job they would like to do.

Most workers are in their present job because of its content, although there are also large numbers who have to work merely for the sake of the pay. In the discussion that follows we shall omit from consideration the small group which we call 'prevented instrumentality' (including both the breadwinners of large families with extremely low income and people with a very well-paid job). The profile consisting of the other types is differentiated according to both class groups and gender.

Table 5.5.
Types of work orientation*

| | | Which would you prefer if you could choose | |
		A boring and inconvenient but well-paid job	An interesting job with low or average pay
What is the main factor which keeps you in your present job:	Wages	Instrumentality (IN) 18 %	Prevented identification (PI) 28 %
	Job contents	Prevented instrumentality (PIN) 5 %	Indentification with contents of work (IC) 45 %

*) 4 % of the respondents said they "don't know"

Table 5.6.

Types of work orientation in male and female wage workers

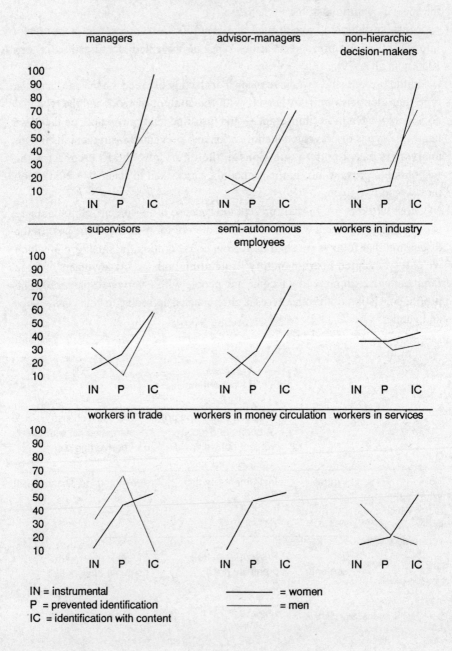

IN = instrumental
P = prevented identification
IC = identification with content

——————— = women
——————— = men

154

Class is clearly an important determinant of work orientation. Only 9 % of all managers have an instrumental work orientation, whereas among industrial workers the figure is 29 %. Accordingly, 71 % of the managers and approx. 25 % of the industrial workers identify themselves with the content of work. The most common orientation in the working class is prevented identification. Those occupying contradictory wage worker locations tend to identify themselves with the contents of work. However, women show this kind of orientation even in working-class locations, although prevented identification increases as we move towards the working class; in the working class it is quite common. The orientation of men tends to be more instrumental.

Of the more concrete manifestations of class, educational level is an important background factor. Two in three highly educated wage workers identify themselves with the contents of work, and in this respect there are no differences between men and women. At lower educational levels, women still tend to identify themselves with the contents of work, although prevented identification is here increasingly common; men in turn show increasing instrumentality.

Work orientations thus distinguish men from women, but this does not hold true beyond a certain social threshold. Is this threshold determined by the favourable reproduction situation that comes with a high position and level of education? Work orientation seems to depend on the sufficiency of income, but there is also a difference between the two genders: the instrumentality of men increases in direct proportion to decreasing income. Women, in turn, seem to become instrumental only when it becomes 'impossible to make ends meet'. A very important point is that the orientation of neither gender is dependent on the income level in itself: the orientation is in the final analysis determined by the relation between income and the needs of the family. Thus one might be tempted to conclude that the higher instrumentality of men is due to their traditional role as breadwinners. Unfortunately this is not true.

Married men are slightly more instrumental than married women, but both identify themselves strongly with the contents of their work. The divorced and widows, who often have greater difficulty in supporting their family, are often prevented from identifying themselves with their work. But between single women and men there seems to be a huge difference: single men are the most instrumental, while single women identify themselves with their work. This cannot be explained by age. About one quarter of young men (under 30) and of those falling in the next age group (30-50) are instrumental. The oldest age group (over 50) is even more instrumental: three in ten. In the older age groups the work orientation of men is in fact divided into identified and instrumental, while prevented identification begins to fall into the background. The situation of women, on the other hand, changes from strong identification typical of the young wage workers to prevented identification and instrumentality, although identification remains the most common attitude.

The above suggests that work orientation is determined by the articulation of class, gender and division of labour. Occupation is the position that integrates all of them.

In the higher white-collar occupations which are relatively unsegregated by gender, the most common attitude is identification with work. In gender segregated occupations, including either higher or white-collar occupations (among men, technicians and supervisors, among women, skilled services and clerical work) identification is still most common, although prevented identification is also more usual. Even in routine service tasks, women maintain the tendency to orientate themselves towards work on the basis of its contents. The orientation of female sales personnel and of female industrial workers is of the prevented identification type. There are two orientation profiles in male blue-collar occupations, the prominent instrumentality of industrial workers and the prevented identification of sales personnel and unskilled workers (instrumentality being the second most common type among sales personnel).

There are no class locations where workers have a strictly instrumental attitude towards their work. In the field structured by class relations and the gender division of labour, however, there emerges a masculine culture which emphasizes the wage employment of the industrial working class. Women are socialized, in a broad sense, to take care of reproduction, to take other people's needs into account; from this aspect, even restrictive, subordinate tasks may have a personal human content. In industrial work such features are rare, and thus female industrial workers feel that they are working because they have to. On the other hand, interesting mental work not only provides people with the opportunity to identify themselves with the contents of work but also requires conscious selection of field of education and occupational socialization. The hard core of the instrumental work orientation is socialization to masculine industrial work. Skilled workers do not stress their qualifications or occupational pride but their wages. In spite of some differences in educational level and autonomy, craftsmen and industrial operatives have a common and consistent view that a man works in order to earn wages. We should, however, remember that this study presented its subjects imaginary and simplified alternatives. A closer, culturally oriented study would probably show that work orientations are actually much more nuanced and also much more contradictory.

Wages, entrepreneurship and income distribution

The connection between wages and performance is vital in the inversion of wage-worker consciousness (Kudera et al. 1979, 96). Wage workers' attitudes towards wages and income differentials are affected by illusions of performance, one's own work, private ownership, justice, etc., engendered at the level of exchange based on the principle of equity. But the consciousness of workers is also affected by the conflicts of interest caused by their mutual competition and their competition with entrepreneurs.

Performance illusions are clearly demonstrated by the finding that 60 % of all Finnish wage earners accept the claim that a fair income distribution is best reached when all people are paid according to their performance. Such illusions are more prevalent among those occupying managerial positions than in other wage earners. These illusions are only slightly less common among managers than among the bourgeoisie and small entrepreneurs.

The belief in individual performance is also reflected in the fact that many wage workers would want to have their own company: one in four wage workers would want to be self-employed. These ambitions are clearly more common among men than women. Every third male worker would want to be self-employed, whereas four women in five are not at all interested. It is worth noting that among women, advisor-managers and non-hierarchic decision-makers are most keen on the idea. Among men the highest proportion of those who want to be self-employed is found in workers in industry and trade.

On the other hand, the contradiction of wage-worker consciousness is reflected in the fact that about 60 % consider the current income differentials in Finland either completely or fairly unjust. Here, the bourgeoisie, small entrepreneurs and those occupying managerial positions clearly differ from the others. In these class groups, the vast majority is of the opinion that income differentials are completely justified or fairly justified. Industrial workers are the most critical: only 26 % of them regard these differences as rather just.

All in all, wage-earners in Finland are bound by performance illusions to the

Table 5.7.

Views on income differentials by class group (%)

	Distribution fair when everyone is paid according to performance	Income differentials are	
		justified	not justified
Bourgeoisie and small employers	90	48	43
Petty bourgeoisie	80	61	31
Large farmers	69	30	48
Middle farmers	50	34	45
Small farmers	76	21	38
Managers	73	57	38
Advisor-managers	66	59	25
Non-hierarchic decision-makers	63	48	50
Supervisors	62	36	58
Semi-autonomous employees	56	39	51
Workers in agriculture and forestry	58	33	67
Industrial workers	58	26	68
Workers in trade	63	43	46
Workers in money circulation	48	39	52
Workers in services	54	25	63
All approx.	62	37	54
Wage workers approx.	60	36	56

forms of consciousness of the surface of bourgeois society. However, in lower class groups there is some criticism of income differentials.

Work time and out-of-work time

The relationship between work and other spheres of life has changed in several ways in the course of the history of capitalism. During the past few decades the most outstanding development in many advanced capitalist countries has been the gradual dissolution of traditional working class culture and the privatization of

Table 5.8.
Entrepreneurship by gender and class group (%)

	Women	Men	All
Managers	18	38	32
Advisor-managers	38	32	34
Non-hierarchic decision-makers	35	25	31
Supervisors	11	29	21
Semi-autonomous employees	20	28	24
Workers in agriculture and forestry	0	11	9
Industrial workers	20	42	33
Workers in trade	29	46	33
Workers in money circulation	11	20	13
Workers in services	12	21	15
All	29	34	27

N=790

the working class way of life. These changes can be roughly described as follows (see e.g. Lockwood 1975).

Traditional working class culture has its roots in tightly-knit working-class communities and residential areas. The basis of this culture has been a strong sense of pride in skills. Workmates have usually lived together in the same area and spent much of their leisure time together, and the members of these communities have helped each other in their problems of everyday life. In a word, there is a strong sense of solidarity about traditional working-class culture.

The more modern, privatized worker differs from the traditional worker at virtually all levels. He considers work a necessary evil and wants to make a strict distinction between working time and out-of-work time. He is not a member of a tightly-knit group of colleagues or of a specific residential community of workmates. In the new working class residential areas, social relations no longer revolve around workmates, neighbours and relatives. Therefore, the privatized worker is oriented, in his job, to the wages, while outside the world of work he is primarily oriented to consumption. He is also primarily a member of the family rather than any broader social community.

The key importance of the family in the way of life of Finnish wage earners is very clear. Almost half of them say that the most important thing in their life is their family, while less than one fifth are interested primarily in their job. This tendency to de-emphasize the personal meaning of work is particularly evident in the lower social classes. The highest scores for work orientation are found in managerial women.

Family orientation has been measured by a familism[6] index. The family is a more important part of the life of all wage worker groups than in the agricultural population. The tendency towards privatization is also underlined by the finding that most Finnish wage earners spend more time with friends in leisure activities than with their nextdoor neighbours. There are no significant differences either between the class groups or the genders on the familism dimension.

However, there is reason to believe that an interview material does not give a very accurate picture of the cultural contents of the family vs. work orientation of men and women. The theory of instrumental work orientation, for instance, looks at the relationship between work and out-of-work time from a very sexist point of view, and ignores the possibility that women may experience even dull and monotonous work as an opportunity to get away from the routines of housework.

It also seems clear that the present material tells nothing about the triangle which according to cultural studies of way of life plays an important part in the life of wage-worker families: work — family — pub. The first and last are traditionally the domain of men: for them, the pub often serves as a refuge from the experiences of exploitation at work and from the family. However, in a questionnaire which asks people to state what they feel are the most important things in their life, it is unlikely that anyone will mention the local pub.

As well as measuring instrumentality with regard to the contents of work, we also constructed an indicator containing the other important aspects identified by Goldthorpe: indifference towards workmates, calculative attitude towards trade union activity, and the feeling of being a fully human being only outside the factory gates.

The results suggest that there are marked differences between the class groups in their instrumentality. The highest degree of instrumentality is shown by all working-class groups and supervisors. In the light of the present material it seems that familism is a broader phenomenon than instrumentality, in that it concerns all wage workers. There can be found no correlation between these two variables.

Earlier studies of privatization have regarded familism as representing the opposite of social activity. Paul Willis (1979), however, has argued that withdrawal into the family may represent a more or less conscious way of showing disapproval or resistance to the capital-dominated labour process and to bureaucratic trade unions. This would mean that the familism of wage workers should not be interpreted as the opposite of class consciousness proper. It is perhaps no coincidence that familism correlates negatively with illusions of common interests both in the working class and among supervisors.

Kudera has argued that the whole notion of industrial workers making a distinction between work and leisure is simply not possible, because their leisure is in any case overshadowed by the world of work; most of their leisure time is taken up by recovery from work. In Finland this is the case in one third of all industrial workers and in one third of workers of trade.[7] In other wage earner groups the proportion is smaller but still over one fifth. The figure is clearly highest in entrepreneurs, where four in five say that they spend most or all of their leisure time recovering from work.

Interest promotion and trade union activity at the workplace level

Unionization levels are very high in Finland; among wage earners over 80 % are members of the trade union. The figures are highest in the class group of supervisors (almost 100 %) and lowest among managers, but even here two in three are members of an interest organization.

In Finland trade union membership is widely regarded as a universal duty of all wage workers, but in reality there are considerable age, gender and class differences in trade union activity. Participation is lower among younger workers, and men represent the clear majority among active members. On the other hand, it would seem that women's unions encourage immediate forms of collectivity to a greater extent than the unions of men.

There are very few union members who give instrumental reasons for their membership. About 15 % of Finnish wage workers say they are members only because they expect the union to fight for better wages. On the other hand, over 80 % believe that workers can effectively further their interests only if they have a united front. However, only 30 % report that there has been real cooperation at their own workplace, and 40 % held that workers are inclined to leave the task of interest promotion to their representatives. This points to an interesting contradiction between the system of representation in the promotion of workers' interests and the principles of mass power. At the workplace level interest promotion is characterized by delegatory arrangements.

The majority of Finnish wage workers agree that the trade union is necessary, but they also tend to be sharply critical of the union. Only one in three holds that the union's recent policies have been successful or rather successful. Most workers feel that their own union has been less successful than the trade union movement as a whole. Critical attitudes are most common in the group of industrial workers, of whom only one quarter are satisfied with the union's policies. Non-hierarchic decision-makers are most critical of the work of their own union.

Industrial workers have been on strike much more often than any other class group. The average industrial worker has been on strike 3.8 times; in other groups the average is one time. Most of these strikes, not surprisingly, have concerned pay levels. The proportion of wage workers who have been involved in strikes concerning working conditions or general social questions is very low indeed.

State citizenship and the political system

One of the main discoveries of the Marxist debate on the bourgeois state in the 1970s was that people's illusions of the form and contents of that state were firmly anchored to the surface relations of bourgeois society (a finding that, incidentally, Soviet scholars already made in the 1920s). The relations represent the bourgeois, capitalist state as constitutional and as neutral with regard to the different social classes. At the same time, the bourgeois state appears as a subject with unlimited power to rule and dominate society. A closer analysis of the bourgeois state reveals, however, that the form of this state is a necessary mediation of exchange relations and that the content of its activity is defined by the reproduction of the capitalist social formation.

People's illusions relating to the form of the capitalist state can be empirically analysed by examining their illusions of parliamentarism, i.e. the idea that voting at general elections is the only way people can hope to influence things in this society. Among wage workers, these illusions are most common in the working class and least common among supervisors.

The view that there are certain interests which are common to all social classes is even more prevalent. Over 70 % of Finnish wage earners agree with the statement that 'continued growth in GNP is in our common interest'. Several variables of this kind were combined to form an indicator of illusions of common interests. These illusions are slightly more common among managerial groups and workers in money circulation than among others. They were least common among workers in agriculture and forestry and in industrial workers.

There are marked class differences in attitudes towards political parties. The proportion of supporters of left-wing parties is highest among supervisors, workers in forestry and agriculture, industrial workers and workers in the service sector. Within the working class, workers in money circulation form a special case in that support for left-wing parties is very low; they are also more reluctant than others to reveal their political stand. With the exception of supervisors, managers support right-wing parties, although to a lesser extent than entrepreneurs.

Political apathy — the view that there is nothing one can do to influence government decisions and policies — is most common among the agricultural population, supervisors and the working class; about half of these groups showed clear signs of political apathy. The lowest scores were found for the bourgeoisie, managerial groups and semi-autonomous employees.

Social criticism in general is described by an index based on a combination of questions concerning attitudes towards income differentials, employment prospects, and the effect of political decisions on the respondent's own interests, on the growth of GNP and on international competitiveness.[8] The results indicate that industrial workers and workers in money circulation and services are the most critical. The scores were lowest for advisor-managers, entrepreneurs and managers.

The results concerning state citizen consciousness appear in a slightly different light when we look at the respondents' attitudes towards state interventions. Here the interview question concerned people's attitudes towards state regulation of private investment, supplemented by the arguments that the state knows exactly what kind of living conditions individual citizens have, that the state should do more to help young people find employment, and that the state should pursue a more active day-care policy. The answers were combined to form an indicator of attitudes towards state intervention.[9] In the economically active population, only the bourgeoisie gave primarily negative answers to the questions. The most positive attitude was found for workers in trade, industry and services. A particularly interesting result is that small employers and the agricultural population seem to be very sympathetic to state intervention.

The action-orientation of different class groups has been measured by the following questions:

Table 5.9.

State citizen consciousness by class group (% and x)

	Illusions of parliamentarism (x)	Illusions of common interests (x)	Left/right wing (%)	Political apathy (%)	General criticism (x)	Attitudes towards state intervention (x)	Action-orientation 1 (%)	Action-orientation 2 (%)
Bourgeoisie	50[a]	-	10/53[a]	31	-2.0	-0.4	0	-
Small employers	55	-		40	-2.1	2.0	8	-
Petty bourgeoisie	57	-	18/30	57	-2.0	1.6	12	-
Large farmers	36	-	0/78	49	-2.0[d]	2.1[d]	14[d]	-
Middle farmers	56	-	0/72	59	-1.1	2.3	18	-
Small farmers		-	11/61					-
Managers	40	0.1	26/48	32	-2.0	1.3	9	33
Advisor-managers	44	0.1	26/43	22	-2.6	1.1	9	34
Non-hierarchic decision-makers	43	0.1	33/52	31	-1.2	2.1	33	78
Supervisors	38	0.5	42/28	49	-0.7	2.3	21	53
Semi-autonomous employees	43	0.6	29/38	35	-0.5	2.0	34	46
Workers in agriculture and forestry	56[b]	-0.1	50/25	50[b]	-0.7	2.0	33	50
Industrial workers		-0.1	46/19		-0.1	2.6	39	56
Workers in trade	42[c]	0.5	28/30	57[c]	-1.1	2.7	31	50
Workers in money circulation		0.8	13/21		-0.2	1.9	26	70
Workers in services	44	0.1	38/23	45	-0.4	2.5	32	58

N = 998

a) Figure includes both bourgeoisie and small employers
b) Figure includes both industrial workers and workers in agriculture and forestry
c) Figure includes both workers in trade and workers in money circulation
d) Figure includes both middle and large farmers

(1) Would you be prepared to take part in a demonstration aimed at securing more jobs in your own town and at improving the situation of the unemployed?

(2) Would you be prepared to go on strike if people were laid off at your own workplace?

The working class and non-hierarchic decision-makers are more willing than others to take part in demonstrations. In these groups, 15 % would participate without hesitation, and a further 15 % would participate if most of their workmates did. Managers, advisor-managers and supervisors are less willing to take such action than other wage earners.

Over 50 % of all Finnish wage workers would go on strike if they had the backing of their trade union. If not, the number of potential strikers is far smaller. Non-hierarchic decision-makers and workers in money circulation seem to be particularly militant. Managers and advisor-managers are more passive, as only one third of them are prepared to go on strike even with the backing of the trade union.

As regards the role of an instrumental work orientation to the development of class consciousness, two main conclusions can be drawn from the above results:

- It seems that the worker who is oriented to the content of his work is an essentially different type than the militant worker: in all class groups a strong orientation to work correlates negatively with critical attitudes and willingness to take action.

- There are clear differences between the class groups in the type or quality of instrumentality. Among managers, an instrumental work orientation seems to be associated with a non-critical attitude and reluctance to take action. Among industrial workers, instrumentality correlates positively with these variables. The instrumental work orientation of managers seems to support the Weberian thesis of weakening class conflicts. On the other hand, as regards industrial workers, the view that an indifferent attitude towards the contents of work is a precondition for a developed class consciousness seems to be more valid.

Understanding of society and future utopias

Several studies have pointed to the tension that prevails between workers' immediate experiences of their working and living conditions and the more abstract thinking that is concerned with the problems and prospects of society as a whole (see e.g. Mahnkopf 1982). At the latter level, there tends to be far greater hesitation and uncertainty. Most workers who are critical at the more concrete level of immediate work experiences find it difficult to form a clear picture and opinion of society at large. Below, we shall discuss the conceptions that are held by Finnish wage earners of society. The aim is to find out how the respondents perceive the class structure of society and how they identify themselves with social classes.

This latter question has inspired sociologists for decades. Since the study by Centers (1946), there has been an influential line of research that has attempted to describe the class structure on the basis of subjective criteria (see e.g. Coleman and Rainwater 1979). However, the vast majority of relevant studies have attempted to describe perceptions of the social structure in different class groups, or to identify the various 'class structure models' that people use in analysing social reality.[10]

Conceptions of society were here studied by two open-ended questions: 'What in your opinion are the main social classes in Finland?', and 'In which class would you include yourself?' The interviewers were instructed to write down the answers verbatim. The answers were then coded in several ways to determine the respondent's basic idea of class structure; his or her criteria of class distinctions; views on how profound these distinctions are; ability to explain his or her concept of class structure; and his or her class identification.

Only about three fifths of the respondents have a more or less clear conception of social classes, and only half present a detailed picture of class structure. One fifth hold that the class division is based on power and relations of production, while one quarter present various stratification or other criteria (such as between the rural and urban population).

Every tenth respondent denies the existence of class differences. One fifth hold that there are clear class differences, and one fifth also hold that there is some kind of stratification in society. The majority (58 %) of those who identify themselves with some social class say that they belong to a deprived group, while 40 % identify themselves with the middle class. The intensity of class identification varies between class groups. Half of the entrepreneurs do not identify themselves with any class, while among middle and small farmers the figure is around 60 %. The same applies to workers in commodity circulation, part-time workers and pensioners, and to a certain extent to advisor-managers and housewives. Supervisors, non-hierarchic decision-makers and industrial workers, in this order, have the clearest picture of class structure and also of the social class they belong to.

On the whole, the more privileged class groups identify themselves with the middle class more often than the less privileged. In the group of those wage earners who identified themselves with some class group, 80 % of the bourgeoisie, 60 % of large farmers, 53 % of managers, 22 % of the industrial workers, and 16 % of the unemployed identified themselves with middle-class or generally affluent groups. All managerial groups identify themselves with the middle class more often than industrial workers. A high level of identification with these groups is also found for non-hierarchic decision-makers (60 %). The class identification of workers in money circulation and services is rather similar to that of supervisors, semi-autonomous employees and advisor-managers.

The results concerning the class identification of the economically non-active population are also interesting. As we saw, only 16 % of the unemployed identified themselves with the middle class or affluent groups. This was also uncommon among part-time workers, housewives and pensioners. By contrast, the majority of students (56 %) identified themselves with affluent groups; this perhaps reflected their anticipated class development.

There are also marked class differences in the criteria presented for class distinctions and in perceptions of the intensity of class divisions.

On the basis of these results on perceptions of the class structure and class identification, it is concluded that this is an inconsistent indicator of consciousness. However, the use of class identification as a general indicator of people's interest in slotting themselves in a given position in society does yield quite interesting results.

Another approach to examining people's conception of society is to look at their social utopias. These have been classified on the basis of the question: 'In what direction would you want to develop our society? Why should it be developed?' One third of the Finnish wage workers are unable to articulate their views on the desirable direction of social development. Half of the workers in industry, trade, agriculture and forestry have some utopias. Critical utopias concerning the whole of society or those referring to socialism are most often presented by non-hierarchic decision-makers. Otherwise these utopias are very rare, particularly among industrial workers: only five % of them have such utopias, which is less than among semi-autonomous employees and workers in money circulation.

As regards the rest of the economically active population, the utopias of the

Table 5.10.

Class identification by class group (%)

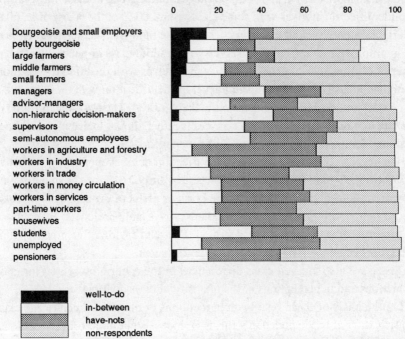

well-to-do
in-between
have-nots
non-respondents

bourgeoisie are clearly opposed to state intervention and characterized by conservatism. The petty bourgeoisie and supervisors, then, are primarily interested in removing social injustices. In the working class the main concern is with unemployment. Workers in money circulation form a special case here in that one third of them have anti-state or conservative utopias.

A comparison of the consciousness profiles of different class groups

In this final section we shall compare the consciousness profiles of three wage worker groups: managers, supervisors and industrial workers. The results described above suggest the conclusion that wage earners have a lot in common in this respect: performance illusions, membership of trade unions, familism, and illusions concerning the form and contents of the state. On the other hand, there are also certain interesting differences, notably on the dimensions of strenuousness of work, work orientation, experiences of strikes, attitudes towards income differentials, party affiliation, degree of criticalness, attitudes towards state intervention, subjective class identification and social utopias. There are also marked differences between class groups in their willingness to take action.

COMPARISON OF THE PROFILES OF CLASS GROUPS

	Industrial workers	Supervisors	Managers
1. Condition and wearing out of labour power	* predominance of experience of wearing out, half experience stress	* one third experience stress	* one fifth experience stress
Autonomy	* no autonomy	* majority has medium autonomy	* almost all have medium autonomy
2. Work orientation	* instrumental attitude (28%) or prevented identification (35%)	* half show identification	* majority (75%) show identification
3. Concept of performance and wages	* over half have illusions of performance and wages * over two thirds regard income differences as unjust	* over half have illusions of performance and wages * over half regard income differences as unjust	* three in four have illusions of performance and wages * over half regard income differences as justified
4. Work and out-of-work time	* women have family as content of life * men have family as content of life * the most instrumental class group	* women have family as content of life * men have family as content of life * the most familistic class group which combines familism and intensive work orientation	* women have work as content of life * men have family and work as content of life
5. Workplace level interest promotion and trade union activity	* high number of strike experiences * three in four are trade union members, every tenth has been a trade union trustee * only one in four regards trade union activity as successful	* few strike experiences * almost all are trade union members, every fifth has been a trade union trustee * half regard trade union activity as successful	* few strike experiences * two in three are trade union members, every tenth has been a trade union trustee * half regard trade union activity as successful

6. State citizenship and political organization as a whole	* over half feel political apathy * every second has an illusion of parliamentarism * over half are willing to take action	* less than half feel political apathy * every second has an illusion of parliamentarism * over half are willing to take action	* less than half feel political apathy * every second has an illusion of parliamentarism * over one third are willing to take action
7. Overall image of society and utopias	* every second has no utopia * every fourth has reformistic utopia or utopia related to elimination of unemployment * 36 % identify with the working class	* every third has no utopia * every third has critical or reformistic utopia and an equal number has moral, anti-state or conservative utopias * 30 % identify with the working class	* every fourth has no utopia * every fourth has critical utopias or utopias related to doing away with injustices; half have conservative, anti-state or moral utopias * 13 % identify with the working class

Excursion: limitations of the survey method in the analysis of consciousness

As we have repeatedly pointed out in the previous chapters of this book, the survey method imposes certain important restrictions on class analysis. Nowhere are these restrictions more evident than in the study of class consciousness. Therefore we conducted a little experiment to test the effect of this method on the picture that emerges of wage-worker consciousness.

We selected nine respondents from the Tampere region for a second, unstructured interview. Rather than repeating our earlier questions on consciousness in a more concrete form, we provided the respondents with certain clues that they could either neglect or pick up and elaborate upon. This strategy, we thought, would give us a truthful picture of what the respondents regarded as the most important things in their life.

The interview covered a number of subject areas that were not included in the questionnaire proper: childhood, growing up, choice of occupation, transition into working life, etc. Also, the respondents' relationship to the trade union and other work-related issues were discussed in considerable detail. We then moved on to housing, family and children, leisure activities, TV viewing, reading newspapers

170

and literature. Next, we asked the respondents to describe their relationship to central social issues, their participation in social activities and political identification. In addition, we discussed matters related to way of life, general life-satisfaction and future prospects.

On the basis of this interview and the questionnaire proper, we produced a consciousness profile of each respondent, which were then compared with each other. The interviews themselves were also compared.

The respondents generally showed a reserved attitude towards our questions relating to social consciousness; as soon as the issue was raised, they seemed to become very tensed up. The same applied to all questions relating to politics, the state and society in general. The reason for this was not that they wanted to hide their opinions, but simply that they had no firm opinions. Our respondents had obviously not given very much thought to these problems, and therefore they felt they did not know enough to talk confidently about them. This interpretation seems legitimate because the respondents showed no hesitation in expressing their political stands.

How do these observations relate to the findings of our questionnaire? It would seem that the more abstract questions in the latter exaggerated the significance of consciousness. It is difficult to say whether the questionnaire forced the respondents into answering questions which were unimportant to them personally, but in any case it is clear that for many of the respondents some questions (e.g. those concerning state citizenship) touched upon subjects that simply were beyond their personal experience.

There is thus a clear tendency for the questionnaire method to exaggerate similarities between the respondents, as if they all had the same abstract areas of consciousness. Questionnaires probably give the most truthful picture of the consciousness of those people who are socially most active, for in this case opinions and attitudes have a firm anchorage in social practice.

The internal differentiation of wage workers and consciousness

In Chapter 3 we discussed various lines of demarcation within the working class which are not included either in Wright's theory or in other class theories. We also stressed that to evaluate the true relevance of these distinctions, we must proceed in class analysis from one level to the next through mediating syntheses. We shall here analyse the relevance of these distinctions in relation to the consciousness of social classes. In other words, we shall try to answer the question as to how far the processes causing internal differentiations within the working class result in a differentiated consciousness.

1. *The core of the working class has no uniform consciousness and action profile.*

There are two antagonistic theses with regard to the consciousness of the core of the working class:

- Many theorists refer to Marx's arguments about the importance of a unified worker front and mass power in the class struggle. It has also been assumed that through industrial work people learn to act in a disciplined and organized manner

- According to the opposite assumption, the core of the working class shows the highest level of integration. This thesis is based on the assumption that capital has a strategic orientation towards integrating the 'spine of production and economy'. In addition, it has been assumed that through its greater mass power the core of the working class gains special economic advantages.

If we define the core of the Finnish working class as consisting of workers employed in large companies (over 500 workers) within the paper processing and metal industries, they account for only 5 % of the Finnish working class. This group, in comparison with the rest of the working class, is characterized by the following features:

- a strong commitment to the organization;
- a lower degree of activity-orientation;
- pronounced class consciousness or critical attitude without organizational activity;
- low organizational activity.

These results are clearly at variance with the traditional Marxist line of argumentation. They suggest that the youngest generation differs very radically from older workers. Young workers show a rather low confidence and interest in traditional forms of wage-worker organization, but on the other hand a high level of consciousness and competence. This result links up very interestingly with the emergence of new forms of social activity and new social movements.

2. *The position of state employees is clearly a relevant factor with regard to consciousness. However, the most decisive factor is in which specific tasks the state employee is engaged.*

The organization-active and critical types are clearly overrepresented among state employees. Wage workers of capital are more often both integrated and willing to take action.

A classification of state employees according to different task types reveals some interesting differences. Workers of the repressive state apparatus are more often organized out of a sense of duty. They are also least critical, even when compared to wage workers of private capital. Those employed in the social state apparatus are almost as action-oriented as wage workers of capital, whereas those employed in the infrastructure are very rarely action-oriented.

In managerial groups there are large numbers of activists, which apparently reflects the political nature of these posts. At the supervisory level, there is a very large proportion of workers showing integration. It is also worth noting that semi-autonomous employees in the social state apparatus form a distinct group, with a clear tendency towards criticism and reformism.

3.   *White-collar and blue-collar workers have different consciousness and action profiles. However, white-collar employees in the working class show a more 'proletarian' profile. Conclusion: if white-collar workers are 'proletarianized', then their distinct consciousness profile is eroded.*

As compared to blue-collar workers, there is a larger proportion among white-collar employees of those who show only formal commitment to organizations. The proportion of action-oriented workers and activists is also lower than among blue-collar workers. In a comparison of higher and lower white-collar employees, it seems that the latter include a greater number of both those who believe in their opportunities for influencing matters and those who are willing to take action.

Nominal organizational commitment is not very common among the white-collar employees of private capital. However, those employed by the private sector seem to be more willing to take action than state employees.

White-collar employees belonging to the working class are more instrumental in their work orientation and more critical and reformistic towards state intervention.

4.   *There are clear differences in consciousness across different labour markets; a stable position in the labour market is conducive to a high degree of organization. Mobility, in turn, generates greater activity and criticism.*

Wage-earners in skilled labour markets and secondary labour markets seem to differ from the average in the same direction. In both there is a high proportion of activists and of the conscious type. Conventional organization is relatively uncommon in both of these sectors, and they include only a small number of those characterized by organizational commitment only.

In the external primary segment, workers are less conscious, but more integrated and nominally committed to organizations. Organizational attachment is most common among workers of internal labour markets, but otherwise their consciousness profile comes close to the average.

5.4. Classes, organizational attachment and the problem of reformism

Our discussion below of the theory of reformism is premised on the view that it combines important aspects of theories on the state, consciousness and trade unionism.[11] The chief reason why we are interested in the theory of reformism does not lie in the history of ideology; nor do we intend to discuss reformism as a certain (party) political or ideological movement. Reformism is here defined as a category describing *the commitment of wage earners to capitalism and its different forms as mediated by wage-worker organization and consciousness* (Andersen 1981).

Modern conceptions of reformism are still largely based on the 'old' theories of reformism that were presented around the turn of the century (Pannenkoek, Lenin, Michels) and that first drew attention to the revolutionary nature of the working class and its organizations. Early studies focussed not only on reformism but also on opportunism, revisionism, anarchism, etc. There were two predominant explanations for the reformistic nature of working-class organizations: the first pointed to the internal differentiation of wage workers, while the latter stressed the tendency for those organizations to be swallowed up by the bureaucratic state apparatus. Wage-worker differentiation, then, was explained by reference to the growth of wage employment, which implied a growth of precapitalist (petty-bourgeois) fractions within the working class and thus increased differentiation, or the emergence of a labour aristocracy (Lenin).

A classical example of the latter explanation is Michels's theory of oligarchy, which points to the tendency for supervisors and managers to move away from working-class organizations and to the emergence of a pragmatically oriented labour bureaucracy. Old theories of reformism were also interested in the significance of the political system (e.g. systems of parliamentary representation) for wage-earner integration into capitalism.

One of the commonest criticisms against this line of theorizing is that it remains detached from the forms of capitalist societalization and from the corresponding forms of consciousness. This in turn means that it tends to explain

174

reformism on the basis of such categories as 'deception' or 'deviation' from what is generally understood as the 'right path'.

As far as class analysis is concerned, the most interesting problems related to the theory of reformism include the nature of reformistic forms of organization and consciousness and the connections of those forms to reproduction in wage workers. One of the most important lines of explanation could be described as *consciousness-theoretical*, which explains the reformism of working-class organizations and their consent to reformistic policy by arguing that the consciousness of individual wage earners is permeated by the general consciousness forms of capitalism.[12] A key role in this process is played by mystified forms of consciousness, which are based on the inversion of capitalist relations of society: on the one hand there is the wage form of labour, which conceals from view the essential difference between necessary labour and surplus labour, and on the other hand there is the notion that labour, capital and landed property are all equal as forms of income. In addition, these illusions give rise to the false impression of 'common interests'.[13] The economic forms of capitalism typically lead to a *consciousness of social partnership*, which is characterized by a transition from class determinants to income groups, a process in which class interests tend to disappear from view together with the profound differences between social classes. All people with some source of income (wage workers, capital owners and landowners) now share the same interest: to keep hold of that source of income, to maximize their respective shares of income and to ensure its continuity.

This line of theorizing which leans on forms of consciousness is directly relevant to our analysis of wage-worker consciousness. However, there is one important weakness: this theory completely neglects the formation of interests at the organizational level. It does not regard membership of the trade union as an important basis for the mediation of reformism, even though it correctly (see e.g. Neusüss and Müller 1971) identifies important limitations in trade union consciousness.

The structural basis for unionization is provided by the reproduction situation of wage earners. In their capacity as sellers of labour power, wage workers are in a situation of mutual competition where they are all out to maximize their own individual need-satisfaction and to safeguard adequate preconditions for individual reproduction. Within certain (very limited) margins, the individual wage earner has the freedom to choose the branch and even employer he or she wants to work with; there is also the freedom to try to economize in the sphere of

175

consumption. In the situation where there is no demand for labour power, the wage earner can work to improve his or her relative position in the competition by upgrading his or her professional qualifications (although the demand for such skills, overall, is very low). Another coping strategy in this situation is for the individual worker voluntarily to lower the preconditions for reproducing his or her labour power. Given the limited options, wage earners typically choose to further their interests of reproduction by joining up with the trade union and by lessening competition between wage workers. The trade union thus becomes a central vehicle in the anti-capitalist struggle to secure wages that better correspond to the value of labour power. Trade union organization does not, however, do away with exploitation; instead, it is one element in the complex social system mediating exploitation.

The promotion of interests through the trade union is chiefly a struggle aiming at a fair(er) income distribution, at changing the proportions in which income is distributed among wage earners and between wage earners and capitalists. Insofar as the trade union is committed to the wage form of labour, this means that the union accepts the performance principle: the principle that the amount of pay depends not on social or historical needs but on output within the production process. And as long as maximum performance is in the interest of both wage workers and capital owners, the capitalist is free to exploit his wage workers without any limit. As far as the wage earner is concerned, increasing performance can in the long run have very serious consequences.

The chief tenets of this line of theorizing on reformism can be summarized in the following two points:

1. the organization of workers in the trade union is an important channel for mediating reformism; and
2. this form of organization (and consciousness) is restricted to the wage form of labour and to the struggle for a fair(er) income distribution.

Both of these aspects are very relevant to integration into capitalism. State-mediated reformism is founded on the idea that the state can safeguard the common interests of both capitalists and wage workers by intervening in the process of social reproduction. Looking at the traditional forms of wage-worker organization, this notion corresponds to the typical distinction in which short-term economic interests are the domain of the trade union, while longer-term social interests remain the responsibility of the state. At the same time, this under-standing of political interests generates a new (inverted) level of consciousness.

Reformistic state-consciousness is based on the view that the state is a neutral agent, that it is capable of promoting common interests, that there is a 'just and fair' social state (Neusüss-Müller 1971). If and when the state has to 'adapt' the task of defending occupational interests according to the capitalists' profit requirements, this may have two kinds of consequences with regard to the formation of conflict frontiers: (1) the conflict between the state and trade unions is intensified, or (2) a new conflict frontier emerges when the state and the trade union leadership join forces to work against rank-and-file union members.

Both these alternatives have their concrete historical preconditions. Strong 'triangle corporatism' (the state and the parties to collective bargaining), the involvement of working-class parties in government, and their commitment to the promotion of workers' interests through organizational channels increase the probability of the latter; an oppositional policy, in turn, increases the probability of the former.

We have already briefly discussed the aspects of reformism theory that are relevant to the study of class consciousness and organization. However, any analysis based on these premises is bound to remain at a fairly general level, where it is impossible to identify the historical conditions determining the reformistic struggle.

The chief tasks of an empirical study of reformism include the following: analysis of the social homogeneity and political and functional unity of wage workers and the working class; analysis of the type of political organization and the nature of membership relations within those organizations; analysis of the consciousness — and particularly the consciousness of social partnership — of rank-and-file organization members, functionaries and top leaders; analysis of reformistic consciousness, political apathy and alienation; and analysis of the interrelationship of action and willingness to take action and different forms of consciousness. In a concrete study we can also examine the changing preconditions for reformistic organization and consciousness, which are related to (1) the differentiation of wage workers along industrial branches and labour market segments, and (2) the connection between class differentiation and other processes structuring civil society.

We do not think it is appropriate to link up the structuration of civil society with the traditional theory of reformism, because the interests involved in the democratic struggles that are related to this structuration do not directly reflect the immediate interests of reproduction among wage earners.

The structure and meaning of involvement in associations can be approached from a number of different perspectives. Associations are political organizations which operate within civil society. On the other hand, associations also have their links to state activity. Associations channel society's resources in certain directions, towards the attainment of certain objectives. At the same time, they are a central mechanism in organizing the way that people see and define their needs and interests. Finally, associations may be important in providing an opportunity for self-realization for a sense of solidarity.

The history of Finnish associations can be briefly described as follows:

(1) With the relatively late appearance in Finland of capitalist relations of society, the capitalist institution of associations only started to develop around the turn of the century. Many of its central features can be explained by the structure of production and capital in this country. The forest and wood-processing industry, and particularly the large monopolies within these sectors, played a very central role in the growth of capitalist organizations. Today these are Finland's most important export industries, which obviously gives added importance to this role.

(2) Compared to most other advanced industrial countries of the west, there is a very large number of associations in Finland. They also seem to be very deeply rooted in Finnish social life.

(3) Associations have a very distinct class nature; this applies equally to trade unions as well as to other organizations (such as cooperatives, sports clubs). This factor can be traced back to the Civil War of 1918 and to even earlier decades.

(4) The split of the Finnish labour movement after 1918 has very profoundly affected associations and activity within associations. The main lines of disagreement are reflected in attitudes towards parliamentary activity (as opposed to direct action or grassroots activity). There are also continuous power struggles in mass organizations.

(5) Membership of associations and organizations is at an extremely high level in Finland. Party organizations, cooperative organizations, and trade unions are the most important channels of organization.

(6) The bourgeoisie has adopted different methods in reproducing its political power in different ages. In the inter-war period, they resorted chiefly to repressive means and to restricting the political freedoms of wage earners. After World War II, all Fascist and military organizations were banned. These main periods can be further divided into more or less distinct stages of development.

(7) In the late 1960s, with the continuing growth of corporatist political structures, there was a radical change in the political organization of society which also affected the position of mass organizations. One important reason behind this change was the need for capital to improve its competitive position on the international markets through wage regulation and by intensifying labour output.

What is the situation in the field today? We shall start our analysis by proposing a distinction between four types of association: parties, trade unions, cooperatives and other organizations.

Farmers, and big farmers in particular (48 %), are the most active participants in party organizations. Looking at the agrarian population as a whole, 30-50 % of them are members of party organizations. The second most active members are managers and non-hierarchic decision-makers, of whom some 20 % are members. Supervisors and semi-autonomous employees come third, with 12-14 % being members. Finally, participation is lowest among the working class proper (8-9 %).

Trade union membership varies from 65 % (managers) to 96 % (supervisors). The groups which most frequently attend trade union meetings are advisor-managers and non-hierarchic decision-makers (26 % and 25 %); here the figure is lowest for workers in trade and circulation (about 5 %).

Participation in cooperative associations is by far most common among farmers, of whom almost 50 % are members of some cooperative association.

As far as other organizations are concerned, the most active group is that of managers: the average manager is a member of two associations, which take up around one hour of his or her time every week. The most passive groups are the working class and small farmers, who spend 6 to 42 minutes in these activities per week.

The following conclusions can be drawn from our results. Different class groups have different channels for taking part in associations and organizations; for instance, farmers (big and medium farmers in particular) are frequent members of party organizations and cooperatives, whereas managers take an active part in other types of associations. On the whole, managers are the most active group and the working class — the largest group within the body of wage earners — are least active. Wage workers in commodity and money circulation (most of whom are women) show the lowest interest in associations. The results also indicate that *formal commitment (membership) is high whereas participation or activity remains low.*

179

Table 5.11.

Participation in associations by class group

Membership of an association (x) = 1
Time spent in association activities (x/h/week) = 2
Membership of a functional community = 3
Member of a cooperative (%) = 4
Votes in cooperative elections (%) = 5
Trade union member (%) = 6
Attends trade union meetings regularly (%) = 7

Trustee in a trade union (%) = 8
Municipal trustee (%) = 9
Member of a party organization (%) = 10
Time spent in party organization activities (x/h/month) = 11
Member of the Central Union of Agricultural Producers (%) = 12
Member of an employers' organization = 13

	1	2	3	4	5	6	7	8	9	10 Right	Centre	Left	11	12	13
Bourgeoisie and small employers	1.0	0.2	12	28	0				9	6	3	0	0.2		28
Petty bourgeoisie	1.3	0.5	5	35	5				13	4	4	4	0.7		9
Big farmers	1.4	0.6	43	39	0				13	9	39	0	0.5	87	
Middle farmers	1.0	0.1	56	47	0				9	2	42	0	0.3	79	
Small farmers	0.7	0.4	33	59	3				13	3	18	10	0.2	59	
Managers	1.8	0.9	13	33	3	65	20	12	11	5	7	7	0.2		
Advisor-managers	2.0	1.4	9	34	3	78	28	12	19	6	6	6	0.8		
Non-hierarchic decision-makers	1.2	1.2	3	33	3	72	25	8	17	6	3	11	0.8		
Supervisors	1.1	1.0	9	32	0	96	23	11	9	0	4	9	0.3		
Semi-autonomous employees	1.2	0.8	5	30	4	76	20	8	12	4	3	11	0.5		
Industrial workers	0.6	0.7	4	24	4	82	14	7	3	0	1	6	0.4		
Workers in circulation	0.4	0.1	3	31	3	75	6	5	4	3	3	4	0.2		
Workers in services	0.7	0.6	2	31	5	85	15	10	4	2	4	8	0.2		

Table 5.12.

Non-vocational organization membership of wage workers
(the respondent's most important membership in a non-vocational association)

Vocational and professional organizations = 1
Related to non-professional interests = 2
Political organizations = 3
Other ideological organizations = 4
Religious associations = 5
Cultural organizations = 6
Sports organizations = 7
N/A = 8
Total = 9

	1	2	3	4	5	6	7	8	9	N
Managers	22	2	1	13	0	4	15	43	100	94
Advisor-mangers	16	3	6	0	0	13	13	50	101	32
Non-hierarchic decision-makers	8	3	14	8	0	6	19	42	100	36
Supervisors	13	2	11	4	4	0	13	53	100	47
Semi-autonomous employees	9	3	8	8	1	3	15	54	101	110
Workers in agriculture and forestry	0	0	0	0	0	9	18	64	100	11
Industrial workers	3	3	3	3	2	2	17	69	102	235
Workers in trade	4	2	2	6	0	4	6	78	102	54
Workers in money circulation	9	0	0	13	0	0	4	74	100	23
Workers in services	3	5	8	8	1	2	9	64	100	129
All	8	3	5	6	1	3	13	60	99	771

The most important organizations are those that work to promote their members' economic interests (trade unions, cooperatives, consumer organizations and other economic organizations); these are followed in rank order of importance by party political organizations. What about the other types of association? What kind of associations do Finns consider important?

When we omit from consideration all professional and occupational organizations, we find some very interesting results. Under the question where the respondents are asked to state the most important non-occupational organization of which they are a member, the majority do not mention any organization at all. This was more common in lower class groups and among women. On the other hand, both political and ideological organizations seem to be rather insignificant. In higher class groups in particular, occupational contacts have some appeal outside the sphere of work as well. However the most significant type of association, especially all among men, is represented by sports organizations.

In sum: the majority of Finnish associations and their activities are aimed at reproducing labour power, at maintaining its saleability. A minor but not insignificant role is played by associations which are active in the fields of self-education, self-realization and social charity.

Moving on to illusions of common interests among Finnish wage earners, we asked our respondents to give their opinion on the statement that an 'increased GNP is in the interest of all people'. Also, we wanted to know what they thought of the statement that 'everyone should sacrifice their own individual interests to improve the country's international competitiveness'. The respondents were divided into groups according to their attitudes by cross-indexing the questions. This gave us nine groups, three of which were particularly interesting.[14]

Those who agreed with both statements are here described as 'integrated', while those who answered the first question in the affirmative and the second in the negative are called 'interest-fighters'. Our interpretations are based on the assumption that the latter type have a strong awareness of the working class's immediate interests in their struggle against capitalists. At the same time, it is held that combined with this awareness there is also a recognition of the possibility of equivalent exchange. This line of thinking starts from the premise that the working class must not sacrifice its interests but continue its struggle for fair wages. Finally, the respondents who did not agree with either statement are described as anticapitalists. We assume that this group does not believe in reconciling class interests as a strategy of safeguarding common interests, but holds that this requires the complete abolition of the capital relation.

In our total sample of economically active Finns, 49 % fell into the category of integrated; 17 % are interest-fighters, and 6 % anti-capitalists. The remaining one quarter are not sure about their position.

Given the clear differences revealed by this analysis in action and consciousness structures, it seems that attitudes towards common interests provide a useful starting-point for an analysis of wage-worker consciousness. On the other hand, there are also clear differences in attitudes towards the specific interests of different class groups; from these differences we should be able to draw relevant conclusions with regard to the power relations of class groups.

We measured the consciousness of class groups on the basis of their attitudes towards class interests: the consciousness of a given class group is considered to the stronger the smaller the proportion of integrated and the greater the proportion of the anticapitalist type. In this analysis it seems that workers of money circulation are the most conscious group of the Finnish economically active population. Every third wage earner in this class group falls in the category of 'integrated', while just over 10 % are anti-capitalists. At the other end of this continuum we have managers, 62 % of whom are integrated and 3 % anti-capitalist. The working class proper includes a smaller proportion of integrated and a greater proportion of anti-capitalists than contradictory wage-worker positions. The low level of consciousness within contradictory positions is explained by the attitudes of managers and advisor-managers; in other class groups there are only minor differences in comparison with the working class. The highest level of consciousness is found in wage-earner groups in which women form the majority; this also seems to be the case among female-dominated industrial workers. Among female industrial workers, almost one third are integrated, while the figure for male industrial workers is 48 %.

There is a very clear difference between the self-employed and wage earners. In the bourgeoisie, 71 % are classified as integrated; the figure for farmers is 60 %. Attitudes seem to be far less militant within the self-employed than in the entire wage-earner population.

In conclusion then, the Finnish bourgeoisie shows a strong class consciousness and has close connections with the top layers of wage earners in managerial positions. The bourgeois way of thinking is also relatively common among the petty bourgeoisie and among the working class. Within the working class, young people and women show the strongest consciousness.

The trade union movement can in principle serve either as an interest organization for wage earners or as a state-controlled mechanism of integration; or as both at the same time. In either case it needs a field organization and people to run it. Below we have divided wage workers into four groups on the basis of their trade union membership: non-members, passive members, active members not in trustee positions and trade union activists in trustee positions.

Less than one quarter of all wage earners (and 17 % of the working class) are trade union activists who have occupied a trustee position. In addition, 10 % of all union members participate on a regular basis in the union's activities even though they do not have trustee positions.

Differences in union activity across class groups and between the genders illustrate the division of positions of trust within the trade union in line with the relations of control and domination in society. The majority of these positions union are occupied by male wage earners in contradictory locations.

A large number of workers in contradictory locations and with (limited) control over the consumption of their subordinates' labour also have (limited) control over the conditions under which their subordinates sell their labour power. The group of supervisors is particularly interesting in this regard: almost half of them (and over half in the case of women) have occupied positions of trust in the trade union.

Analysis of participation in trade union activities by gender suggests that women usually vote for men in trustee elections. Where this is not possible, they will vote for their female supervisor; and where they have to settle for a female worker, it is most often someone with a strong consciousness who is elected.

This same analysis also indicates that the verb 'elect' is more relevant in female-dominated than in male-dominated fields. The majority of trade union activists who do not have a trustee position and a minority of those who do are women. In female-dominated fields participation in trade union activities (e.g. in the election of trustees) is relatively high even among members who do not hold positions of trust. In male-dominated fields, activists typically vote for each other. The gap between activists and the rank-and-file is less marked among women than among men; the necessary exception to the rule is formed by workers in trade. Although this group is female-dominated, it comes quite close to male-dominated groups in terms of trade union activity and consciousness.

Non-members, passive members, active members and activists differ from each other not only in terms of their social composition. When we shift the focus of our analysis from wage workers to the working class as a whole, other differences begin to surface as well. In the working class, active members differ from the other groups in their entire life situation. The differences between members and non-members can be explained by a variety of factors in addition to the level of unionization itself. However, the differences between working-class union passivists and activists in consciousness and reproduction situation, as well as the differences between active members in positions of trust and other activists, are due in part to the nature of trade union activities.

The phrase 'interest promotion at the workplace level' implies certain assumptions about the relationship between trade union activity and wage-worker consciousness. At the company level, wage earners work to defend their interests against the employer and his interests. The workers who take part in this effort obviously belong to the group of interests-fighters. The election of a trade union trustee implies delegation of the everyday tasks involved in the interest struggle. If a given problem cannot be resolved through negotiations between the workers' and the employer's representatives, then workers occupying positions of trust will resort to the use of mass power. Thus the activist occupying such a position is an interest-fighter. Another obvious conclusion is that those who believe workers and employers have common interests will remain passive members in the interest struggle.

The interests of the working class are therefore chiefly defended and promoted by workers who accept the existence of specifically working-class interests. Those who believe that the working class and the bourgeoisie have important interests in common should remain passive members. Finally, a trade union activist should be an interest-fighter or even an anti-capitalist. However, all of these assumptions are wrong.

An interest-fighter's attitude strongly correlates with participation in trade union activity. However, this attitude is not predominant among trade union activists in positions of trust, but among active members who do not occupy such positions: 38 % of the latter are interest-fighters. The proportion of the 'integrated' is even greater among activists in positions of trust (47 %) than among passive members (39 %). The consciousness profile of active members in positions of trust comes closer to that of non-members than to that of other trade union members.

Among workers occupying positions of trust in the trade union, shop stewards show the highest level of consciousness. A good illustration of the trade union's integration mechanisms is provided by the finding that the least conscious group consists of those who have been representatives at the union congress, among whom 69 % are integrated and none anti-capitalists. Other occupants of positions of trust are more conscious than congress representatives, but less conscious than shop stewards. However, there is no group which reaches the same high level of integration as passive members.

The predominance in the working class of conscious but passive union members and union activists with a positive attitude towards capitalism is more clearly visible within the so-called traditional core of the working class than in the working class taken as a whole (IMSF 1973, 47, 59, 147-149). If we look at the core of the working class as defined by IMSF (workers of material production in industries of scale), there are no anti-capitalists among union activists, while the proportion of the integrated is 57 %. Among trade union passivists in the core of the working class, anti-capitalists represent 14 % and the integrated 46 %.

Almost half of the passive male union members are integrated; the figure for active union members is 43 %, and for union activists 60 %. Among women the situation is exactly the opposite: 36 % of the passive members, 35 % of the active members, and 28 % of the activists are integrated; and 9 %, 0 % and 16 %, respectively, are anti-capitalists. The respective figures for male workers are 10 %, 7 % and 6 %. So within the core of the working class we see clear differences not only between male passivists and male activists, but also between male and female activists.

Party affiliation in the working class also correlates with worker consciousness and integration, as measured by attitudes towards common interests. Even within the same party union activists and passivists often have completely different attitudes. The differences between union passivists and activists occupying positions of trust are most outstanding among supporters of the Social Democratic Party, where 43 % of the activists and 75 % of the passivists are integrated. On the other hand, there are also marked differences across parties. In the SDP, 17 % of the activists are interest-fighters, while the figure for the Communist Party is 53 %. In other words, there are clear differences in this regard between the two strongest parties in the trade union movement, although among supporters there are hardly any differences: 43 % of SDP supporters and 40 % of CP supporters are integrated, while 8 % of the former and 7% of the latter are anti-capitalist.

When we include in our analysis the factor of political party support and gender, our conclusions that were based on an examination of activists in trustee position and activists not occupying trustee position, need to be modified some-what. That is, from the differences observed we may conclude that the adequate, 'spontaneously' contradictory interest-fighter takes an active part in the trade union movement, is elected to a position of trust, and in the process of defending workers' interests he 'discovers' various realities and turns into a conservatist, an integrated worker with a positive attitude towards capitalism. It seems that communists and women can cope with the change from an active member to an activist much better than other groups. Regardless of gender, communists often remain interest-fighters and adequately contradictory in their relationship to the 'surface forms' of capitalism. And regardless of political views, women may even develop through their participation in trade union activity from interests-fighters to anti-capitalists.

The processes taking place in the individual's consciousness in interest promotion at the workplace level reflect a very typical course of development: a realistic and action-oriented interest-fighter whose performance illusions and criticism are adequately contradictory to the 'surface relations' of capitalism, accepts a position of trust in the trade union movement and eventually becomes an 'integrated' worker who has maintained his or her performance illusions and pessimism but who at the same time has lost his or her criticism and willingness to take action. The underlying reasons for this development should be sought from the social situations related to and reproduced by trade union activity.

Insofar as the union activist controls the conditions under which other workers sell their labour power, he or she is in a similar position as the supervisor who controls the consumption of labour power. The union activist is caught in the middle between the interests of workers and the employers, and at the same time between trade union management and rank-and-file members. The latter will be pushing the activist to influence the management, who control the 'wholesale price' of labour power; management in turn will use activists to try to keep the rank-and-file members quiet.

In a purely theoretical analysis this process of separation would eventually lead to a situation where union management decides on the value of their members' labour power without any interference on the part of the rank-and-file; so far we have not seen this happen, nor is it really possible. However, there does seem to be a trend now towards the separation of the 'wholesale prices' of labour power as defined by the state from the field prices of individual jobs. This trend is interesting in two respects. First, it has become more or less legitimate[15], and second, it seems that this is the direction in which we should seek to uncover the connections between performance illusions and illusions of common interests which are mediated by trade union activity.

Performance illusions and illusions of common interest have an empirical connection which is mediated by trade union activity. Illusions of common interests are more prevalent among union activists than among passive members. On the whole the former do not differ to any significant extent from passive members in terms of illusions, but it is important to note that activists who most often have illusions of common interests also tend to have performance illusions. The reinforcement of performance illusions among union members in general is due to the nature of trade union activity at the grassroots level, which concentrates on maintaining fair rates for individual performances. The selective conversion of performance illusions into illusions of common interests is due in part to the successes achieved in this same activity: every time an activist succeeds in settling a disagreement on wages, he or she creates a performance illusion. Successful interest promotion at the workplace level is conducive to performance illusions and converts activists' performance illusions into illusions of common interests. On the other hand, failure in this task has similar effects.

The connection between control over the conditions for selling labour power and performance illusions explains in part why the consciousness profile of trade union activists closely resembles that of certain contradictory wage-worker positions. One of the jobs of union activists is to make sure that individual workers receive adequate compensation for their performance in the form of fair wages. Wage workers in contradictory positions whose job it is to control the use of labour power, make sure that these fair wages are met by a fair performance.

There are rather clear differences in the reproduction situations of worker groups who participate in the trade union. Non-members form a group where all indicators of resources (with the exception of education), standard of living and social participation draw a classical portrait of the underprivileged worker. On the other hand, union activists in positions of trust show all the typical signs of the well-to-do worker (with the exception of education).

The differences between non-members and union activists are not particularly interesting from the point of view of our analysis of trade union activity, since they are explained by several factors that are related to membership itself. Non-members are either young people who have just entered the labour market, or older workers often with temporary jobs. Non-membership is due in many cases to the nature of work, to union rules, or other factors related to the nature of the employment relation. Part of the non-members in our sample would probably have exactly the same life situation even if they were members of the union. On the other hand, some of the differences between union activists and the rank-and-file can be explained by reference to the nature of trade union activity.

Social participation tends to be higher among working-class union activists than among passive members. On average, the passive member is involved in 0.4 organizations, while the figure for activists is 1.2. Among passive members, 3 % occupy municipal positions of trust; here the figure for activists is 6 %. Eighteen percent of activists and 7.5 % of passive members are members of a political party. Activists also take part in employer-sponsored recreation activities slightly more often than the rank-and-file.

Most of the working-class union activists are men, and a substantial proportion are well-paid skilled workers. However, the higher proportion of these affluent worker groups among union activists does not explain the differences in the reproduction situation of activists and passive members, for these differences are also visible within the genders (examined by occupational groups), labour market groups, etc. There are no variables in the empirical material that would explain the good reproduction situation of all activists as compared to that of passive members. Vocational education partly explains the wage differences between female activists and passive members, but training levels among male activists are even lower than among passive members. With the exception of trade union activity, there is no variable that explains the differences in reproduction situation between male activists and passive members.

A comparison of the working class and activist wage earners in contradictory positions reveals certain internal differences within the working class and certain similarities across the working class boundary. The income levels of working-class activists come closer to those of certain passive members in contradictory positions (supervisors, non-hierarchic decision-makers) than to the incomes of working-class union passivists. The consciousness of working-class union activists resembles that of the average contradictory positions. In view of their high level of unionization and activity, left-wing union activists are rather similar to right-wing wage workers in contradictory class positions who are not union members.

The consciousness of working-class activists comes closer to that of working-class non-members rather than to the consciousness of passive members. Non-members constitute a underprivileged right-wing working-class group with a positive attitude towards capitalism. The wage-worker elite, in turn, consists of workers in contradictory positions who are not members of the trade union (and who may even be members of bourgeois organizations). In terms of their consciousness and degree of action-orientation and criticism, they resemble working-class non-members, but in view of their high income level, activity and degree of organization, the exact opposite is true.

Working-class activists and non-member managers seem to constitute two functional elites. One is formally attached to the working class, the other to the bourgeoisie. There are certain similarities in the consciousness profiles of these groups and minor differences in their reproduction situation. Both, however, stand clearly above the ordinary worker, and both pretend to be concerned about the fate of society at large.

5.5. Classes and parties

Political parties play a key part in mediating the process of interest-formation. The important question is, what kind of interests do they mediate, what sort of goals do they aim at. Party structures and supporter compositions vary over time. The history of the current party system in Finland goes back to the turn of the century, when the conservative Coalition Party and the Agrarian (Centre) Party were formed and the labour movement split up into a reformistic (the Social Democratic Party) and revolutionary camp (the Communist Party).

The SDP split up in the 1950s and the Communist Party in the 1980s. The 1980s also saw the appearance of the Greens on the Finnish political scene, as in most other West European countries. The first popular front government was set up in Finland immediately after the war, but the cooperation between Communists, Social Democrats and the Agrarian Party lasted only for a few years. Following the 1966 parliamentary elections, the same three parties again cooperated in popular front governments, but in the 1980s the Communists were ousted. After the 1987 elections, the SDP and the conservative National Coalition Party joined forces to set up a 'black and red' government. In the 1991 parliamentary elections the Social Democrats suffered a major setback and their place in government was taken over by the Centre Party; SDP now became the biggest opposition party.

In any analysis of political parties and interest-formation, it is important to look not at the names of the parties but at the actual contents of their respective policies. Also, we must consider the issue of how far those policies are feasible within the given structural conditions. If, for instance, a certain party is working to promote the interests of the working class but structural conditions for any real improvements are absent, then tensions are bound to escalate. If in this situation the practical policies of this party do not essentially differ from those of other parties, then its chief task will be to adapt or integrate workers into the political systems; if it fails in this, the party will lose its popular support. In the opposite case, the party policy will coincide with its supporters' interests, and the main problem will be in canvassing support under 'normal bourgeois' conditions.

The following analysis of classes and political parties is primarily concerned with differences between the social composition of supporters (and to some extent party members); we want to find out whether it is legitimate in Finland to speak of 'class parties'. But we have an even more important question than that. A study of classes and the social composition of party supporters contributes most directly to our understanding of the formation of hegemony. Here, the fundamental question is: what is the *organizing role* of political parties in and between different classes and class groups?

For several reasons the analysis that follows is rather restricted. First of all we must bear in mind that parties are by no means the only factor which organize classes and class groups: organizations, mass communication, and bourgeois publicity are other directly relevant factors. Secondly, it remains unclear how far the organizing role of political parties also leads to organization with respect to immediate collectivity or to the formation of subcultures. In this case focus is on the differences in the consciousness of party supporters: we will be trying to answer the question of whether the differences in the social and class compositions of party supporters also imply differences in their consciousness. It is also important to note that we are interested in differences in the consciousness of party supporters, not in differences in the actual policies pursued by parties.

First, we shall look at the composition of party supporters in terms of class groups. Most supporters of the conservative Coalition Party are wage earners occupying managerial positions and semi-autonomous employees. Together, these two groups represent half of the supporters of the Coalition Party. On the other hand, it is interesting to note that every fourth supporter of the Conservative Party belongs to the working class. The support by the bourgeoisie and non-agrarian entrepreneurs for the Coalition Party is clearly more significant than in the case of any other party.

Almost half of the supporters of the Centre Party are agrarian (and 18 % of them are small farmers with less than 15 hectares of land).

The working class is the most significant supporter group for both the Social Democrats (60 %) and the People's Democratic League of Finland (62 %). The proportion of industrial workers is higher among PDLF supporters than among SDP supporters. Almost one third of the support to these parties comes from managerial groups and semi-autonomous employees (35 % in SDP and 30 % in PDLF).

As we can see, different parties depend to a great extent on different class groups for their popular support. However, this does not yet say anything about how parties can 'organize' class groups. In order to answer this question, we must look at the distribution of class groups in terms of their support to different parties.

The majority of the bourgeoisie and small employers are supporters of the Coalition Party (73 %). Most farmers support the Centre Party. Half of the support of non-agrarian small entrepreneurs goes to the Coalition Party; the rest is more or less equally divided between other parties. Working-class parties seem to attract small entrepreneurs (36 % of them are supporters). Among farmers, the Coalition Party receives most support from big farmers (over 19 hectares). The support for the Centre Party is strongest among middle farmers (10 to 19 hectares). The support for the SDP and the PDLF is strongest in the smallest farm size category, where SDP's support is 3 % and the support for PDLF 13 %.

Excluding the group of supervisors, the Coalition Party seems to be the most attractive party for managerial groups (35-47 %), followed by the SDP (18-26 %; 26 % among managers). Support for the SDP is strongest among supervisors. In the group of semi-autonomous employees, there is most support for the Coalition Party (about one third); the remaining support is equally divided between small bourgeois parties, the SDP and the PDLF.

Most of the working class supports its 'own' parties: 38 % vote for SDP and 24 % for PDLF. The SDP has the greatest relative support among industrial workers and workers in services. The relative support of the Coalition Party is greatest among workers in money and commodity circulation (15 and 13 %). The support of the Centre Party among workers of services amounts to 11 %, and among workers in money circulation to 9 %. In absolute terms support for the PDLF is strongest among industrial workers and workers in services (16 and 11 %).

Table 5.13.

Support for political parties by class group (% of those who responded)

Bourgeoisie = 1
All petty bourgeoisie = 2
All farmers = 3
Non-agricultural petty bourgeoisie = 4
Managers = 5
Advisor-managers = 6
Non-hierarchic decision-makers = 7
Supervisors = 8
Semi-autonomous employees = 9
Working class = 10
Total economically active population = 11

	1	2	3	4	5	6	7	8	9	10	11
PDLF	—	7	5	17	5	15	14	20	18	24	17
SDP	12	5	1	19	26	18	22	43	23	38	27
Centre	8	58	73	9	17	7	10	14	8	10	18
Coalition	73	17	7	50	41	47	35	18	34	14	24
Others	7	13	14	5	11	13	19	5	17	14	13
Total	100	100	100	100	100	100	100	100	100	100	100
N	32	175	115	60	98	32	36	47	114	460	994

193

However, in the group of workers in commodity and money circulation, the PDLF has far less support than the Coalition Party. The majority of workers in money circulation and half of the small entrepreneurs are either reluctant to express their political views or are unsure. Managerial groups, farmers and industrial workers are most positive on their political views.

The memberships of the Coalition Party and small bourgeois parties are dominated by entrepreneurs to a greater extent than other parties. On the other hand, the membership of the Coalition Party also contains a surprisingly large proportion of working-class members: one quarter. In this respect the Coalition Party differs quite clearly from the small bourgeois parties. Most members of the Centre Party are farmers. The highest proportion of wage workers is found in the membership of the SDP, where only 3 % of the members are entrepreneurs. As expected, the memberships of both the SDP and the PDLF consist mainly of the working class, but there are certain differences in the relative shares of managerial wage earners and semi-autonomous employees: the share of these groups is clearly higher in the SDP (14 %) than in the PDLF.

Finally, we shall briefly examine the following two questions: (1) How do supporters of different parties differ from each other in terms of their consciousness profiles; and (2) Are there any differences in the consciousness of party members on the one hand and party supporters on the other?

The former question is related both to the alleged convergence of different political parties and to the role of existing party structures in the formation of consciousness. The latter question, in turn, should throw some light on the ideological similarities between members and supporters and on the influence exerted by different parties on consciousness.

Summarizing the differences between supporters of different parties, we may note that PDLF supporters are, first, distinguished from other party supporters by their anti-capitalist, critical attitude; and second, PDLF and SDP supporters are together distinguished from other supporters. The former applies to general criticism and performance illusions, as well as to illusions of common interests; the latter, in turn, applies to instrumentality and attitudes towards state intervention. The major exception to these rules is found in attitudes towards parliamentarism. The view that voting at general elections is the only way individual people can influence things, is most common in the Coalition Party and the SDP. The illusion of parliamentarism is weakest among supporters of the Centre Party.

However, the differences across different groups of party supporters are not very considerable in terms of illusions of parliamentarism, performance, or common interests. On the other hand, attitudes towards state intervention and general criticism in particular vary quite clearly.

Political apathy and experiences of social powerlessness are common to supporters of different parties. The only exception is that PDLF supporters are somewhat less apathetic than others.

As regards willingness to take action (going on strike for a worker who has been given notice and taking part in a demonstration against unemployment), there again were rather clear differences between party groups. PDLF supporters show the strongest willingness to take action, followed by SDP supporters. Both of these groups differ clearly from the supporters of the Centre Party and the Coalition Party. Willingness to take action in the case that a worker has been given notice is lowest among supporters of the Centre Party; in the case of taking part in a demonstration against unemployment, willingness is lowest among the supporters of the Coalition and the Centre Party.

5.6. The results and a theory of consciousness

In this chapter we have developed an antieconomistic and antireductionistic starting-point for the analysis of class consciousness, in which we nevertheless take into consideration the relevance of Marx's critique of political economy to consciousness formation. Our theoretical position can be summarized in the following thesis:

The most general determinants and contradictions of wage-worker conscious-ness are based on the general form-determinants of capitalist wage labour. In the consciousness of wage workers there are both elements that are attached to the surface forms of bourgeois society (ownership, individuality, freedom, etc.) and critical elements arising from the class nature of society. However, the formation of class subjects cannot be directly derived from Marx's theory of capitalism. Subjects are not given at the level of production relations, nor is their constitution determined by these relations only. It is important to stress the role of civil society and various hegemonic apparatuses.

Another important starting-point for our analysis has been the idea of proceed-ing in class research through mediating syntheses which link together different levels of analysis. In the present case this meant that we empirically analysed the relevance of alternative theories of class structure and assumptions of the internal differentiation of wage workers to the formation of consciousness.

Looking at the various assumptions that exist of the formation of consciousness in different class theories, it seems that the theory on the differentiation of managerial positions by Erik Olin Wright receives strongest support from our analyses; on the other hand, the assumptions by Nicos Poulantzas that the old and new petty bourgeoisie come very close to each other are clearly overruled. Likewise, the material does not lend support to the theory by PKA, which says that the working class differs in its consciousness from the middle class. However, PKA has a very useful theory on differences of consciousness within the working class.

As far as the differentiation of wage-worker consciousness is concerned, specific determinants related to state employment and state functions are also significant. However, in our analyses we found no evidence of the existence of what has been described as the core of the working class. As to white-collar employees, our results indicate that their specific consciousness may dissolve in the process of 'proletarianization'. Labour market segmentation also leads to different consciousness profiles. The most important observation in this respect is that criticism arising from experiences of secondary labour market does not lead to active participation in working-class organizations.

A concrete study of the consciousness of Finnish wage workers shows that wage earners in different positions have many features in common: performance illusions, familism and illusions concerning state and its form. On the other hand, wage-worker consciousness contains many aspects related to class position from work orientation to utopias. Social classes also differ from each other in terms of their channels of organization.

Finnish parties are largely class parties, but less obviously so than formerly. Nevertheless the consciousness profiles of party supporters still differ from each other rather clearly. It is also important to observe that trade union activists and passive members have different consciousness profiles: working-class men seem to be sharply divided between passive men with a critical attitude towards capitalism and trade union activists showing a positive attitude. Female union activists, on the other hand, seem to be more conscious than passive members.

All in all, it is an important observation that consciousness, organization and willingness to take action constitute distinct dimensions of consciousness which do not necessarily coincide with each other.

When we look at the various factors which structure wage-worker conscious-ness, a significant dimension related to the level of civil society comes forward: that is, activity in political parties. Another interesting finding is the observation that women and young workers show strong social criticism and a relatively low level of commitment to conventional organizations. There is good reason to ask whether these findings are indicative of an emerging conflict at the level of civil society. The answer will largely depend on how different social movements — both the traditional labour movement and neoconservatism — can articulate these contradictions.

6   Class division and the significance of classes

6.1. Class research as an articulated whole

As we pointed out in the Introduction, this study is based on Marx's class theory: we start from the assumption that classes are determined on the basis of production relations. At the same time, however, our concept of class analysis as an articulated whole means that we must retain a certain degree of theoretical openness within the Marxist research tradition; we do not believe that the relative strengths of different research traditions can be determined without a serious comparison of these at all levels of class analysis. Also, although Marx's concepts of the theory of capitalism provide an important starting-point for class research, it must be borne in mind that Marx himself does not present any systematic elaboration of class theory in his own production. Therefore it is necessary in our concrete research work to combine different theoretical approaches and empirical lines of argumentation.

A careful distinction between the different conceptual levels of class theory means we can also evaluate the relevance of Weber's arguments. Weber does not lend support to arbitrary stratification theories that fail to see the basic differences between such concepts as class and status. However, Weber's market theory remains in certain fundamental respects extremely vague. Weber can only describe the monopolization of resources as a basis of class structure. He presents no conceptualization of the capitalist exploitation that occurs at the level of production. On the other hand, it is also clear that Weber's theory does not provide us with the tools we need to resolve the problems related to the theory of forms of consciousness and organization.

198

By contrast, it would seem that the neo-Weberian research tradition which is concerned with social closure has an important contribution to give to class analysis, particularly to questions related to the mechanisms of maintaining and seizing class locations. However, from our point of view the analysis of social closure is mainly relevant for our efforts to develop a theory of civil society.

Analytical Marxism is the latest influential approach in Western Marxism (see Blom and Kivinen 1990). It is an attempt to tackle the classical problems using new theoretical tools of analytical philosophy. However in many respects the starting-points of analytical Marxism are very traditional and orthodox. The problems are most evident in the case of Marx's theory of capitalism. For analytical Marxism, Marx is above all a theorist of history. This means that the tradition fails to take into account the most important result of the 'capital-logical' research of the 1970s according to which traditional Marxism — which evolved after Marx's death within the Second International — seriously deforms Marx's thought. Much in the same way as the Second International, analytical Marxism hinges on those stages of Marx's thinking in which he was least critical of Ricardo: in other words, on the materialist concept of history as presented in the *German Ideology* and on Marx's theory of capitalism, which he developed in the late 1840s and early 1850s. The hard core of Marx's theorizing which is contained in *Capital* and various preliminary works — the critique of political economy — is largely ignored.

The approach we have adopted in this study to class analysis has uncovered many important problems of mediation and also many new conceptual solutions:

(1) We have seen that most studies and lines of theoretical argumentation have focussed only on certain aspects of the total problem field. It follows that these theories have failed to thematize the mediation problems occurring at different levels, and are therefore also of little help in trying to understand the problems involved.

(2) Different theories of the same problem field are by no means always consistent with one another. For example, we have repeatedly pointed to the profound and real conceptual differences between the German and French/Anglo-Saxon traditions concerned with the problems of class structure. The same applies to many other issues as well.

(3) There is also considerable variation in how far theorists have advanced in the conceptualization of different problem fields. It is quite obvious that the concepts employed in the analysis of class structure, for example, are more

developed than those relating to the sphere of civil society.

(4) The relationship between different levels of class analysis should not be understood merely as relations between certain scientific constructs. For example, Marx's theory of capitalism, the critique of political economy, plays a role not only in the analysis of class structure but also in the analysis of the structuration of class situation and class consciousness.

(5) Different problems of mediation are not of equal theoretical relevance. In. addition to class structure and the constitution of 'class society', other important mediations include that from class position to the analysis of the internal contradictions of class situation; and the analysis of the relationship between class situation and class consciousness.

(6) Problems of mediation consist not only in abstract relations of certain factors, such as critical vs. uncritical class consciousness; the key issue is the way in which the structuration of class situation 'affects' the internal structure of class consciousness. According to this concept apparatus structuration is not only a solution to the problem of mediation between the actor and structure, as Anthony Giddens has it. It refers to the different relations of determination of different kinds of structures.[1]

(7) Problems of mediation cannot be resolved merely on a theoretical and speculative basis; there must exist a solid empirical basis to that solution. The question of the significance of class division and the increasing internal differentiation of social classes can only be answered through an analysis which tackles many different problems at the same time. In accordance with its methodological guidelines, our Project has proceeded in its analysis of the Finnish class structure along successive cycles, from determining class positions to analysing the structuration of class situation (situation in work and reproduction), and further to discussing differences in consciousness and organization. The following is an attempt to synthesize these three stages and their interconnections.

Before we proceed to summarizing the empirical results of our study, a few words are in order on the special characteristics of our theoretical approach. The Comparative Project on Class Structure and Class Consciousness has published a large number of national reports (Ahrne 1982, Colbjörnsen et al. 1987, Erbslöh et al. 1987, Marshall et al. 1988),[2] which open up interesting insights both into the nature of the societies concerned and into the relevance of different class theories. Nevertheless the approach we have developed here is quite unique. As well as elaborating our own theory of the 'scope logic' of class research, we have stressed that class theories do not necessarily address the same problems: the most relevant aspect of any class theory is its relationship to different theoretical constructs. This means that the theoretical solutions adopted in class analysis are intricately bound up with various other theoretical issues and debates which on the surface seem to give precedence other themes. To clarify our point, we shall briefly comment on certain major lines of research that have evolved over the past few years.

(1) Since Braverman, research on the labour process has produced a number of sophisticated theoretical distinctions which concern managerial strategies, forms of labour control, and power resources related to the 'politics of production'. Most of the empirical research on labour processes has consisted of historical or case studies. However, it would be a serious mistake to regard this line of research as historically or qualitatively more sensitive or as a more concrete alternative to class theory. In fact there is an important conceptual link between labour process theory and class theory, which is related to the understanding of the processes of class relations and thus to the definition of Wright's class groups. Rather than postulating labour process research as an alternative to class theory, the question we have to ask is what kind of implications does post-Bravermanian theory of the labour process carry for the definition of class criteria on the basis of the processes of class relations. Markku Kivinen (1989)[3] has attempted to demonstrate that this strategy leads to a definition of the new middle classes which is more historical than that arrived at on the basis of Wright's premises, and which explains the structuration of class situation more adequately than Wright's theory.

(2) In recent years many sociologists have considered French cultural studies and particularly the theory of Pierre Bourdieu (1986) to represent an important challenge to traditional class research.[4] Bourdieu has indeed presented some very penetrating analyses of certain aspects of the structuration of class situation and consciousness. Bourdieu's theory shares many similarities with the work of Nicos Poulantzas,[5] whose relevance has been widely discussed in this study. Both writers

(1)   adopt an anti-economist approach to constructing their class theories;
(2)   emphasize the importance of class struggle and class practices;
(3)   aim at developing a power-based class theory; and
(4)   aim at revealing the mystification connected to mental labour.

Poulantzas's consistent adherence to structuralism prevented him from saying anything relevant about the way in which class practices are formed. Bourdieu, on the other hand, proposes a concept apparatus which is supposed to form the basis of a whole new theory of social action. It is here that he presents his new theoretical concepts of *habitus* and *distinction*.

The concept of economy is in many ways the weakest point in the work of both Poulantzas and Bourdieu. For Bourdieu, economic capital means above all an asset that is used by individual people or families in their reproduction strategies. As Markku Kivinen (1989) has argued, it is perfectly legitimate to study capital from such a perspective, and in doing so it also seems reasonable to draw an analogy between cultural and economic resources. In particular, such a perspective is justified when we are concerned to study the reasons for why certain people drift into certain positions. However, it is totally inadequate for purposes of explaining the constitution of those positions and the relationships between those positions.

In sum then, Bourdieu's theory provides a new and interesting explanation for the relationship between positions and people and between positions and dispositions. The former is particularly important in explaining the phenomenon of social mobility, the latter in analysing class consciousness. By contrast, Bourdieu's theory does not seem to offer a viable alternative to theories based on the politics of production when it comes to explaining the constitution of positions.

(3) The theory of civil society is an attempt to respond within the confines and along the boundaries of the Marxist tradition to the dilemma represented by the growing plurality of subjects of social resistance (Urry 1981, Cohen 1982).[6] A common denominator of the different versions of the theory is the avoidance of class reductionism. Although the theorizing concerning various levels of domination within civil society is in many ways open-ended and vague, we would still agree with the must fundamental starting-point. A basic shortcoming of Marxist theory of the constitution of society is the absence in that theory of an any thematization of the sphere of civil society. Collective and individual subjects (Hänninen 1982) cannot be reduced to character masks and accordingly, the theory of civil society cannot be reduced to the critique of political economy.[7]

However, the rejection of class reductionism does not mean we can abandon Marx's theory of capitalism and his class analysis in the study of modern society or in outlining perspectives of emancipation. A relevant study of classes cannot start directly from the subjects of civil society; before proceeding to that level of analysis, we must first go through several intermediate steps. From an analysis of class structure, we have to proceed to the structuration of class situation and further to an analysis of the basic structures of consciousness and forms of collectivity and organization. The abandonment of class reductionism should not lead to discarding the study of class structure.

(4) It is obvious that theorizing on the change in reproduction type also has important implications for class theory. If we really are moving from Fordism to post-Fordism, or from organized to disorganized capitalism (Hirsch and Roth 1987, Lash and Urry 1987), this should also lead to changes in class structure.[8] The theoretical starting-points we have elaborated here provide a useful way of specifying this question, which currently remains open and which can only be resolved by empirical research. Is it possible to argue that the entire field of class relations is undergoing a process of change (rather than just the situation of individual class groups) in such a way that it is legitimate to speak of a *new type of structuration* of class relations? It is exactly in this context that we feel we can also answer the question of how far it is justified to describe the current develop-ments in society as indicative of new kind of individualization (Beck 1986).[9]

6.2. Class structure

Finland is very clearly a wage-earner society. About 80 % of the economically active population are in wage employment; the remaining 20 % are self-employed. The growth of wage employment has led to a commodification of social relations, but it would be wrong to describe Finland as a 'transcapitalized' society; the large size of the petty bourgeoisie is alone sufficient to invalidate such an argument. As regards the self-employed population, there are three types of relations which complicate the analysis of the stage of development of different groups:
1. detachment from wage labour;
2. liberation from the concrete labour process; and
3. relations of subordination between different groups (here problems are caused by vertical integration and subcontracting relations, by the question of the factual independence of the petty bourgeoisie and small employers and, finally, by the relationships of these groups to state).

Compared to other advanced capitalist countries, the self-employed popula-tion in Finland is characterized by the large size of the smallholder population (the agricultural petty bourgeoisie). The life of farmers has been changing very dramatically with the mechanization and increasing specialization of agriculture. There is a very high degree of internal differentiation within the group of farmers.

In the future, we can expect to see an increasing number of farms, even larger ones, to undergo a process of semi-proletarianization, while the share of small semi-proletarian farms will decline. On small and middle-sized farms, semi-proletarianization will take place through an increase in part-time farming, and on large farms through intensified vertical integration.

There is also a high degree of internal differentiation within the non-agricultural self-employed population, which is basically due to the position of the private business company in the structure of production and to the scale and profitability of capital. Business companies are increasingly dependent on large corporations, banks and the state. Our results indicate that there is a qualitative difference between the bourgeoisie and the petty bourgeoisie, between which there are a number of transitional groups.

Small entrepreneurs, small employers and the bourgeoisie are all relatively heterogenous groups in terms of their social background, although only small numbers come from a working-class position. However, when we look at their generational mobility, we see that the tradition of entrepreneurship is rarely handed down from generation to generation.

Our Project has had little to say about the internal differentiation of the bourgeoisie according to different types of capital and according to the size and monopolistic position of capital. However, when we examine the research material that is available on the subject it seems clear that our picture of a bourgeoisie with a very heterogenous background would be radically altered if we focussed on the representatives of big capital. In Finland, production and business are highly concentrated, and the internal differentiation of the bourgeoisie is very clear.

In Wright's theory, the petty bourgeoisie is a social class based on simple commodity production. Small employers are a contradictory class location between the bourgeoisie and the petty bourgeoisie. The contradictory nature of small employers is most clearly reflected in their continuous movement between different classes. However, we would argue that the class position of the petty bourgeoisie is contradictory in an even more fundamental sense, for in this group we have a confluence of the determinants of both (small) owners and workers. This means that the definition of the petty bourgeoisie as a non-contradictory class position comparable to the bourgeoisie and the working class, is in fact a highly problematic solution. Another problem stems from the specific character and the alleged independence of the petty bourgeoisie. Small-scale production and small business companies in general are increasingly bound up with an dependent on the capitalist mode of production. Although subcontracting relations have not developed in Finland to the same extent as in other advanced capitalist countries, and although there is considerable variation across different fields, these relations are now increasing. Similarly, the dependence of private enterprises on banks (loans) and on the state (which buys their products, grants and guarantees loans, and regulates taxation) considerably restricts the independence of small entrepreneurs.

Old Marxist predictions say that we will see a decline of entrepreneurship. However, in recent debates and particularly in the discussion on dual economies it has been argued that private entrepreneurship will actually increase and that (state) support for this development would solve unemployment and various other economic problems. Indeed the decline assumption is not as such a valid argument. However, we can expect to see changes in the nature of private entrepreneurship (its position in the productive structure, independence, necessary qualifications, etc.) and in its social significance.

All wage workers share the same basis of reproduction: the selling of labour power and wages. The relationship between capital and wage labour is one of exploitation and domination. The execution of the functions of capital (supervision and control of labour power) is not the responsibility of the individual owner-capitalist, but of the hierarchic organization with its division of labour. This means that some wage earners bear the functions of capital. These managerial positions, from company managers to supervisors, represent one fifth of the economically active population, and they may also imply participation in economic exploitation. However, it is extremely difficult to establish how far wages for work done exceed the actual value of that work, or a surplus which comes from tasks related to the reproduction of labour power. On the basis of the wide income differentials we find in the managerial groups, it seems that such a surplus does indeed exist.

The working class is distinguished from contradictory managerial positions by the fact that it has no functions of domination (nor decision-making authority over investments or control over the use of physical capital or the labour power of others). In the narrow definition (excluding semi-autonomous employees and supervisors), the largest group among the working class is that of industrial workers (54 %), followed by workers in services (29%). Workers in trade represent 12 % of the working class and workers in money circulation 5 %. The

Table 6.1.
Internal differentiation of wage workers

Performance level	60%	(42%)	Leading	21% (15%)
Performance level non-autonomous (narrow working class)	46%	(32%)	Actual managers deciding on matters at the level of the	
Productive workers	34%	(24%)	whole organization	10% (7%)

majority of the working class is employed in middle-sized or large companies. The monopolistic section employs 12 % of the working class. State employees account for over one third of all wage earners. Only 60 % of them are employed in state functions related to the reproduction of capital. One third of all state employees occupy supervisory locations, leaving the remaining two thirds in performance-level jobs tasks.

The statistical category of 'white-collar employees' represent 57 % of all wage earners in Finland. Over 60 % of white-collar employees are women. They are chiefly occupied in performance-level tasks (59 % belong to the working class), while 38 % are in managerial positions. In the social division of labour, white-collar employees are mainly engaged in services and money circulation (79 %).

A class analysis based on individual class positions tends to give an exaggerated picture of class differences. The following lists some of the reservations we have had to make at different stages of this project:

1. Only half of the families, the main units of reproduction, are class families. For instance, 26 % of all the families in our sample were purely working-class families. In other words, there are typically different class positions within the individual family. The implications depend mainly on the distance between those positions.

2. About one third of the Finnish population aged between 18 and 65 are economically non-active. This finding underscores the key role of the state as a reproductive source and at the same time points to the limitations of the economic character mask as a category mediating consciousness and organization. The economically non-active population does not have a common class position; instead, it is internally differentiated in several different ways.

3. With the exception of farmers, 'self-recruitment' is relatively uncommon.

Over half of all managerial wage earners and industrial workers have a wage-earner background. On the other hand, only one third of the latter are second-generation industrial workers. Self-recruitment is even more uncommon among workers in circulation and services. In contrast to these results which strongly suggest an ongoing process of structural change, it seems that we will see a rapid growth in the future of second-generation wage earners. Industrial workers in particular typically enjoy a rather stable position throughout their career.

4. The connection between the processes determining class position and the factors structuring civil society have a significant impact on class position. The most important connections are related to regional differences in class structure (which are still very considerable in Finland), the relation between class and generation (or age), the influence of gender (both the predominance of women in the working class and the predominance of men in managerial positions, the differential location of men and women in different economic sectors and the gender differentiation of occupations), and the link between party identification and class positions related to political organization. As far as class consciousness and the organization of classes are concerned, the structuration of civil society is a significant level in the constitution of subjects.

6.3. The structuration of class situation

Key factors in the structuration of class situation are the individual worker's work and reproduction situation and the relationship between work and out-of-work time. There is considerable variation between individual workers in terms of their working conditions and the structuration of their work situation. Working conditions are essentially structured by class position, so much so that it is legitimate to speak of a hierarchic system of working conditions from the working class to managers. Within this system, negative jobs aspects tend to accumulate in working class positions and positive aspects in contradictory locations. The differences are based on the nature of work and forms of supervision. The working class is subjected to external control, which is achieved by means of specialization, task fragmentation, bureaucracy, direct supervision, heavy restrictions and the linking of performance to the preconditions for reproduction. External control is heaviest in the case of industrial workers. The control to which workers in money circulation are subjected has a different dynamics, in that the development of labour power and social integration is also taken into account. The supervision of managerial groups, then, is basically a process of intensive socialization.

How wide are the class differences in working conditions? Most aspects in the structuration of working conditions — the polarization of the mental and physical stress at work, opportunities for personal and professional growth, the range and degree of task routinization, methods of control and managerial strategies, opportunities to orientate oneself towards the contents of work (as opposed to an instrumental orientation) and differences in pay levels — all lend support to the following generalizations:

1. Managerial wage earners and semi-autonomous employees differ from the working class in terms of their working conditions and the nature of their work.

2. A hierarchic structure of working conditions is also in evidence within managerial locations, which implies that working conditions are bound up with the control hierarchy. On the other hand, semi-autonomous employees are in many respects better placed than supervisors (this applies above all to task scope and job contents).

3. There are also clear differences in the structuration of work situation within the working class: a narrow task scope, strict control and other negative aspects are most typical of industrial workers and least typical of workers in money circulation and services (similar differences are also seen within the industrial division of labour in that shopfloor workers are clearly in a poorer position than other groups).

On the whole the internal differences among wage earners follow a hierarchic logic within managerial groups, and there are also differences in the structuration of working conditions between working-class positions. The differences are most clearly visible in the differentiation of the working class from other wage-worker groups (including semi-autonomous employees) and in the differentiation of industrial workers from the rest of the working class in terms of control, work intensity and job contents.

The results also indicate that working conditions vary considerably between the bourgeoisie and the petty bourgeoisie (including both farmers and other entrepreneurs). The differences are chiefly found on two dimensions: the wearing out of labour power and opportunities for personal and professional growth. There are differences both between the bourgeoisie and small employers, and between these two groups and the petty bourgeoisie. In a comparison of entrepreneurs with the working class, we note that the former are characterized by a wide scope of tasks and high autonomy in the concrete work process, but also by the long working hours and by a relatively poor reproduction situation.

There are two reasons why it would be wrong to speak of a one-dimensional proletarianization of the working conditions of white-collar employees:

1. The working conditions of managerial white-collar employees differ from those of both the working class (above all industrial workers) and performance-level white-collar employees.

2. Different aspects in the working conditions of performance-level white-collar employees have been proletarianized to different extents. Thus the results lend support to the assumption of the proletarianization of the so-called lower middle class. The proletarianization of the working conditions of performance-level white-collar employees is most clearly visible in the high degree of routinization and in the lack of job autonomy. The scope of tasks, the opportunities for self-development, the wage form and career prospects show lesser signs of proletarianization.

Labour market segmentation is one mediating aspect in the relationship between the class position and working conditions as well as in the reproduction conditions of wage workers. The Finnish labour markets are highly segmented, even though there are many features which distinguish them from the labour markets in other countries (such as the predominance of women in the labour market outside the primary segment and the predominance of men among secondary labour power). A large proportion of secondary labour power is typical of small enterprises in the competitive segment, while a large proportion of labour power outside the primary segment is characteristic of the monopolistic segment and state companies. The differential structuration of working conditions according to labour market segments suggests that we have in Finland a dual labour market.

Our comparison of the relative strengths and weaknesses of different class theories in explaining the structuration of class situation leads into the second phase of measuring the relevance of class theories.

All the class theories we have discussed in this study (Wright, Poulantzas and Projekt Klassenanalyse)[10] give adequate evidence that working conditions are hierarchically structured. Comparing Poulantzas and PKA with Wright, the latter must be credited for uncovering the differences in the structuration of working conditions as a result of the internal differentiation of wage earners. This applies most particularly to the differences *between contradictory locations*.

Figure 6.1.
Differences in the confluence of class position and consciousness

An example of how class position, class situation, and consciousness coincide: the proportions of (1) the non-integrated, (2) those identifying themselves with the working class or other have-nots, and (3) left-wing supporters according to their income among wage-worker groups arranged in order of affluence (relative indicators formed into a continuous curve), monthly income (FIM/month), and relative instrumentality.

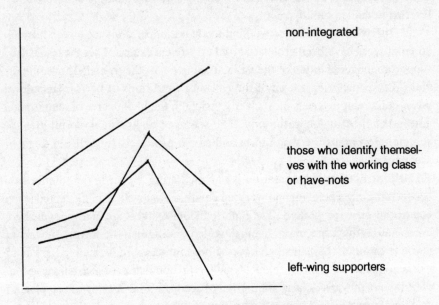

non-integrated

those who identify themselves with the working class
or have-nots

left-wing supporters

	non-hierarchic		workers in money circula-	
managers	decision-makers	industrial workers	tion	
				Income
4994	3411	2965	2512	Whole group
4453	2845	2600	2525	Those who identify themselves with have-nots
				Instrumentality
1.1	1.1	2.8	2.2	Whole group
1.2	1.6	2.8	2.1	Those who identify themselves with have-nots

210

Projekt Klassenanalyse, on the other hand, lays bare the differences in the structuration of working conditions and reproduction situations as a result of the *internal differentiation of the working class*. In particular, analyses based on PKA's method clearly reveal that the position of machine workers is inferior to that of productive workers and unproductive workers. In addition, PKA takes into account the differences between state employees engaged in different functions.

One major problem with the work of PKA — again in comparison to Wright — is its distinction between working class and middle class which is based on form of income. This distinction is not directly relevant to the structuration of class situation. What is more, differences in the structuration of working conditions reflecting managerial hierarchy play an important role in the case of state employees, too. As we already pointed out, there are certain clear differences between state employees engaged in different fields. Those involved in the maintenance of the general conditions for production come rather close to the working class in terms of their working conditions. The working conditions of employees in the administrative apparatus, in turn, tend to resemble those of unproductive workers. State employees engaged in the reproductive sector display a more distinctive pattern in the structuration of working conditions, which combines high stress with high qualifications, interesting job contents with a wide scope of tasks; at the same time opportunities for advancement are poor.

In sum: class theory has an important role to play in explaining difference in working conditions and reproduction situations. The theory proposed by Erik Olin Wright makes a valuable contribution in revealing hierarchic differences related to positions of domination. This aspect remains without due attention in the work of both Poulantzas and PKA. The main problem with Wright's theory is that he has failed to analyse the internal differentiation of the working class and state employees. That machine workers are distinguished from unproductive workers and aggregated personnel (which can be compared to managerial locations in Wright's theory) suggests that, in the analysis of the structuration of working conditions, the general determinants of class theory can be elaborated in more detail through a study of how and to what extent different forms of labour have been subordinated to capital. Not all aspects of work and reproduction situation are directly structured by class location. Gender creates the dimension of social division of labour, which is intricately intertwined with class relations. Although this type of study can only provide a preliminary and somewhat superficial description of the processes of control and social reproduction, it is obvious that

211

even in the traditional sections of the working class women's labour is subjected to heavier control and is even more fragmented than the work of men. Gender also plays a selective role in the hierarchy of wage-earner positions. If we look at the whole range of work that is done in society, women are generally in a more stressful situation in that it remains their responsibility to do most of the daily household chores. Gender socialization to the social division of labour also maintains differentiated work orientations. In the field structured by class relations, there is a strong male working-class culture whose traditional predominance is now being tested by female-dominated groups.

6.4. Consciousness and organization

Different class groups have different types of consciousness profiles, even though there are also certain interesting similarities. Basically, the consciousness of all wage earners may be described as contradictory, but the relative weight of critical elements and bourgeois values varies across different groups. Different areas of consciousness and organization also vary in terms of how solidly they are based on personal experience; work orientations, for instance, will typically have a more solid experiential basis than views on alternative ways of organizing society. Further, different elements in consciousness have different functional roles. There is certain element of instability in consciousness: activity in organizations, willingness to take action and a critical attitude towards capitalism do not necessarily coincide. Compared to the structuration of class situation, the structuration and determination of consciousness is more mediated by nature.

The consciousness and organization of individual class groups is more coherent in some matters than in others. In addition, the internal differentiation of class groups may depend to different extents on the combined effect of factors structuring civil society (gender, generation, political identification) and class location. Similarly, the role of class location may be visible in clear class differences in their orientation to economic interests.

Our basic methodological tenet was that the mediation from the analysis of class situation to the analysis of consciousness and organization at once implies a break. On the basis of our results we can present a preliminary interpretation of the nature of this mediation and break. There are three basic types of mediation, which also have a major impact on the size and nature of differences in the consciousness and organization of class groups.

1. *Elements of consciousness and organization which depend more or less directly on class location or are mediated on the basis of the mutual relationship between the structuration of class location and class situation.* Central to this mediation are such factors as activity in organizations, (lack of) coherence of concepts of society, class identification, work orientations and confidence in one's opportunities for social influence.

Education and cognitive capacities are of crucial importance on many of these dimensions. In particular, education is bound up with the coherence of social conceptions and faith in one's chances to influence matters. Cognitive capacities are also related to activity in organizations, probably through the link between education and positions in organizations.

2. *Phenomena related to class location but largely mediated and channelled by the prevailing political organization.* The most important of these factors are political identification and organization, reformistic consciousness, and (in a more mediated sense) willingness to take action and a critical attitude towards society. According to our results, these phenomena do not necessarily have to do with traditions mediated by social relations, since they do not seem to be of any great significance to consciousness. Instead, we would seem to be talking of continuous learning process which is regulated by political organization. The political organization of society can institute general alternatives for consciousness and work as a central mediating mechanism of consciousness. The results also suggest that at least trade union organization is an important mediator of common interests and reformistic consciousness.

There is a tendency for willingness to take action and criticism to increase when we move from the bourgeoisie down through the managerial level to the working class, and also with leftist political identification and activity. These features are common to the consciousness of supporters of the communist party and social democrats. The mediating role of organizations is also visible in a certain 'trade union threshold' for willingness to take action, in that people seem to be willing to take action if they have the backing of the trade union. It is also interesting to observe that this threshold is somewhat clearer among the working class than among managerial groups.

3. *There are certain aspects of consciousness which are common to different social classes in relation to the nature of society, the form of social relations and frames of experience.* A study which is concerned with class differences is bound

to underestimate these common features. This conclusion is inevitable if we look at structures that are common to all members of society, such as the physical and cultural environment, the rhythm of everyday life, etc. Marquardt distinguished in his theory of consciousness those frames of experience that are specific to social classes from those that are shared by all classes. The latter are characteristic of out-of-work time, above all the members of society as consumers, users of mass culture and receivers of mass communication. It is important to repeat that we are here talking about common frames of experience; patterns of consumption, the use of out-of-work time and lifestyles are still very much differentiated. However, it seems that the common basis of these frames of experience have a more profound significance than Marquardt assumed. Certain basic cultural codes are always bound up with everyday life in a relatively stable, unchanging way. Suburbs, fake collectives produced by TV, rhythms of consumption, etc. produce uniformity. In research this is perhaps most clearly visible in the general appreciation of work and family relations.

Among the most central features that are common to the consciousness of different class groups, mention can be made of illusions of performance and common interests, the place of work as the most important thing in life, familism, trade union membership and, on the other hand, passive organization relations (in the trade union, parties, co-operatives, as well as other associations), political apathy and a sense of powerlessness in social issues. These features reflect the general structuration of society in different ways. Illusions of performance and common interests are to do with the inversion of social relations and the concealed nature of capitalist society. The appreciation of work and familism is related to the same premise in a more mediated way, but also to the prevailing cultural and institutional fabric.

Political apathy and the sense of powerlessness may be indications both of the closed nature of the political system and the lack of social alternatives, as well as of the lack of preconditions for individual activity (all of these are most typical of working-class locations). In its most simple form, the lack of alternatives is reflected in the nature (or complete absence) of ideas concerning the development of society. Many members of society have no utopias at all; this is the case with the majority of industrial workers, for example. As for those who have an alternative conception of society, only a handful have some utopia involving social criticism.

Party identification, if understood as an aspect of consciousness, combines

214

class location and class interests with the alternatives offered by the political system. Parties still recruit their members and supporters from different classes.

Popular support for the political left does not correspond to the Wrightian hierarchy. The clearest exceptions are formed by the bourgeois attitudes of the workers in money circulation and the leftist attitudes of supervisors. The *political division* within class groups varies considerably. Only farmers and the bourgeoisie can be described as class groups which are organized within one and the same party. Among all other class groups, the support for the most popular party is under one third. The relationship between the support for leftist and non-socialist parties is balanced among other groups than farmers, the bourgeoisie and industrial workers. The political division does not directly correspond to the class division. However, it is impossible within the confines of the present study to dwell upon this question in further detail. It is also difficult to say whether the similarities in class location and political views is 'too high' or 'too low', whether different parties represent different class interests, what are their chances of realizing these interests in their practical policy. Or do the interests of wage-earner groups, small entrepreneurs and small farmers, for instance, really differ from each other so significantly?

Women and young workers show a common aversion towards traditional channels of organization. Our results also indicate that in all groups there is a specific female consciousness. Both of these examples draw attention to such contradictions between organization, willingness to take action and consciousness which presumably result from the subordinated position of women and young people, and from the political and cultural asynchronism of these groups; they are very clearly marked off from skilled workers. Until the late 1960s, an active and masculine occupational and political culture was based on professional skill and pride, but now this basis is being eroded. The activity and critical attitudes of women and young people are largely based on a different development which combines a threatened position with uncertain future prospects and alienation from the traditional channels of organization.

In the light of these results, it is quite clear that a class theory cannot as such serve as a theory of consciousness and organization. Class theory is very useful for purposes of analysing consciousness and organization, but it is not sufficient for that purpose. There are also differences in the relevance of different class theories in this respect. The rather crude assumption in Wright's theory that working-class consciousness increases when we move from managerial locations

215

down to the working class, holds true for critical consciousness in social issues and for increased willingness to take action. However, it does not hold good for membership of organization.

Projekt Klassenanalyse's assumptions with regard to consciousness seem to be valid in the case of the internal differences within the working class; in particular, they give an adequate description of the differences between machine workers and aggregated personnel. On the other hand, the theory does not seem to be valid when it comes to the differences between the working class and the middle class.

Our results do not lend support to the theory of Poulantzas. The old and the new petty bourgeoisie have different consciousness profiles.

Looking at the differences in the consciousness and action profiles of class groups from the point of view of class boundaries, both Poulantzas's and Projekt Klassenanalyse's definitions of the working class seem to be too narrow. Wright draws this boundary between managerial locations and the working class (including semi-autonomous employees). However, this boundary makes some sharp turns, particularly in the class groups of supervisors and semi-autonomous employees. In addition, industrial workers differ in their consciousness and experience profile in many respects from other working-class groups. The main reason why semi-autonomous employees are closely related to the working class lies in the fact that they resemble workers in services. Workers of money capital are distinguished from other working-class groups.

As we have already pointed out earlier, there are a number of aspects of consciousness which are common to all class groups. This greatly complicates the definition of firm boundaries between class groups.

Moving forward in accordance with our strategy of consecutive cycles of class analysis, leaving behind the basic concepts of class theory, *social category* can be understood as a large group of people distinguished from other groups by other criteria than those at the level of production relations, but which involves a specific structuration of working conditions and consciousness. In this approach, labour market segmentation and state employment, for example, would seem to produce several social categories within the group of wage workers which cut across class-based distinctions. It is clear that these specific social categories have to be taken into consideration in a discussion of the constitution of class subjects.

Our results can be divided into two parts. First, the results do not lend support to the assumption that the core of the working class (defined as workers in the large enterprises of the monopolistic segment, the paper industry, wood-process-ing industry and metal industry) is the most conscious or, conversely, the most integrated faction of the working class. State employees form a clearly distinct group, and their internal differences are of importance. The most visible differen-ces are to do with critical consciousness and willingness to take action. State employees in the administrative (repressive) apparatus are the least critical, while those employed in the reproduction sector are more critical and willing to take action than others.

There are also differences in consciousness across labour market segments. A stable position in the labour market correlates with high organization membership, while mobility correlates with activity and critical attitudes.

The consciousness and action profile of white-collar employees differs from that of blue-collar workers. There are also clear differences between upper and lower white-collar employees. Those white-collar employees who on the basis of class criteria fall under the working class are more 'proletarian' than others. They are characterized by a more instrumental work orientation, a more critical con-sciousness, and a more reformistic state conception. On the basis of the results, we may assume that the proletarianization of white-collar employees is under-mining their specific white-collar consciousness.

In conclusion, it may be noted that at least state employment, the division of tasks between state employees, and labour market position play a certain role in the structuration of wage-worker consciousness. The white-collar position is also of some significance; the clearest indication of this that upper white-collar employees are distinguished from other wage workers. Finally, it is important to bear in mind the limitations of our study: if we included in the analysis the cultural preconditions for consciousness, for instance, they would also have relevance for the differentiation of wage-worker consciousness.

6.5. Class theory and class differences

What can now be said about class differences in Finland on the basis of our examination at different levels of class analysis: class location, the structuration of class situation and consciousness and organization? In a rather crude generalization, we might note that the bourgeoisie is distinguished from the rest of the entrepreneurial population. Small employers represent a transitional group where there are in evidence various contradictory elements. The petty bourgeoisie is differentiated into two sections, viz. agrarian and non-agrarian. The class situation of small entrepreneurs is characterized by various proletarian features, which are not yet visible in their consciousness and organization. The contradictions in the class situation of the petty bourgeoisie include reproduction difficulties, self-exploitation and the loss of independence.

Contradictory wage-worker locations are very heterogeneous not only in terms of the structuration of class situation and consciousness but also in organization. The class location and organization of some managers resemble those of the bourgeoisie. The differentiation of a core group of managers from other managerial locations lends some support to the theories of the growth of a 'service class'. Non-hierarchic decision-makers appear to be a very unstable group.

Semi-autonomous employees and supervisors are located between managers and the working class. The contradictions in the class situation of the semi-autonomous employees (a high level of education and qualifications but no functions of domination and poor prospects of promotion) are reflected in a relatively critical consciousness and willingness to take action, as well as in leftist political consciousness and organization. However, the consciousness of semi-autonomous employees also differs from the consciousness of the working class, above all when it comes to experiences of work.

Supervisors come closer to the working class than semi-autonomous employees in terms of the structuration of class situation. They show a distinctly proletarian consciousness, but that consciousness remains passive and formal. Willingness to take action and critical consciousness are lower among supervisors than among semi-autonomous employees. It might perhaps be legitimate to argue that the consciousness of semi-autonomous employees is approaching that of the working class. Supervisors (at least for the time being) form a group that is formally committed to the working class but is also uncritical and rather passive. The crisis of the social state and the degradation of mental labour may lead to increased contradictions in the class situation of semi-autonomous employees and give new impetus to their activity and critical consciousness. Automation, which will reduce the tasks of supervisors, may prove to generate revived activity and socio-critical consciousness among supervisors.

The class situation of the working class is relatively coherent. The negative aspects are still most pronounced among industrial workers, and particularly among shopfloor workers in immediate production. Positive aspects (which are mainly related to the opportunities for personal and professional growth) are most conspicuous among workers in money circulation and in services. The consciousness of the working class is not as coherent as its class situation. Workers in money circulation differ very clearly from the others both in terms of their organization and their political identification. However, their low degree of traditional organization and leftist political identification is combined with elements of critical consciousness. In terms of its consciousness, this group almost represents the opposite of the group of supervisors. As far as the structuration of class situation is concerned, workers of commodity circulation come closer to industrial workers than workers in services, but in consciousness terms the situation is the exact opposite.

It is important not to not exaggerate these differences in consciousness. Many aspects of consciousness that are closely related immediate experiences are in fact rather similar across different working-class groups. The differences are most pronounced in those aspects of consciousness and organization which are most strongly affected by the prevailing political organization and bourgeois publicity. In many groups (and particularly among workers in money circulation and in trade) the situation is characterized by an interesting contradiction. In one scale of the balance there is the proletarianization of working conditions and reproduction situation, in the other there is the alienation from working-class organizations and political culture based on skilled labour. The latter aspect is also related to the bourgeois atmosphere of the workplace and to the fact that the subordinated position of women is taken for granted.

We have already pointed out that class differences will be de-emphasized when we take into consideration the family level and the economically non-active population. We have also stated that the factors structuring civil society (differences based on sex, gender or political organization and regional differences) are linked to class structure. We can no longer dwell upon these aspects here, but will have to content ourselves with the conclusion that the inclusion of these factors in our analysis narrows down the relevance of class theory.

6.6. Classes, social change and hegemony

We shall now move on to the fourth and final level of class analysis, i.e., to a study of the relationship between class subjects and the state. We have repeatedly stressed in this study that the analysis of class structure, class situation and consciousness differs in essential respects from the analysis of the discursive constitution of class subjects.

During the 1980s social scientists have offered a wide range of scenarios of social development: from the post-modern society, that development is taking us either to a 'risk society' and the 'second modern', to post-Fordism, to flexible specialization and a flexible work organization, to information society, or to the collapse of organized capitalism. Below, we shall present our vision of the changing structural preconditions for social activity and organization in Finland.

Structural change is always an ongoing process. However, there are some recent studies on Finland which provide a useful starting-point for evaluating the current situation and for predicting the course of future development. Nevertheless the picture we provide will inevitably remain somewhat sketchy.

Although the process of structural change since World War II has been proceeding more rapidly in Finland than in any other OECD country, we are still lagging behind the most advanced capitalist countries. This is evident in a number of different features. The growth of entrepreneurship has still been relatively modest. During the 1980s there have been no significant changes in the size of the working class. The petty bourgeoisie, on the other hand, has been growing smaller at an accelerating rate, but it still remains a larger class group than in other advanced capitalist countries, particularly in the agricultural sector. Intermediate management in business companies has not grown smaller as in most other countries. Also, contrary to most expectations, job autonomy has tended to increase in Finland.

In short, it seems that there have been no dramatic qualitative changes. This, however, is not the whole truth. There are also signs of new trends in development which are significantly affecting the entire social structure and the constellation of social forces.

The 1980s saw a rapid internationalization of the Finnish economy with the growth of many multinational corporations in the country. Developments in this field have followed the revised Gershunyian model. The information society has been gradually unfolding, although in quantitative terms it still remains fairly insignificant in Finland. The growth of capital and consultation services has most clearly followed the pattern suggested by this model. However, these developments have been less important overall than the growth of numerical flexibility in the private service sector, the breakthrough of computer technology in office work and in the most advanced sectors of the economy, such as the electronics industry. According to Raimo Lovio, who has done intensive research in this field, the tendency is for companies to split up into individual profit units, while maintaining the group structures as juridically independent units. At the same time, a growing proportion of necessary support services are subcontracted. Consequently we have seen a considerable increase in the number of small subcontractors. If this development is going to continue, then we are also bound to see profound changes not only in company and work organizations, but also in the class and stratification structures: administrative and technical groups at the intermediate level will continue to grow, the top levels of corporate hierarchies will become increasingly horizontalized, top management will grow in quantitative terms, intermediate management will be reduced.

Welfare state services have been spared from any dramatic cuts during the 1980s; in fact the numbers of those employed in this sector has tended to increase throughout the decade. There have also been significant changes in work organization within the public sector, including the introduction of the management-by-results strategy. In terms of income distribution, the role of the social state has also remained more or less unchanged.

It is extremely difficult to anticipate the future course of development in the field of social policy. All in all social integration increased in Finland during the 1980s. This is reflected in the lack of social criticism and in the growth of indifference in general. On the other hand, the struggle for a fair(er) income distribution within the labour market organizations was stepping up again.

The conclusion one is tempted to draw from these observations is that, overall, the ongoing structural change is proceeding and will continue to proceed rather gently, although at the same time there are emerging new and perhaps increasingly stronger elements of transformation.

Currently, however, the definite focus of attention is in Europe and the internal European markets. It is quite possible that these will eventually determine the working conditions and material standard of living of the Finnish wage earner — and possibly even the future development of civil society.

Notes

Notes to Chapter 1

1. The most significant representatives of stratification theory in the 1940s were Talcott Parsons (1940) and Kinsley Davis (1945). For an example of a stratification study based on subjective criteria, see Coleman et al. (1979). For evaluations of stratification theory, see Therborn (1983).

2. The first study in this tradition was by Mauke (1980). The most significant representative of this tradition in the 1980s has been Projekt Klassenanalyse (1973; 1975; Bischoff 1976; Bischoff et al. 1982). PKA's most important consciousness study was produced by Bierbaum et al. (1977a).

3. PKA was not of course the only school to adopt this strategy: in the early 1970s a number of similar 'capital-logical' investigations were made into consciousness; see *Class consciousness and the mode of reproduction of bourgeois political dominance*, in Blom 1983.

4. Another central concern has been the immiserization of the working class; see Wagner (1976) and Rasmussen (1978).

5. The main work of IMSF is *Klassen und Sozialstruktur der BRD I-II* (1973/74). IMSF's theoretical position and criticisms can be found in IMSF (1971) and (1974). These reports also contain analyses of wage worker consciousness and organization. The major work by IMSF on consciousness is Heiseler et al. (1978a). See also Heiseler et al. (1978b), Priester (1978), Werner (1979) and Werner (1982). The class analysis presented by IMSF is criticized by PKA in various contexts; see esp. PKA (1975). The work of both IMSF and PKA are evaluated and discussed e.g. by Armanski (1974), Armanski et al. (1975), Hagelstange (1975), and Kievenheim (1976).

6. Other important studies are Carchedi (1977) and Crompton and Gubbay (1978). Wright's position on the difference between these theories and his own conception can be found in Wright (1980). One of the most recent reviews of this discussion is presented by Abercrombie and Urry (1982)

7. Braverman's work on *Labor and monopoly capital* (1974) has represented an important watershed and object of discussion. Other significant contributions include Mendner (1975),

Edwards (1979) and Littler (1982). For more on the question of Fordism and neo-Fordism, see Aglietta (1979).

8. Mallet (1975; original French edition 1963). Touraine (1974; in French 1965) argues that the executive and service personnel of large organizations form a core group of resistance against capitalism (ibid., 66). For the debate on the 'new working class', see Deppe et al. (1971) and Lange (1972).

9. The problem was originally formulated by Gramsci, and it has been discussed e.g. by Poulantzas; see Jessop (1982), 142-219. For more recent thematizations, see Hirsch (1980) and Urry (1981a).

10. A well-known representative of this position is Edward Thompson, who presents his views e.g. in *Making of the English working class* (1968) and in his polemic against Althusser and structuralistic Marxism (1978). An analysis of this discussion and a critique of Thompson can be found in Anderson (1980).

11. See e.g. Lefebvre (1975), Negt and Kluge (1976), Krovoza (1976), Volmerg (1976) and Schmidt (1978).

12. See Projekt Ideologie-Theorie (1979) and (1980). PIT attacks PKA and criticizes its economistic theory of consciousness, in which consciousness is merely a reflex of economic movement (1980, 492-493). PIT says its own position represents Gramscian anti-reductionism (ibid., 494).

13. See Haug and Maase (1979) and Johnson (1980).

14. The research carried out by the Birmingham school is described e.g. by Clarke et al. (1980). For a recent discussion on the work by Projekt Ideologie-Theorien, see Hänninen and Paldán (1983).

15. The most interesting studies are those by Aglietta (1979) and Hirsch (1980), who attempt to associate the tendencies towards capitalist reorganization with changes in the forms of the subordination and control of wage labour and in the forms of labour power reproduction, and to link these further with changes in the political and ideological mode of reproduction.

16. On the object of class analysis, see e.g. Neumann (1976) and Mortensen and Christiansen (1975). Several works that are concerned with the problematics of the object proper of class research attempt to find a connection between objective and subjective factors; see e.g. Autorenkollektiv (1976). From a slightly different perspective, the same issue has been dealt with within the context of the problem of the object (scope logic) of Marx's political economy and the limitations of its explanatory power as a scientific construct (see Funder et al. 1975). The essential problem — as many writers correctly point out — lies in the mediation between different objects and levels of analysis. This draws our attention to the validity of different methods at different levels of analysis.

17. A useful history is presented by Hill (1981); see also Wright (1978), 64-74.

18. This problem has usually been discussed in connection with 'the dual constitution of consciousness' (objective preconditions and subjective structures of relevance), or in the context of the biographical method. See Hack (1977) and Hack et al. (1979).

Notes to Chapter 2

1. A detailed analysis of these developments towards capitalization and increasing wage employment is presented in Kosonen 1981, 139-186. According to Kosonen, a total of 34,300 working years were lost in forestry and agriculture between 1950 and 75. At the same time, there was an increase of 315,000 working years in industrial production, most of which was due to the growth of the metal industry. On the whole the changes in the division of labour in post-war Finland have been bound up with process of industrialization. Employment in commodity and money circulation also increased during the period mentioned by 230,000 working years. This was reflected above all in the improved employment situation in trade and commerce in the 1950s and 60s. In the service sector, the general tendency has been for personal services to give way to customer services, such as holiday and accommodation services. Another important factor in the growth of the service sector has been the increase in services provided by the state (health care, social welfare), above all in 1965-1975. In 1955-75 there was an overall increase of 280,000 working years in the service sector.
2. On the operationalization of class criteria, see Wright et al. 1982.
3. For descriptions of the material of these international projects and the class structures of the countries concerned, see Wright et al. 1982 and Ahrne 1982.

Notes to Chapter 3

1. Kadritzke (1982, 221) says that this idea is closely intertwined with the development of sociology as self-deception (and the deception of others).
2. See e.g. Goldthorpe (1982); Crompton and Gubbay (1978); Renner (1982); Fritsch (1976).
3. See e.g. King and Raynor (1981) and Bechofer et al. (1978); cf. also Abercrombie and Urry (1982).
4. On levels of abstraction and dialectical determination, see Carchedi (1977).
5. See Blackburn and Mann (1979), who also make the important observation that segmentation is functional not only from the point of view of capitalists but also for certain sections of the working class.
6. The problems are obvious e.g. when we analyse Wright's class group using PKA's criteria. In this case 51 % of the semi-autonomous employees are wage workers of capital and 48 % belong to the middle class. In the former category, 28 % are machine workers, 4 % are aggregated personnel, and 14 % are unproductive workers. In the middle class, the proportion of state employees is 45 %, and 3 % are workers of organizations. See Kivinen (1983).
7. Wright fails to recognize the methodological problems related to the conceptualization of strategies, cf. Friedman (1977, 265-267). Friedman distinguishes between two main types of capitalist strategy: direct supervision and responsible autonomy. Their usage varies from time to time and they are applied in different ways to different worker groups. According to Friedman, responsible autonomy is mainly applied to worker groups which have considerable potential for resistance.
8. Markku Kivinen has argued that a theory of the middle classes cannot be based on the assumption that mental (autonomous) labour is a residual criterion which is relevant only in

the case of wage earners excluded from managerial positions. On the contrary, the focus of concrete research should be on how managerial position and different forms of mental labour are combined as class criteria (Kivinen 1987a and Kivinen 1987b).

Notes to Chapter 4

1. Braverman published his work in 1974 and Mender one year later in 1975. Of the two, Braverman's work is far better known and far more influential even outside the English-speaking world. On the whole it may be noted that German research on the labour process has concentrated on elaborating the concept of qualification, while the Anglo-American tradition has been more concerned with the concept of control. See Lappe 1986.

2. Theories that define the middle class on the basis of productive and unproductive labour (e.g. PKA, Nichols) or which emphasize the ideological and political differences between the working class and the new petty bourgeoisie (e.g. Poulantzas) do not include the proletarianization hypothesis in any form. On the other hand, it is usually present in theories concerned to describe the heterogeneity of the middle strata. Wright makes a distinction between such processes as the separation of ownership and possession, the development of complex hierarchies, and the proletarianization of the content of work (1978, 64-74). He does not, however, offer any explanation for the changing position of white-collar workers.

3. The index of skill development was constructed on the basis of three questions. The respondents were asked: To what extent are you able to use your skills and capacities at work. The answers were coded as follows: to a very great extent (5 points); to a great extent (4 pts); to a certain extent (3 pts); not very much (2 pts); not at all (1 pts). The same scale was used in coding the answers to the two other questions: To what extent do you need to learn new things at work; To what extent do need to develop your skills at work?

4. The coding of the autonomy variable is explained in Järvelä-Hartikainen, Kivinen and Melin (1982). The types of autonomy were coded before the class structure variable was formed.

5. In his dissertation Markku Kivinen shows that the shortcomings of Wright's theory of autonomy have far-reaching consequences for the whole systematics of class theory. He proposes a conceptualization of types of autonomy as forms of mental labour, linking these with specific power resources at the level of 'politics of production'. Kivinen specifies four major consequences of the critique of Wright's theory of autonomy: (1) As Wrights considers autonomy a relevant class criterion only in the case of those wage earners who have no decision-making authority, the thematization of different types of autonomy gives reason to suspect that autonomy is not a residual criterion after all. This means that, in order to determine their significance as class criteria, different combinations of forms of mental labour and dominance must be analysed in a concrete setting. (2) The theory of types of autonomy also gives new significance to the problematics of mental and manual labour. It is necessary to make a distinction between several different kinds of mental labour, only part of which can be considered to be related to the traditional intelligentsia problematics or to 'mental production' at the level of the social division of labour. (3) Reference to different types of autonomy implies that there must be other processes of class relations than the three mentioned by Wright. (4) When the processes of class relations are problemized in the theory of types of autonomy, this means that the purely structural determination of classes is also

questioned. The class struggle, power resources and strategies are taken into account already in defining the forms of mental labour at the level of the labour process itself. (Kivinen 1987, 53-54)

6. Craftsmen represent a group whose power resources are based on the conception and knowledge that are assimilated in the labour process (Burawoy 1979, 276-278). The strategy is to monopolize these resources both in relation to the management and unskilled workers. A central vehicle in this strategy is the trade union (see e.g. Penn 1982, 90).

7. However, Wright has no theoretically justified concept of the strategy of professionalization. See Larson 1977, esp. pp. 47-48.

8. Crompton and Jones (1984, 234), for example, emphasize that this type of autonomy differs in principle from professional autonomy.

9. On the restrictions of caring and reproduction autonomy in the application of the strategy of professionalization, see Larson: ibid., 196.

10. See Littler (1982); Mickler et al. (1976); Nichols and Armstrong (1976); on the methodological premises see e.g. Altman et al. (1979); Baron and Bielby (1980); Wilkinson (1983); Burawoy (1985); Salomon (1986).

Notes to Chapter 5

1. For historical reviews on the study of worker consciousness, see Deppe and Lange 1970, Deppe 1971, Voss 1980, and Blom 1980. Studies dealing with new social movements are being published at an accelerating rate. A useful background analysis is presented by Roth 1980; see also Hirsch and Roth 1986.

2. For more on this approach and its critique, see Tjaden-Steinhauer 1975. For an example of more recent studies, see Bulmer 1975.

3. According to Lockwood (1966) the traditional worker types were 'proletarian trad-itionalist' (whose identity is based on solidarity of work and living community, who divides the world in to 'us' and 'them') and 'yielding' traditionalist (who conforms to the paternalist relations of the workplace, has good relations to his foremen, and who examines social relations as an integral status system).

4. The average coercions of the wage-worker character mask are: the selling of labour power, subordination to capitalism in the labour process, dependence on wages, and maintaining the condition of one's labour power and qualifications. The main problem is the level of abstraction at which the concept of character mask is used: there are certain historical and social differences between wage workers which are not revealed at a general level of abstraction. As far as the differences are real and significant, they cannot be understood without mediating conceptualizations.

5. Goldthorpe et al. 1968. The work orientations of industrial workers in Finland are analysed Antti Kasvio, 1983. Kasvio, however, arrives at the conclusion that orientation towards wages among Finnish industrial workers is not closely related to an orientation to consumption, as was the argument in Affluent Worker, but rather an objective necessity for wage workers. In fact, the Finnish respondents considered security and permanence of employment more important than wages.

6. The familism index was constructed as follows:

H14: Different things are of different importance to different people. How important are these things to you personally:

A) Family

    1) very important

    2) important

    3) neither important nor unimportant

    4) not very important

    5) quite unimportant

B) Next-door neighbours

C) Human relations in leisure

D) Human relations in associations or organizations

E) Cultural events (e.g. theatre, cinema and concerts)

F) Reading literature

G5: Most people have something that gives their life a special meaning. What is this something in your case?

H14	Points
1-2 only family	1
1-3 only family	2
1-4 only family	3

G5:	Points
Family first, then home etc.	3
Only family and home	3
Family and home first, then something else	2
Family and home second in order of importance	1

7. The question of recovery reads: Many people think that out-of-work time is used mainly for recovery from work, necessary household duties and preparation for the next day. To what extent is this true in your case?

8. The index of criticism is an effort to analyse different types of criticism appearing on the level of everyday experience. The variable is constructed on the basis of the following questions:

B12: To what extent do you consider income differentials in our society justified?

1) fully justified	-2
2) quite justified	-1
3) rather unjust	+1
4) fully unjust	+2
5) Don't know	0

B16: It is said that you can always find employment if you really want to. Is this true in present-day Finland?

1) true	-2
2) quite true	-1
3) not quite true	+1
4) not at all true	+2
5) don't know	0

K8: Political decisions are said to be basically compromises. To what extent do you think that political decisions during the past few years have served your interests?

1) fully	-2
2) quite well	-1
3) to some extent	0
4) not very well	+1
5) not at all	+2
6) don't know	0

L6: It is said that the continuous growth of the national economy in the interest of us all. What do you think of this?

1) fully agree	-2
2) agree to a certain extent	-1
3) disagree to a certain extent	+1
4) disagree	+2
5) don't know	0

L8: It is often said we should all sacrifice our own individual interests to safeguard our national competitiveness. What do you think?

1) agree	-2
2) agree to some extent	-1
3) disagree to some extent	+1
4) disagree	+2
5) don't know	0

9. The index of attitudes towards state intervention reformism was constructed as follows:

L12: In your opinion, should the state take a more active role in regulating private investment?

L13: Should the state be better informed about the living conditions of individual peole?

L14: Should the state take a more active policy in helping young people find employment?

L15: Should the state take a more active policy with regard to children's day care?

L12-L15 Points
1) yes+1
2) no-1

10. Bott 1954; Popitz et al. 1957 and Goldthorpe et al. 1969. For recent studies, see Jackman and Jackman 1983.

11. For a definition of the concept of reformism and theories of reformism, see Olofsson 1979, 24-26; Buci-Glucksmann and Therborn 1982; Mortesen et al. 1979. So-called historical interpretations of reformism have emphasized the rationality of social democracy either for the bourgeoisie or the working class or social democracy as (the best available) conscious choice to guarantee the standard of living in a situation with few options, see Andersen 1981, 36-48.

12. A good example of this is Marquardt 1974. For a critique see Blom 1983a, 43-45.

13. Flatow and Huisken 1973. For a more general discussion on the concept of general interest see Blom 1983b.

14. The situation arises from the fact that 'don't know' answers cannot be combined with other answers. Another problem was that part of the respondent's considered 'common' as

228

synonymous with 'divided into equal portions'. Therefore, the empirical boundary is somewhat obscure.

15. Here we try to problemize the question as to what extent trade union activists represent the ordinary people below and to what extent the managing group of the trade union above. A survey easily produces a mechanistic answer: so and so many per cent say that it represents those who are above and so and so many that they represent the people at the grassroots level. In reality people are not so sure and a certain percentage of the respondents seems to answer in one way or the other.

Notes to Chapter 6

1. See Giddens 1973.
2. Ahrne 1982 deals with Sweden, Colbjörnsen et al. 1987 with Norway, Erbslöh et al. 1987 with Germany and Marshall et al. 1988 with the United Kingdom.
3. See Kivinen 1989a.
4. Bourdieu 1986.
5. Poulantzas 1975.
6. Since the publication of Urry's and Cohen's books, there has been very lively debate in Finland on civil society; even political parties have been adopting concepts from the academic debate.
7. See Hänninen 1982.
8. Both Hirsch and Roth (1987) and Lash and Urry (1987) predict that the class structure will become more fragmented and the relative size of the working class will decline.
9. See Beck 1986.
10. See also the more detailed discussion in Luokkaprojekti 1984.

Bibliography

Abercrombie, N. & Urry, J. (1983) Capital, Labour and the Middle Class. London.

Aglietta, M. (1979) A Theory of Capitalist Regulation. London.

Ahrne, G. (1982) Report on the Swedish Class Structure 1. Comparative Project on Class Structure and Class Consciousness. University of Wisconsin. Department of Sociology. Working Paper Series 4. Madison.

Ahrne, G. & Leiulfsrud, H. (1984) Den svenska klassstrukturen och de offentligt anställda. Sociologiska institutionen. Oslo.

Ahrne, G. & Wright, E.O. (1983) Class and Social Organisation in the United States and Sweden: A Comparison. Acta Sociologica 3-4/1983.

Alestalo, M. (1980) Yhteiskunta, luokat ja sosiaalinen kerrostuneisuus toisen maailmansodan jälkeen. In: Suomalaiset (Valkonen, T. et al.) Porvoo.

Althusser, L. (1968) Om det teoretiska arbetet. Häften för kritiska studier 4/1968.

Altman, R. & Bechtle, G. & Lutz, B. (1978) Betrieb — Technik — Arbeit: Elemente einer soziologischen Analytik technisch-organisatorischer Veränderungen. Frankfurt.

Andersen, H. (1981) Reformismen og dens organisatoriske former. Københavns universitet. Sociologisk institut. Arbejdspapir 3.

Anderson, P. (1980) Arguments within English Marxism. London.

Armanski, G. (1974) Staatliche Lohnarbeiter im Kapitalismus. Probleme des Klassenkampfs 16/1974.

Armanski, G. et al. (1975) Notizen für Klassenanalyse der BRD durch das PKA. Probleme des Klassenkampfs 17-18/1975.

Autorenkollektiv (1975) Georg Lukács: Verdinglichung und Klassenbewusstsein. West-Berlin.

Bader, V. et al. (1976) Einführung in die Gesellschaftstheorie: Gesellschaft, Wirtschaft und Staat bei Marx und Weber. Frankfurt.

Bader, V. et al. (1975) Krise und Kapital bei Marx I-II. Enschwege.

Baron, J. & Bielby, W. (1980) Bringing the Firms back in: Stratification, Segmentation and the Organisation of Work. American Sociological Review 45/1980.

Bechofer, F. et al.(1978) Structure, Consciousness and Action. British Journal of Sociology

4/1978.

Beck, U. (1986) Risikogesellschaft. Auf dem Weg in eine andere Moderne. Frankfurt.

Becker, U. (1986) Kapitalistische Dynamik und politisches Kräftespiel. Zur Kritik des klassen-theoretischen Ansatzes. Frankfurt.

Bendix, R. & Lipset, S. (1953) (eds.) Class, Status and Power. Social Stratification in Comparative Perspective. London.

Bierbaum, C. et al. (1977b) Bewusstseinsformen des Alltagslebens. Beiträge zum wissen-schaftliche Sozialismus 3/1977.

Bierbaum, C. et al.(1977a) Ende der Illusionen? Bewusstseinsänderungen in der Wirtschaftskrise. Frankfurt.

Bischoff, J. (1976) (hrsg.) Die Klassenstruktur der Bundesrepublik Deutschland. Westberlin.

Bischoff, J. et al. (1982) Jenseits der Klassen. Hamburg.

Blackburn, R. & Mann, M. (1979) The Working Class in the Labour Market. London.

Blom, R. (1980) Associational Commitment and the Political Organization of Society. Sosiologia 1/1980.

Blom, R. (1983a) Classes and the State. University of Tampere. Department of Sociology and Social Psychology. Research Reports 2.

Blom, R. (1983b) On the Scope Logic of the Theory of Class. In: Classes and the State (Blom, R.) University of Tampere. Department of Sociology and Social Psychology. Research Reports 2.

Blom, R. & Kivinen, M. (1989) Analytical Marxism and Class Theory. In: Organization Theory and Class Analysis. New Approaches and New Issues (ed. Clegg, S.). Berlin.

Bott, E. (1954) The Concept of Class as a Reference Group. Human Relations 3/1954.

Bourdieu, P. (1986) Distinction. A Social Critique of the Judgement of Taste. London.

Braverman, H. (1974) Labor and Monopoly Capital. New York.

Buci-Glucksmann, C. & Therborn, G. (1982) Der Sozialdemokratische Staat. Die 'Keynes-ianisierung' der Gesellschaft. Hamburg.

Bulmer, M. (1975) (ed.) Working Class Images of Society. London.

Burawoy, M. (1983) Between the Labor Process and the State: The Changing Face of Factory Regimes under Advanced Capitalism. American Sociological Review 5/1983.

Burawoy, M. (1979) Manufacturing Consent. Chicago.

Burawoy, M. (1985) The Politics of Production: Factory Regimes under Capitalism and Socialism. London.

Burawoy, M. (1978) Toward a Marxist Theory of the Labor Process: Braverman and Beyond. Politics and Society 3-4/1978.

Burris, V. (1986) The Discovery of the New Middle Class. Theory and Society 15/1986.

Carchedi, G. (1987) Class Analysis and Social Research. Oxford.

Carchedi, G. (1977) The Economic Identification of Social Classes. London.

Carchedi, G. (1986) Two Models of Class Analysis. Capital & Class 29/1986.

Carchedi, G. (1983) Problems in Class Analysis. London.

Centers, R. (1946) The Psychology of Social Classes. A Study of Class Consciousness. Princeton.

Chandler, A. (1977) The Visible Hand. Massaschusets.

Chandler, A. & Daems, C. (1980) Managerial Hierarchies. Cambridge.

Clarke, J. et al. (1980) (eds.) Workingclass Culture. Studies in History and Theory. London.

Clarke, S. (1982) Marx, Marginalism and Modern Sociology: From Adam Smith to Max Weber. London.

Clegg, S. (1990) Organization Theory and Class Analysis. Berlin.

Clegg, S. et al. (1985) From Class Bearers to Civil Subjects: Ideology, Interests and Identity. Paper presented at the International Meeting of the Comparative Project on Class Structure and Class Consciousness. University of Tampere. Department of Sociology and Social Psychology. Working Papers 13.

Cohen, J. (1982) Class and Civil Society: The Limits of Marxian Critical Theory. Oxford.

Colbjörnsen, T. et al. (1987) Klassesamfunnet på hell. Oslo.

Coleman, R. & Rainwater, L. (1979) Social Standing in America. New Directions of Class. London.

Cottrell, A. (1984) Social Classes in Marxist Theory. London.

Crompton, R. & Gubbay, J. (1978) Economy and Class Structure. New York.

Crompton, R. & Jones, G. (1984) White-Collar Proletariat. Deskilling and Gender in Clerical Work. London.

Dahrendorf, R. (1959) Class and Class Conflict in an Industrial Society. London.

Davis, K. (1945) A Conceptual Analysis of Stratification. American Sociological Review 2/1945.

Deppe, F. (1971) Das Bewusstsein der Arbeiter. Köln.

Deppe, F. et al. (1971) Die neue Arbeiterklasse. Frankfurt.

Deppe, F. & Lange, H. (1970) Zur Soziologie des Arbeiter und Klassenbewusstseins. Das Argument 9-10/1970.

Diligenskij, G. (1984) Massove obshestvenno-politiceskoe soznanie rabocego klassa kapitalisticeskih stran: problemy tipologii i dinamiki. Rabocij klass i sovremennyj mir 1-2/1984.

Doeringer, P. & Piore, M. (1971) International Labor Market and Manpower Analysis. Lexington.

Eckart, M. et al. (1979) Frauenarbeit in Familie und Fabrik. Frankfurt.

Edwards, R. (1975) Contested Terrain. The Transformation of the Workplace in the Twentieth Century. London.

Edwards, R. et al. (1975) Labor Market Segmentation. Toronto.

Elger, T. (1982) Braverman, Capital Accumulation and Deskilling. In: The Degradation of Work? Skill, Deskilling and the Labour Process (ed. Wood, S.). London.

Erbslöh, B. et al. (1987) Klassenstruktur und Klassenbewusstsein in der Bundesrepublik Deutschland. Universität Duisburg Gesamthochschule. Duisburg.

Flatow, S. & Huisken, F. (1973) Zum Problem der Ableitung des bürgerlichens Staates. Probleme des Klassenkampfs 7/1973.

Friedman, A. (1986) Developing the Managerial Strategies Approach to the Labour Process. Capital & Class 30/1986.

Friedman, A. (1977) Industry & Labour. Class Struggle at Work and Monopoly Capitalism. London.

Fritsch, W. (1981) Zwischen Reaktion und Gesellschaftlichen Fortschritt. Die Mittelsichten und die nordeuropäischen Zentrumpartien in der Klassenanseinandersezung. Greiswald.

Fuder, B. et al. (1975) Bevidsthedssociologi, elementer til en teori om bevidsthedsdamels i det borgerlige samfund. Århus.

Game, A. & Pringle, R. (1984) Gender at Work. London.

Giddens, A. (1973) The Class Structure of Advanced Societies. London.

Goldthorpe, J. (1982) On the Service Class, its Formation and Future. In: Social Class and the Division of Labour (ed. Giddens, A. & Mackenzie, G.). Cambridge.

Goldthorpe, J. et al. (1968) The Affluent Worker: Industrial Attitudes and Behaviour. Cambridge.

Goldthorpe, J. et al. (1969) The Affluent Worker in the Class Structure. Cambridge.

Gordon, D. et al. (1982) Segmented Work, Divided Workers. The Historical Transformation of Labor in the United States. Cambridge.

Gronow, J. (1978) Formaali rationaalisuus ja pääomasuhde. Max Weberin 'Wirtschaft und Gesellschaftin' ideaalityypit ja ymmärtävän sosiologian metodi. Helsingin yliopisto. Sosiologian laitos. Working Papers 9.

Hack, L. (1977) Subjektivität im Alltagsleben. Frankfurt.

Hack, L. et al. (1979) Leistung und Herrschaft. Frankfurt.

Hagelstange, T. (1976) Probleme der Klassenanalyse. Anmerkungen zur Studie des IMSF. In: Zur Theorie des Monopols. Staat und Monopole (I). Argument Sonderband 6. Berlin.

Hartikainen, H. (1979) Ekonomiakritiikki, subjektiviteetti ja käyttöarvot. In: Keskustelua pääomalogiikasta ja kapitalismin tutkimisesta (ed. Takala, T.). Tampereen yliopisto. Yhteiskuntatieteiden tutkimuslaitos. Sarja B 27.

Haug, W. & Maase, K. (1980) (hrsg.) Materialistisk Kulturtheorie und Alltagskultur. Argument Sonderband 47. Berlin.

Heiseler, J. et al. (1978b) Arbeiterbewegung und Krise. In: Marxistische Studien. Jahrbuch des IMSF. Frankfurt.

Heiseler, J. et al. (1978a) Jugendliche im Grossbetrieb. Studie zum gewerkschaftlichen und politischen Bewegung arbeitender Jugendlicher. Frankfurt.

Hill, S. (1981) Competition and Control at Work. London.

Hirsch, J. (1980) Der Sicherheitsstaat. Das 'Modell Deutschland', seine Krise und die neuen sozialen Bewegungen. Frankfurt.

Hirsch, J. & Roth, R. (1986) Das neue Gesicht des Kapitalismus. Hamburg.

Hirszowic, M. (1981) Industrial Sociology. London.

Hoff, J. (1985) The Concept of Class and Public Employees. Acta Sociologica 3/1985.

Honneth, A. (1981) Moralbewusstsein und soziale Klassenherrschaft. Leviathan 3-4/1981.

Honneth, A. & Joas, H. (1988) Social Action and Human Nature. Cambridge.

Hänninen, S. (1982) Aika, paikka ja politiikka. Tutkijaliiton julkaisusarja 17. Helsinki.

Hänninen, S. & Paldán, L. (1983) (eds.) Rethinking Ideology. A Marxist Debate. Argument Sonderband 84. Berlin.

IMSF (1974) Klassenstruktur und Klassenbewusstsein in der BRD. Frankfurt.

IMSF: Klassen- und Sozialstruktur der BRD 1950-1970.

-Teil I (1973) Klassenstruktur und Klassentheorie Theoretische Grundlagen und Diskussion. Frankfurt.

-Teil II (1974) Klassen- und Sozialstruktur der BRD 1950-1970. Sozialstatistische Analyse. Erster Halbband. Frankfurt.

-Teil III (1975) Die Intelligenz der BRD 1950-1970. Frankfurt.

Jackman, M. & Jackman, R. (1983) Class Awareness in the United States. Berkeley.

Jessop, B. (1982) The Capitalist State. Oxford.

Jessop, B. (1985) Nicos Poulantzas. Marxist Theory and Political Strategy. New York.

Jessop, B. (1990a) Regulation Theories in Retrospect and Prospect. Economy and Society 2/1990.

Jessop, B. (1990) State Theory. Putting Capitalist States in their Place. Cambridge.

Johnson, R. (1980) Three Problematics: Elements of a Theory of Working-class Culture. In: Working-class Culture. Studies in History and Theory (ed. Clarke, J. et al.). London.

Jones, B. (1975) Max Weber and the Concept of Social Class. Sociological Review 4/1975.

Jonston, L. (1986) Marxism, Class Analysis and Socialist Pluralism. London.

Järvelä-Hartikainen, M. et al. (1982) Vertailevan luokkarakenne- ja luokkatietoisuustutkimuksen otos, aineisto ja aineiston edustavuus. Tampereen yliopisto. Sosiologian ja sosiaalipsykologian laitos. Tutkimuksia 50.

Kadritzke, U. (1982) Angestellte als Lohnarbeiter. Kölner Zeitschrift für Soziologie und Sozialpsychologie. Sonderheft 24/1982.

Kanter, R. (1977) Men and Women of the Corporation. New York.

Kasvio, A. (1983) Teollisuustyö ja elämäntapa. Acta Universitatis Tamperensis. Ser. A 134.

Kauppinen-Toropainen, K. & Hänninen, V. (1981) Case Studies on Job Reorganisation and Job Redesign in Finland. Institute of Occupational Health. Reviews 6. Helsinki.

Keane, J. (1988) Democracy and Civil Society. London.

Kerkelä, H. (1982) Suomen luokka- ja kerrostumarakenteen kehityspiirteitä 1900-luvulla. Tampereen yliopisto. Sosiologian ja sosiaalipsykologian laitos. Tutkimuksia 47.

Kern, H. & Schumann, M. (1984) Das Ende der Arbeitsteilung? Rationalisierung in der industriellen Produktion. München.

Kerr, C. (1954) The Balkanization of Labour Markets. Cambridge.

Kievenheim, C. (1976) Zur Diskussion der Klassenstruktur. Das Argument 96/1976.

King, G. & Raynor, J. (1981) The Middle Class. London.

Kivinen, M. (1987b) The New Middle Classes and the Labour Process. Paper presented at the International Meeting of the Comparative Project on Class Structure and Class Consciousness. Madison, Wisconsin, August 1987.

Kivinen, M. (1989a) The New Middle Classes and the Labour Process. Acta Sociologica 1/1989.

Kivinen, M. (1989b) The New Middle Classes and the Labour Process. Class Criteria Revisited. University of Helsinki. Department of Sociology. Research Reports 223.

Kivinen, M. (1987a) Parempien piirien ihmisiä. Näkökulma uusiin keskiluokkiin. Tutkijaliiton julkaisusarja 46. Jyväskylä.

Kivinen, M. (1983) Työn autonomia ja luokkatietoisuus. In: Tutkimuksia luokkateoriasta (Blom et al.). Tampere.

Knights, D. & Willmot, H. (1990) The Labour Process Theory. London.

Kolbe, H. et al. (1976) Arbeiterklass im Kapitalismus. Berlin (DDR).

Kortteinen, M. & Lehto, A. & Ylöstalo, P. (1986) Tietotekniikka ja suomalainen työ. Helsinki.

Kosonen, P. (1981) Yhteiskunnallisen työnjaon muutos ja pääoman uusintaminen. Helsingin yliopisto. Sosiologian laitos. Tutkimuksia 219.

234

Kreckel, R. (1980) Unequal Opportunity Stratification and Labor Market Segmentation. Sociology 4/1980.

Krovoza, R. (1976) Zum Sozialisationsgehalt der Kapitalistische Produktionsweise. In: Produktion, Arbeit, Sozialisation (hrsg. Heinz, W.R. & Leithäuser, T.). Frankfurt.

Kudera, W. et al. (1979) Gesellschaftliches und politisches Bewusstsein von Arbeitern. Eine empirische Untersuchung. Frankfurt.

Laaksonen, O. (1962) Suomen liike-elämän johtajisto. Helsinki.

Laclau, E. (1983) Transformation of Advanced Industrial Societies and the Theory of the Subject. In: Rethinking Ideology: A Marxist Debate (eds. Hänninen, S. & Paldán, L.). New York.

Laclau, E. & Mouffe, Ch. (1985) Hegemony and Socialist Strategy. Towards a Radical Democratic Politics. London.

Lange, H. (1972) Wissenschaftliches-technische Intelligenz. Neue Bourgeoisie oder neue Arbeiterklasse? Eine sozialwissenschaftliche Untersuchung auf Verhältnis von sozialer Differenzierung und politischen Bewusstsein. Köln.

Lappe, L. (1986) Technologie, Qualifikation und Kontrolle. Die Labour-Process Debatte aus der Sicht der Deutschen Industriesoziologie. Soziale Welt 2-3/ 1986.

Larson, M. (1977) The Rise of Professionalism. Berkeley.

Lash, S. & Urry, J. (1987) The End of Organized Capitalism. Cambridge.

Lefebvre, H. (1975) Kritik des Alltagslebens 3: Grundrisse einer Soziologie der Alltäglichkeit. München.

Lilja, K. (1983) Workers' Workplace Organization. Their Conceptual Identification, Historically Specific Conditions and Manifestations. Acta Academiae Oeconomicae Helsingiensis. Ser. A 39. Helsinki.

Littler, C. (1982) The Development of the Labour Process in Capitalist Societies. London.

Lockwood, D. (1958) The Blackcoated Worker. A Study in Class Consciousness. London.

Lockwood, D. (1966) Sources of Variation in Working Class Images of Society. Sociological Review 14/1966.

Lockwood, D. (1975) Sources of Variation in Working Classs Images of Society. In: Working Class Images of Society (ed. Bulmer, M.). London.

Loveridge, R. & Mok, W. (1979) Theories of Labour Market Segmentation — a Critique. London.

Luokkaprojekti (1984) Suomalaiset luokkakuvassa. Jyväskylä.

Lutz. B. & Sengenberger, W. (1977) Arbeitsmarktstrukturen und öffentliche Arbeitsmarktspolitik. Komission für wirtschaftlichen und sozialen Wende 26. Göttingen.

Mahnkopf, B. (1982) Das kulturtheoretische Defizit industrie-soziologischen Forschung. Prokla 46/1982.

Mallet, S. (1969) La nouvelle classe ouvrière. Paris.

Marquardt, O. (1974) Konjunkturforløb og klassebevidsthed. Jyske Historiker 1/1974.

Marshall, G. et al. (1988) Social Class in Modern Britain. London.

Marx, K. (1976) Capital I. New York.

Mauke, M. (1970) Die Klassentheorie von Marx und Engels. Frankfurt.

Melin, H. (1990) Managers and Social Class. In: Organization Theory and Class Analysis (ed. Clegg, S.). Berlin.

Mendner, J. (1975) Technologische Entwicklung und Arbeitsprozess. Frankfurt.

Mickler, O. & Dittrich, E. & Neumann, U. (1976) Technik, Arbeitsorganisation und Arbeit. Eine empirische Untersuchung in der automatisierten Produktion. Studienreihe des Soziologischen Forschungsinstituts SOFI. Göttingen.

Moore, B. (1978) Injustice: The Social Bases of Obedience and Revolt. London.

Mortensen, N. & Christiansen, E. (1975) Arbejderbevägelse og arbeiderbevidsthed — oplaeg til en teoretisk afklaringsprocess. NSU Stencilserie 9. København.

Mortensen, N. et al. (1979) Affirmation eller emancipation. Om reformismediskussionen, det 'nye venstres' politiska identitet og nødvendigheden af en marxistisk kritik. Kontext 36-37/1979.

Mouffe, C. & Laclau E. (1985) Hegemony and Socialist Strategy. London.

Murphy, R. (1986) The Concept of Class in Closure Theory: Learning Rather than Falling into the Problems Encountered by Neomarxism. Sociology 2/ 1986.

Murphy, R. (1985) The Structure of Closure: A Critique and Development of the Theories of Weber, Collins and Parkin. British Journal of Sociology 1/1985.

Negt, O. & Kluge, A. (1972) Öffentlichkeit und Erfahrung. Zur Organisationsanalyse bürgerlicher und proletarischer Öffentlichkeit. Frankfurt.

Neuendorf, H. (1980) Der Deutungsmusteransatz zur Rekonstruktion der Strukturen der Arbeitsbewusstsein und Persönlichkeitsentwicklung. Köln.

Neumann, G. (1976) Methoden der Klassenanalyse. Köln.

Neusüss, C. & Müller, W. (1971) Die 'Sozialstaatsillusion' und der Widerspruch von Lohnarbeit und Kapital. Probleme des Klassenkampfs 1/1971.

Nichols, T. & Armstrong, P. (1976) Workers Divided. London.

Offe, C. (1985) Bemerkungen zur spieltheoretischen Neufassung des Klassenbegriffs bei Wright und Elster. Prokla 1/1985.

Offe, C. & Wiesenthal, G. (1980) Two Logics of Collective Action: Theoretical Notes on Social Class and Organizational Form. In: Political Power and Social Theory (ed. Zeitlin, M.). Greenwich.

Olofsson, G. (1979) Mellan klass och stat. Lund.

Osterland, M. (1973) Lebensgeschictliche Erfahrung und gesellschaftliches Bewusstsein. Anmerkungen zur soziographischen Metode. Soziale Welt 4/1973.

Parkin, F. (1979) Marxism and Class Theory: A Bourgeois Critique. London.

Parkin, F. (1980) Reply to Giddens. Theory and Society 9/1980.

Parsons, T. (1940) An Analytical Approach to the Theory of Stratification. The American Journal of Sociology 6/1940.

Penn, R. (1982) Skilled Manual Workers in the Labour Process. In: The Degradation of Work (ed. Wood, S.). London.

Piore, M. (1975) Notes for a Theory of Labor Market Stratification. In: Labor Market Segmentation (Edwards, R. et al.). Lexington.

Pollert, A. (1991) (ed.) Farewell to Flexibility? Worchester.

Popitz, M. et al. (1957) Das Gesellschaftsbild des Arbeiters. Tübingen.

Poulantzas, N. (1976) The Crisis of the Dictatorship. London.

Poulantzas, N. (1975) Klassen im Kapitalismus heute. West-Berlin.

Priester, K. (1980) Krisenentwicklung und Arbeiterbewegung. Bericht über ein Kolloquium des IMSF.

Projekt Ideologie-Theorie (1980) Klassencharakter und Ökonomische Determination des Ideo-logischen. Ein Beitrag zur Diskussion. Das Argument 122/1980.

Projekt Ideologie-Theorie (1979) Theorien über Ideologie. Argument Sonderband 40. Westberlin.

Projekt Klassenanalyse (1978) Materialien zur Klassenstruktur der BRD. Hamburg.

Projekt Klassenanalyse (1973) Materialien zur Klassenstruktur der BRD I-II. West-Berlin.

Projekt Klassenanalyse (1974) Oberfläche und Staat. West-Berlin.

Przeworski, A. (1977) Proletariate into Class: the Process of Class Formation from Karl Kautsky's The Class Struggle to Recent Controversies. Politics and Society 7/1977.

Rasmussen, F.D. (1978) Arbejderens situation, de sociale problemen og revolution. København.

Renner, K. (1982) The Service Class. In: Austro-Marxism (ed. Bottomore, T. & Goode, P.). Oxford.

Roemer, J.E. (1982) A General Theory of Exploitation and Class. Cambridge.

Rose, D. & Marshall, G. (1986) Constructing the (W)right Classes. Sociology 3/1986.

Roth, R. (1982) Neue Soziale Bewegungen. Literatur Rundschau 7/1982.

Schmidt, L. (1978) Socialisationskritik og politisk praksis. København.

Scott, J. (1979) Corporation, Classes and Capitalism. Hutchinson.

Semjenow, W. (1972) Kapitalismus und Klassen. Die Erforschung der Sozialstruktur in der modernen kapitalistischen Gesellschaft. Berlin.

Sève, L. (1972) Marxisme et theorie de la personalite. Editions sociales. Paris.

Stark, D. (1980) Class Struggle and the Transformation of the Labour Process. A Relational Approach. Theory and Society 9/1980.

Suomen tilastollinen vuosikirja (1989) Tilastokeskus. Helsinki.

Söderfeldt, B. (1980) Att mäta klasserna i Sverige. Häften för kritiska studier 3/1980.

Tainio, R. (1982) Internal Strategy of Management in Industrial Organizations. Helsingin kaup-pakorkeakoulu. Julkaisuja B 56. Helsinki.

Therborn, G. (1938) Why Some Classes Are More Successful than Others. New Left Review 138/1983.

Thompson, E. (1968) Making of the English Working Class. London.

Thompson, E. (1978) The Poverty of Theory and an Orrery of Errors. In: Poverty of Theory and Other Essays (Thompson, E.). New York.

Thorbek, S. (1980) Mellansikten ø den nya småborgerskapet. Häften för kritiska studier 2/1980.

Tjaden-Steinhauer, M. (1975) Gesellschaftsbewusstsein der Arbeiter. Umrisse einer theoretischen Bestimmung. Köln.

Touraine, A. (1974) Old and New Social Classes. In: The Post-industrial Society (Touraine, A.). London.

Urry, J. (1981) The Anatomy of Capitalist Societies. The Economy, Civil Society and the State. London.

Vester, M. (1970) Die Entstehung des Proletariats als Lernprozess. Frankfurt.

Volmerg, U. (1976) Zum Verhältnis Produktion und Sozialisation, am Beispiel industriellen Lohnarbeit. Im: Produktion, Arbeit, Sozialisation (hrsg. Heinz, W.R. & Leithäuser, T.). Frankfurt.

Vonderach, A. (1974) Kapital und Klasse. Giessen.

237

Voss, G. (1980) Arbeitssituation und Bewusstsein. Frankfurt.

Wagner, W. (1976) Verelendungstheorie — die hilflose Kapitalismuskritik. Frankfurt.

Weber, M. (1978) Economy and Society. Berkeley.

Werner, D. (1982) Die Sozialpsychologie der Arbeiterklasse und die 'neuen sozialen Bewegungen'. In: Marxistische Studier, Jahrbuch der IMSF 5. Frankfurt.

Werner, D. (1979) Zwischen Sozialpartnerschaft — Ideologie und Klassbewusstsein. In: Marxistische Studien, Jahrbuch der IMSF 2. Frankfurt.

West, J. (1982) (ed.) Work, Women and the Labour Market. Boston.

Wilkinson, B. (1982) (ed.) The Dynamics of Labour Market Segmentation. London.

Wilkinson, B. (1983) The Shopfloor Politics of New Technology. London.

Willis, P. (1979) Learning to Labour. How Working Class Kids Get Working Class Jobs. Westmead.

Wright, E.O. (1976) Class, Crisis and the State. London.

Wright, E.O. (1985) Classes. London.

Wright, E.O. (1982) The States of Political in the Concept of Class Structure. Comparative Project on Class Structure and Class Consciousness. University of Wisconsin. Department of Sociology. Working Paper Series 3.

Wright, E.O. (1980) Varieties of Marxist Conception of Class Structure. Politics and Society 3/1980.

Wright, E.O. (1985b) Wo liegt die Mitte der Mittelklasse? Prokla 1/1985.

Wright et al. (1982) The American Class Structure. Madison.

Zimbalist, A. (1983) (ed.) Case Studies on the Labour Process. New York.

Zoll, R. et al. (1981) Arbeiterbewusstsein in der Wirtschaftskrise. Köln.

Biographical notes

Raimo Blom is Professor of Sociology at the University of Tampere. He has published widely on class and comparative structural analysis, as well as on the theory of the state and law. He is author of *State and Classes* (1985), and co-author of *Classes and Social Organization in Finland, Sweden and Norway*. Professor Blom has been in charge of the Finnish component of Erik Olin Wright's project on class structure and class consciousness since 1981. He was Editor of *Sociology* in 1975-77 and of *Acta Sociologica* in 1985-87. *Address:* Department of Sociology and Social Psychology, University of Tampere, PO Box 607, 33101 Tampere, Finland.

Markku Kivinen is Professor of Sociology at the University of Lapland. He has published on political sociology and class analysis. He is author of *The New Middle Classes and the Labour Process — Class Criteria Revisited* (1989). He is also co-author of *The Reality of Social Classes in Finland* (1985). Professor Kivinen has been involved in E.O. Wright's project on class structure and class consciousness since 1981. He was Editor of *Acta Sociologica* in 1985-87. *Address:* Department of Sociology, University of Lapland, PO Box 122, 96101 Rovaniemi, Finland.

Harri Melin is Assistant Professor of Sociology at the University of Tampere. He has published on class analysis and trade union studies. He is co-author of *The Reality of Social Classes in Finland* (1985) and of *Classes and Social Organization in Finland, Sweden and Norway*. Assistant Professor Melin has been involved in E.O. Wright's project on class structure and class consciousness since 1981. He was Editor of *Acta Sociologica* in 1985-87. *Address:* Department of Sociology and Social Psychology, University of Tampere, PO Box 607, 33101 Tampere, Finland.

Liisa Rantalaiho is Professor of Sociology of Work at the Department of Public Health, University of Tampere. She has published several articles in the field of sociology of work and women's studies. She edited the book *Men's Science, Women's Jobs* (in Finnish; 1989). Professor Rantalaiho was the first Editor of *Naistutkimus* (1988-90), Finland's first journal specializing in women's studies. *Address:* Department of Public Health, University of Tampere, PO Box 607, 33101 Tampere, Finland.